Business
and Its
Environment

Business and Its Environment

Essays for Thomas C. Cochran

Edited by
Harold Issadore Sharlin

Contributions in American Studies,
Number 63

GREENWOOD PRESS
Westport, Connecticut • London, England

096366

Library of Congress Cataloging in Publication Data
Main entry under title:

Business and its environment.

(Contributions in American studies, ISSN 0084-
9227 ; no. 63)
Bibliography: p.
Includes index.
1. United States—Commerce—History—Addresses,
essays, lectures. 2. United States—Social con-
ditions—Addresses, essays, lectures. 3. Cochran,
Thomas Childs, 1902-   . I. Cochran, Thomas
Childs, 1902-   . II. Sharlin, Harold I.
III. Series.
HF3031.B78   338.0973   82-6143
ISBN 0-313-21438-7 (lib. bdg.)   AACR2

HF
3031
.B78
1983

Library of Congress Catalog Card Number: 82-6143
ISBN: 0-313-21438-7
ISSN: 0084-9227

First published in 1983

Greenwood Press
A division of Congressional Information Service, Inc.
88 Post Road West, Westport, Connecticut 06881

Printed in the United States of America

10 9 8 7 6 5 4 3 2 1

Contents

*Business
and Its
Environment*

Thomas C. Cochran

Introduction

HAROLD ISSADORE SHARLIN

Thomas C. Cochran has been so persistently original throughout his career that contemplating an intellectual retrospective of his work is like hoping that a snapshot of an arrow in flight will give some sense of its complete trajectory. While this introduction was being written a new Cochran book with a fresh look at industrialization was published.[1] An inventory of Professor Cochran's original ideas could never be complete; even the diverse essays that follow fail to indicate fully the breadth of his originality. The tribute entailed in this collection is an apt reflection of Professor Cochran's own insistence that his students be experimental and venturesome.

Whether in the classroom or through the published word, Professor Cochran's main role in life has been that of teacher. That role is best filled, a well-known teacher of scientists said 140 years ago, by conducting students "to an eminence from which they might contemplate the fields of original research before them."[2] In order to be an effective guide, the teacher must have reached that eminence through her or his own work. Professor Cochran reached that eminence through his conviction that history should be more useful and have a broader perspective. That conviction was manifest over and over again in the long list of his publications, which form a goodly portion of any catalog of original twentieth-century ideas.

Professor Cochran has constantly urged the use of business history as the most logical general approach to American history. The approach, he has said many times, offers a much broader perspective than that of national politics—the approach usually assumed to represent "general history." In 1967, in his presidential address to the Organization of American Historians, he quoted the introduction to *The Age of Enterprise*, first published in 1942. "Boss" Croker knew how ubiquitous business was: "Ever heard that business is business? Well, so is politics business, and reporting—journalism, doctoring—all professions, arts, sports,—everything is business."[3]

For a lobbyist, that argument means that public policy should follow where market decisions lead. Although most intellectuals would reject "Boss" Croker's coarse description of American life, ideas derived from business underlie much of American history, and those ideas explain much about the course of social change. The point that Professor Cochran has been making is that the ideas and practices taken from business include all activity undertaken for profit and involve institutions that dominate the social environment. Political history, he has argued, lends itself to "a coherent internal narrative," but that kind of history does not deal with the causes of social change. Business, particularly in the United States, he has insisted, is a powerful agent for such change. Conversely, business decisions are very much conditioned by the social environment. Everything basic to American society can be included in a history written about business and its environment.[4]

Business must be treated on its own terms. Because of its pivotal place in society, however, business and its immediate setting form an exceptional tool for understanding social change. The integrative value of business history is related to its general nature. Professor Cochran has broadened the meaning of the term *business* so that it applies as well to an agrarian society: "A large percentage of American farmers were also businessmen, and even the frontier was a mixed area of business and agriculture." Farmers bought and sold land, arranged loans and leases, and dealt in commodity futures. Thus, the dichotomy that Frederick Jackson Turner and Thomas Jefferson saw between the farmer and the urban businessman existed only in the ideal sense. In reality, farmers had many of the same interests and depended on the same institutions as merchants and manufacturers.[5]

In *The Age of Enterprise* and other writing, Professor Cochran has argued that "in the nearly four hundred years of American history, business would seem to have been as continuously present and important as any social institution other than the family and its social or religious rituals."[6] The business attitude, more than anything else, united American colonists and separated them from the traditional landowning outlook of Europe. As Professor Cochran has viewed the estrangement from Europe, this "business ingredient in colonial culture" reduced the differences between farmer and merchant and also served as a means of transition in the American view from "the static views and limited goals of European agricultural workers, serfs, tenants, or small land owners." Business attitudes have continued to close the gap between rural and urban Americans. Rural sociologists in 1950 acknowledged that they were in a fast disappearing field,[7] and the term *agribusiness*, as it is used today, symbolizes the elimination of any gap.

Business activity became institutionalized, Professor Cochran has said, through law. "More specifically," he wrote, "businessmen wanted protection for dispersed decision making based on the market.... They conceived of the law, ...

as a positive force in economic growth."[8] By formalizing and generalizing local custom, the law helped make business the common strain in American history and also made business the universal force in today's economic and social environment. Governments—federal, state, and local—have taken advantage of the pervasiveness of business as a means of expanding political control of many facets of American life.

The government-business relationship, as it has developed, is conclusive evidence of the Cochran thesis that business is the key to understanding American history and the key to analyzing present public policy. President Eisenhower's term, *military-industrial complex*, falls far short of what Professor Cochran meant when he wrote of the "union of business and government." Eisenhower was mainly worried about the role of military procurement in American economic life, whereas Professor Cochran's theme has been that every aspect of social and economic change has been influenced by business attitudes and the activities of private enterprise. Government has shared in spreading this influence, has attempted to redirect this influence through regulation, and has contended with private business influence by using public enterprise to control private enterprise. There are three areas of joint government-business influence: (1) where government supplies the institutions and the infrastructure that support business enterprise; (2) where government regulates business in "the public interest"; and (3) where government undertakes such enterprises as defense and electric power. Every important area of American life is touched by this joint influence.

This pervasiveness of the government-business force in American society has been a major concern for a group of writers among whom Professor Cochran has been the leading historical spokesman. These writers have revived the term *political economy*. As one of the most influential of them, Charles E. Lindblom, has said, after the difference between despotism and libertarianism,

the greatest distinction between one government and another is in the degree to which market replaces government or government replaces market. Both Adam Smith and Karl Marx knew this. Hence, certain questions about the governmental-market relation are at the core of both political science and economics, no less for the planned than for the market systems.[9]

Professor Cochran brings a special historical perspective to the perception of our society of an enlarged government and supersized corporations as the dominant but inescapable facts of American life. To political economists the large corporation "does not fit" into the "democratic theory and vision."[10] The opposite view is that government has grown to the point of threatening our individual liberties.[11] Those who regret either too large government, or too large private enterprises, or both, suppose that once the course of history is determined it can only be reversed by reversing the way power is used. This hope for a reversal of the current of history is a call to return to the halcyon days when the individual could do everything.

One finds Professor Cochran, on the other hand, accepting rather than regretting historical change. His attitude is the one expressed in the *Rubaiyat* toward the "moving finger." But there is still choice; the future can be planned. Once having identified the basis of change, he would direct our future course by better and more conscious control of the forces of social change. His thesis that business is a common strain in American history is far removed from the commonly expressed pessimism and fatalism. In advocating the development of business as a theme in American history, Professor Cochran, through his writing, reveals a pragmatism in the best and the original sense of the word.

General concepts used in thinking about history, because abstract, are the most difficult to transmit in a way that enables them to become tools for other historians. Many who have sat in Professor Cochran's classes or read his books and essays have been convinced of the need to emphasize business as a common strain in American history, but that idea has found relatively few followers among historians. His separate landmark ideas, such as the effect of the Civil War on industrialization and role playing have, on the other hand, raised debate and caused some to apply the ideas to their own work. The spread in the use of these unit ideas is a more easily measured indicator of Professor Cochran's influence on the profession.

History in the Cochran mode enables one to understand how change has occurred and to imagine how change can be controlled in the future. To be able to imagine change, the focus needs to be on the micro as well as the macro level, and he has done much to promote an appreciation of the combined effect of the individual and the institution as agents of change.

The paragon of the agent of change, the entrepreneur, has been an object of study for some time,[12] but Professor Cochran has given the entrepreneur and the entrepreneurial way of effecting change a historical context. His study of railroad leaders is a landmark that describes the ideas and policies of selected railroad entrepreneurs. By doing comparative studies of Puerto Rican and Argentine business leaders, Professor Cochran has shown variations in the activities of the entrepreneur as an agent of change.

Ideas such as Joseph A. Schumpeter's theoretical analysis of the entrepreneur's role were given historical context by Professor Cochran's work. Schumpeter developed an ideal type in drawing his picture of the entrepreneur. His theoretical analysis of the entrepreneur as someone "carrying out new combinations" created a new personality in the drama of economic growth: the entrepreneur as innovator. But Schumpeter's entrepreneur is a theoretical abstraction without reference, except in a general way, to real people and events.[13] Schumpeter used the separate terms *inventor* and *profit seeker* to differentiate their activities from those of the entrepreneur who may introduce a new good or a new method of production, or who may open a new market, adopt a new source of raw materials, or carry out a reorganization of an industry.[14] Schumpeter had said that innovation, the entrepreneur's contribution, came after the inventor's creative work, and Cochran found the historical evidence that supported the usual distinction between inventor and entrepreneur. He wrote, "Skilled workers might be the chief inventors, but it was the entrepreneur who was generally the architect of progress."[15] Schumpeter listed one of the "new combinations" that an entrepreneur might create as the "opening of a new market, that is, a market into which the particular branch of manufacture of the country in question has not previously entered."[16] So that to be innovative an entrepreneur did not even require new technology. Cochran made this generalization historically distinctive in his book on the Argentine entrepreneur whose innovation was to adopt foreign technology to Argentine culture.[17]

The control of the development of new technology was accomplished by the entrepreneur in what Schumpeter characterized as the carrying out of a new organization or what Cochran has called the institutionalization of technological advance by means of the corporate-run research laboratory.[18] Thus the entrepreneur is only occasionally a technologist, although the two roles can be combined. In either role he can promote technological change. The different historical contexts in which Cochran has examined the role of entrepreneur give a clearer indication of how the entrepreneur acculturates technology. The Argentine businessman, railroad leaders, as well as nineteenth- and twentieth-century American businessmen were entrepreneurs who determined the direction of technological change. Their role in controlling this change comes out in stark relief against the historical context.

Another generalization that Professor Schumpeter made about entrepreneurs was that they were not identical with capitalists, the possessors of wealth; Schumpeter went further by insisting that accumulated wealth (savings) was not essential to innovation. In fact, the more general case, he found, was one in which the innovation was accomplished by redirecting employed resources rather than by engaging unused means of production.[19] Or, one might say, the accumulation of capital is a necessary part of innovation, but the impetus for change comes from the entrepreneur. That view of the role of the entrepreneur tells, in a general way, why change occurs; but Professor Cochran's historical context explains the differences that arise between countries and periods. The Schumpeterian thesis has a number of elements in addition to those described above. The historical context shows the correlation between different combinations of those elements and varieties of innovation. So Cochran has been more interested in "where and how capital was invested" than in its accumulation because he believed that the way capital was invested is more important than the absolute quantity of voluntary savings.[20]

The idea that history does make a difference as far as entrepreneurship is concerned, that time and place make a difference, and that the difference clarifies the entrepreneurial roles is a hallmark of Professor Cochran's writing. As a consequence of many years of thinking and writing, he was able to demonstrate the importance of historical context in his *Business in American Life*. He wrote that American society was not simply the result of an "industrial revolution" but that the effect of the culture and its entrepreneurs was to make industrial change a distinctly American phenomenon.

The business entrepreneur, the agent of change, continued to be differently conditioned than his European counterpart. He expected to use government rather than fear it, to find social leaders friendly rather than hostile to his plans, and to regard his personal success as of primary value to his community. These and other environmental influences gradually molded types of entrepreneurial personality in the industrial society of America that differed from those of England, France, or Germany.[21]

Two streams of thought converge in Professor Cochran's interpretation of the entrepreneur: his views on business history and his use of role model. The first stream is his idea that the most important characteristic of American history is that it is the story of a business civilization and that the entrepreneur is the dynamic in that civilization. The entrepreneurial spirit, the consequence of many forces in American culture, was the spirit that accounted for the United States' technological leadership in the world. Fundamental changes in American institutional structure and culture seem to have dampened the exercise of that spirit and, more than any other factor, to account for this country's technological lag.

A second stream of Professor Cochran's thought is the idea of role model. He did not invent the concept, but he has found unique use for the idea and has been a tireless promoter of such analysis: as a "corrective" for economic theorizing that depersonalizes by eliminating people from economic activity;[22] as a means of relating individual action to institutions;[23] and as a way of explaining social change and the equilibrating forces that operate in society.[24]

As a useful analytical and explanatory tool in historical study, role theory functions in a more universal way than such theories as the economic interpretation of history or the frontier theory, which are types of theory limited to time and place and waver in the face of changing circumstance. A social role is the type of activity that others expect from a person occupying a certain status. (Professor Cochran's deviant social role has served as a model for those in the historical profession who seek to develop new theories rather than simply adopt other historians' ideas.)

A proponent of social role theory, he has sought to define and explain its uses as well as to apply the theory to his own research. In 1953, he described the theory: "In the broad view, a particular social role is a product of the type of personality common in the society interacting with the physical and cultural setting."[25] He then analyzed letters written by sixty-one railroad leaders and showed that their actions and decisions were set by the limits of their social role. Professor Cochran's use of role theory in this case was an incisive tool for understanding better the behavior of such a varied group. The railroad leaders were neither theoreticians nor moralists, yet they may have endorsed such novel ideas as social Darwinism while, in other respects, behaving in an orthodox manner in order not to jeopardize their business interests. (For a more recent illustration of this type of behavior, see Ronald Bayor's chapter in this volume.) The railroad leaders' social role was a product of the American environment; in Cochran's view they were "simply carrying out on a large scale the aims and cultural beliefs of American business society." In turn, business roles were a force "in shaping other goals and sanctions in American culture,"[26] a force more pervasive than even the frontier.[27]

Furthermore, the role model as examined in such different cultures as Puerto Rico, Argentina, and the nineteenth-century United States provides the necessary link between the individual's actions and the cultural institutions.[28] The use of role theory is not far from the technique of conceptualizing technological change, which Alfred D. Chandler, Jr., does in his *Strategy and Structure*. The difference between Professor Chandler's approach and Professor Cochran's is that in Chandler's history a few creative entrepreneurs such as Isaac Singer, Gustavus Swift, and James B. Duke develop a corporate structure that others emulate,[29] whereas Cochran's role players include the emulators. In such cases, there is no movement of historical proportions, he seems to be saying, without the diffusion through a culture of the original creative entrepreneurial idea. The Harrimans and the Vanderbilts may have been center stage, but the sixty-one railroad leaders made the American railroad system work. (See James Soltow's chapter in this volume for a modern example of an entrepreneurial role model.)

In Professor Cochran's role theory, the individual obviously acts in ways dictated by culture and class. That idea is partly a way of deflating the star system in history. Causality in history is no longer a saga of giants but rather a movement of social forces. No one would deny the Fords, the Edisons, the Swifts, and the Singers their rightful credit as innovators, but through Cochran's examples we learn what makes change a process rather than a matter of creative spurts.

Professor Cochran's history is a process impelled by ordinary as well as extraordinary people. The industrial revolution, for example, may have been begun by the British because they were "a people fascinated by wealth and commerce," or the technological advance of the industrial revolution may have been a matter of "challenge and response."[30] But what do these ideas say that help policy makers deal with the present American technological lag, if indeed there is a lag? The usefulness of role theory to policy is that the theory tells why the individuals, who are the point sources of movement in the economy, behave as they do. Policy must affect these thousands of role players who, Professor Cochran has said, make up the "entrepreneurial personality in the industrial society of America."[31]

It is one thing for a policy maker, using the star system of history, to try to establish the right economic and social conditions in which an Edison, a Ford, or a Carnegie will flourish and promote technological innovation. The policy that would result from this view would constitute a fruitless effort to establish the extraordinary atmosphere in which creative genius operates best. Or the policy maker, using role theory, the Cochran view, could pay heed to the broad cultural base. The former is the economic "trickle down" theory applied to cultural change, whereas the latter, the role theory, places emphasis on the general causes of social and economic change. (Policy makers did not affect the development of electric power until the technology was well diffused through the economy. See my essay in this volume on New York's electricity.)

The list of Professor Cochran's landmark ideas in historical research is uncommonly long considering that historians have established reputations on a single idea, such as the frontier theory or the economic interpretation of the Constitution. He has been the originator or promoter of such important concepts as the distinctiveness of the entrepreneur, role theory, the use of the social sciences in history, war as an inhibitor of industrial growth, and the social interchange of business and its environment.

Professor Cochran's persistent originality has placed him in the forefront of historical research and made him one of the very few who work comfortably as both humanist and social scientist. He was among those who turned away from history as the story of kings, politicians, and generals. The course he charted was not that of the "new history," which was more interested in giving due credit to unsung, exploited groups than in determining the causes of social change. His interest in the environment of business, both the influences on businessmen and the way business culture affected the social environment, was not a matter of improving the self-regard of businessmen who, after all, have their own public relations departments. What he has been contending is that the drama and widespread influence of national politics have produced a strong bias toward writing the history of events in Washington, D.C. Yet, he asserts, the most pervasive forces for change reside in those "institutions directly connected with the transmission of the culture from one generation to the next."[32] Business culture has a most pervasive influence on society through those institutions, such as child rearing, education, religion, and ways of making a living that are the transmitters of culture. The institutions that he would concentrate on are the largest common denominator of American society.

Professor Cochran began at least as early as 1942 referring to "the story of business enterprise itself, the story of its institutions and their impact on American society,"[33] and he has persisted in the promotion of that idea. In 1972 he wrote that the characteristics of political history "readily lead to the writing of a coherent internal narrative that may have little reference to underlying or gradual social change. In contrast, the institutions of business are inextricably intertwined with their social environment."[34]

The subject of business institutions and their impact on society is not merely one of those minor neglected areas of history but rather the necessary material for analysis of American social change. The pervasive and sinewy character of business enterprise makes the approach an ideal means to attain Professor Cochran's objective, which has always been to understand the cause of social change. The subject is business enterprise; the method is analysis; the object is history that has utility in the formulation of public policy. Those who pursue this approach, Professor Cochran has said, will substitute "analysis for narrative, . . . scope for extensive detail, and . . . the rhetoric of science for that of drama." The result may not be popular literature, but it will possess utility. If history is to be analytical and rely less on the devices of literature, then history will have to employ the analytical tools of social science. The social science approach to history is one of those landmark ideas that Professor Cochran has promoted throughout his career.[35]

Professor Cochran has been typecast as an economic historian, but his particular analytical approach makes use of all the social sciences. In preparation for the research for a history of the Pabst Brewing Company, he asked Arthur H. Cole what questions economists would ask of business records. In preparation for the research on railroad leaders, he consulted with economists, political scientists, sociologists, and social psychologists; in planning for the Norristown project, he asked anthropologists, sociologists, and demographers for suggestions on how to conduct the interdisciplinary research.[36]

The Norristown project was in the forefront of interdisciplinary research in the United States. In 1951 Professor Cochran along with Dorothy S. Thomas, professor of sociology and Anthony F. C. Wallace, professor of anthropology, both at the University of Pennsylvania, began the Seminar in Technological Change and Social Adjustment. The seminar introduced graduate students to an extraordinary situation in which students actively participated in joint research that involved faculty as well as other students. Each student chose his or her topic and shared experiences as well as exchanged advice on their projects. The situation sounds like any other graduate seminar except that in the Norristown seminar historians, anthropologists, and sociologists, students as well as faculty, were engaged in the lively exchange.

The project—investigating technological innovation and its effects—was innovative itself. The different behavioral sciences, including history, sociology, anthropology, law, economics, and psychology, were brought together in a collaborative project that studied a real town and the serious question of how people adjust to technological change.[37] (See Stanley Bailis's chapter in this book for a historical-sociological model of how people adjust to change.)

Those fortunate few who attended and worked in the Norristown seminar had the opportunity to watch Professor Cochran and other active scholars think through research problems. The experience was as close as a graduate student in the behavioral sciences could get to the master-apprentice relationship that is common in the graduate training of physical scientists. The ideal of training physical scientists and mathematicians for research careers is best expressed as training those students so as to conduct them, as mentioned before, "to an eminence from which they might contemplate the fields of original research before them."[38] History graduate students, those not lucky enough to have studied with Professor Cochran, are usually left to reach that eminence on their own.

One of the landmark ideas associated with Professor Cochran, perhaps because it was so controversial, was that the Civil War had an adverse effect on American industrialization. He first proposed the theory and then had to defend it. The idea has gained currency.

"Did the Civil War Retard Industrialization?"[39] was a lesson to historians on how they can err if they neglect the rudimentary rules of historical context:

causation is a main object of history; and periodization is a convenience and must not be considered in historical isolation.

Professor Cochran examined the prevalent belief among historians that the Civil War was the major cause of industrialization in the United States, and he found that this misconception arose because "few writers have examined the available long-run statistical series before adding their endorsement to the conventional interpretation."[40] The argument on this issue was between a historian who has made full use of retrospective economic data and historians who had not.

The social sciences, which include economics, sociology, psychology, and anthropology, Professor Cochran has said, "tend to emphasize the uniform characteristics of social processes rather than the unique elements of each situation. This calls attention to the importance of long-run mass phenomena or trends rather than individual events."[41] The unique elements of each situation, placed in the proper context, are what should concern historians. Social scientists may be interested in spans of time, but these spans are cantilevered, that is, anchored at one end only, either in the present or the past. The historian builds suspension bridges from the past to the present.

The question of economic growth, for example, interests economists such as Simon Kuznets, who has assayed 200 years of economic change from 1770 to 1970. Dr. Kuznets found that in that time the American economy grew 1000 times larger. This emergence of the United States from an agrarian to an industrialized state can be attributed, according to Dr. Kuznets, to a high growth rate in population combined with substantial growth rates of per capita product and an initially high per capita income.[42] Growth over time can be attributed to these factors, but it then remains for the historian to search for causes that underlie these factors.

When Professor Cochran wanted to test the proposition that the Civil War promoted economic growth, he examined some of the foundations of that growth over a long span of time before and beyond the Civil War period. For example, he studied the long-term trends in short-term bank loans because short-term loans were the basis of business expansion, and the fact that short-term loans were down was quantitative evidence that economic growth was also down. Another measure of growth, immigration, was down during the Civil War from an extensive span of growth during all the other decades of the nineteenth century.[43]

Farm mechanization, an aspect of industrialization, was not increased during the Civil War, Professor Cochran observed. The cause of this setback in mechanization he ascribed to wartime destruction and to such events as the suspension of the McCormick company's manufacturing due, as the company said, to "the uncertainties of the times."[44] That 250,000 reapers were sold from 1861 to 1865 Cochran explained as being "a quite ordinary increase for a young industry." To these observations were added data on the decline of pig-iron production and railroad building. The whole argument over whether the rate of industrialization increased or decreased due to the Civil War could only be settled if the cause of the change was ascertained, and this was Professor Cochran's objective, as it would have to be for all historians.

With all these social science indicators available, why did historians persist in the error that the Civil War promoted American industrialization? Historians took "random" statistics, such as the manufacture of 90,000 reapers in 1864, without placing these statistics in their proper, that is, historical perspective. The reaper manufacturer himself saw 1864 as an aberration, and historians would have seen the same thing had they looked at a longer time series.[45]

Periodization became the snare for those historians who specialized in the Civil War and did not take a long enough time span to acquire proper perspective. Eventually the time span must be anchored in the present. Historical context views the past *relative* to the present and, therefore, the past is made *relevant* to the present. Why else study the industrial revolution in nineteenth-century Britain or America, or interpretations of the Fourteenth Amendment? The hallmark of his contribution to historical scholarship has been his use of social science techniques in a historical context. He is original because he never forgets that he is a historian first.

What was it like sitting in a graduate class given by a persistently original historian like Professor Cochran? The model he presented as a guide to the student's own research and writing was that of a historian seeking to explain the causes of gradual social change. What is needed in historical writing today, the student was told, was not to narrate the stories of great men, women, and events of the past written under an intuitively devised label, such as Jacksonian Democracy, Era of Good Feeling, or Irrepressible Conflict, but to address historically issues of present concern, such as the effect on enterprise of government regulation, the causes of economic growth and stagnation, and the social adjustment demanded by growing urban centers. In short, Professor Cochran has said, historians have to be closer to the methods and concerns of social science than to the grand style of storytelling used by the Spenglers and Toynbees.[46] Those views were first expressed in 1948, and in 1964 he wrote:

A society sure of its values has needed history only to celebrate the glories of the past, but a society of changing values and consequent confusion also needed history as a utilitarian guide. Hence the social science approach to history...arose largely from the inner destruction of values, from the loss of historical certainties of nineteenth-century Americans.[47]

Professor Cochran taught students to break the mold of intuitive themes in a narrative setting and to offer a wider choice than either standard periodization or specified topics. Such choices made students uneasy. Most students want to be told what to do rather than invent their own fields of research. A teacher who dominates students' thinking and prescribes rather than provokes runs the risk of causing students to be "mere parroters of what they have learnt, incapable of using their minds except in the furrows traced for them."[48] John Stuart Mill was grateful to his father for pressing him to find his own intellectual path, and, as a teacher, Professor Cochran was not one to retrace furrows.

***

The theme, "Business and Its Environment," of this tribute to Thomas Childs Cochran was chosen to provide contributors, all of whom were influenced by Professor Cochran's teaching, a wide choice of topics that could be treated analytically by applying social science concepts or methods and that could be useful to policy makers, either explicitly or implicitly. No limits were placed on the choice of topics. After all, the man we wanted to honor had ranged as far as to write the *Auction Bridge Handbook* (1926). In allowing the Festschrift theme to be interpreted broadly, the intention was to illustrate the number of opportunities still to be explored by following Professor Cochran's lead. The editor, within these nonrigid constraints, did not enforce any narrow rules of format or interpretation. Each contribution represents a very individualistic approach to a research topic in the contributor's own distinctive voice.

The eight essays that follow are paired into four groups, each of which illustrates one or more of Professor Cochran's landmark ideas. The first pair, essays by James J. Flink and Bernard Mergen, give two separate historical contexts for the idea that the state has by historical development become a permanent part of the environment for business, which Dr. Cochran calls "the union of business and government."

Dr. Flink's essay, "The National Parks: The Business of the Environment," is about one unusual aspect of the business-government relationship and also deals with the issue of who will have access to the national parks. A related question is how government policy has interpreted the idea of conservation of natural resources historically. The history of government policy toward national parks places the theoretical question of preservation versus wise use of national resources in a context that tests each theory against the social issue of class privilege. Does a preservationist policy favor the upper classes?

Dr. Flink shows that it does through rules of access to the national parks. Tourism is the point of union between government and business. Government intervention has done much to make the parks accessible to a wider, although still limited, group of people. Government control of the business environment for tourism has had an influence on both conservation policy and social change. "Antomobility" has meant that parks are more available, and, according to Dr. Flink, government policy has not resulted in the destruction of a natural resource, contrary to preservationist ideology.

Dr. Mergen's essay, "The Government as Manager: Emergency Fleet Shipbuilding, 1917-1919," illustrates the familiar principle that government attempts to control one segment of the economy inevitably involve the government in other areas. The historical context, in this case World War I, provides evidence that government efforts to control one factor of production, labor, cannot be a simple matter of influencing the quantity and character of that factor. The government simply wanted to find more people to build more ships, but the public involvement in private enterprise forced the government to deal not only with wages and hours but also with housing. In addition, the government became enmeshed in the whole technological transition of shipbuilding through the attempt to have a stable supply of labor. Dr. Mergen concludes that "wartime decisions influenced the character of labor relations in shipbuilding for the next twenty years."

The second pair of essays by James H. Soltow and Harold Issadore Sharlin deal with two separate aspects of the role of entrepreneur: as a determinant of the character of the business environment, and as an architect of progress. These essays illustrate Professor Cochran's argument that "environmental influences gradually molded types of entrepreneurial personality in the industrial society of America that differed from those of England, France, or Germany."[49]

Dr. Soltow's essay, "Structure and Strategy: The Small Manufacturing Enterprise in the Modern Industrial Economy," begins with the hypothesis that, in small business, "structure, or organizational form, is an important determinant of strategy, or the kind of activity carried out by the firm." His analysis of metal fabricators and manufacturers of machinery gives a historical context to Professor Cochran's theory that economic growth depends more on where and how capital is invested than on the absolute quantity of savings.

Since the small entrepreneur prized independence most, financing of his business was arranged so as not to jeopardize his control, and these companies continue to be owner-managed. By finding a niche in the large-scale domestic markets, the small entrepreneur "contributed toward an elaborate division of labor by firms in the United States," Dr. Soltow reports. This corporate division of labor is not a holdover from the preindustrial era, rather the division represents an adaptation to an advanced technological era. Dr. Soltow's depiction of the small entrepreneur's role gives credence to Professor Cochran's idea that the American entrepreneurial tradition has created an economy quite different from Europe's and that in many ways the United States' condition is competitively superior.[50]

In the second essay of this group, "New York's Electricity: Establishing a Technological Paradigm," the role of the entrepreneur in technological innovation is explored. I have often wondered at Professor Cochran's statement that "business decisions, usually in an unplanned way, have been the most important source of physical change."[51] What does "unplanned" mean? Does it mean that impulsive, adventurous business decisions are the cause of technological change or that important physical changes occur because business men and women plan market strategies that have unanticipated results? In other words, is technological change produced as a side effect? Does the idea of "unplanned" agree with Professor Cochran's statement that the entrepreneur was "the architect of change"? Using the word *architect* implies a purposeful effort to control the outcome of technological change.

The idea of technological paradigm that is developed in my essay might be said to deal with this puzzle of planned versus unplanned. The technological paradigm is the innovative way of matching a technology with a market. Pairing results, as Schumpeter has said, through creation of a new good, a new method of production, that is, through new technologies, or adapting an established technology to a new market. The entrepreneur, in most cases, is less interested in technological feasibility than in market potential.

Thus, in the case of Niagara power described in my essay, the entrepreneurs knew little about the engineering aspects of alternating versus direct current electric power, but their search was for an immediate market for Niagara power, and this requirement seemed to settle the issue in spite of engineering advice to the contrary. Their choice was a.c. over d.c. The technology was chosen because it fit the market potential. The technological change was "unplanned" in that the technology was determined not determining. But the Niagara entrepreneurs were "architects of progress" just the same because their decision fixed a technological paradigm that has remained unchanged for almost a century. The question raised by this essay is, How can the technological paradigm, which is a guide to business strategy, be prevented from becoming an obstacle to further progress?

The third pair of essays confront a paradox in Professor Cochran's thinking. If businessmen are products of their culture and are molded by that culture, how can they be agents for social change? Or, to state the paradox in terms of role theory, since the individuals who establish the role model are products of their culture, how is the role model changed? Role theory seems to account for a stable society but not for social change. Professor Cochran acknowledged the problem as being that theory can account for changes in the role playing by leaders of society, but the theory does not explain the interaction between role playing and the general spread of social change.[52] In the first essay of this pair, Stanley Bailis has a suggestion for explaining that interaction. He uses a model for explaining what he calls the habit of habit change, and he tests his model against the unusual source of historical data—the autobiography.

In Dr. Bailis's essay, "Modernization and Habitual Change: A Model Explored Through American Autobiography," the important crises that produced modernization were World War I and the Depression. But in the case described by Ronald H. Bayor, social change, in the form of racial integration, is the cause, not the effect. His essay is about the diffusion of social change through a community by businessmen who were as orthodox in their social beliefs as Professor Cochran's railroad leaders.

Professor Cochran's words, written in 1956, can serve as an introduction to Dr. Bailis's essay: "Innovators may well have had personalities that could be called normal to the culture," that is, the environment forced change and the culture taught people to adapt to change.[53] Dr. Bailis describes this ability to adapt to change as one in which "departing from roles becomes the virtual practice." The model that Dr. Bailis develops is designed to answer why individuals acquire an "increased readiness to change." The model explains how people can acquire the habit of habit change, how that way of thinking can become a role, how the habit of habit change spreads in a society, and how the spread of attitude can produce a societywide cultural change.

The model is tested against autobiographies of Bernard Baruch and Marriner Eccles. Both men earned a great deal of money by departing from established ways of doing business. In the role of speculator, Baruch acquired the habit of habit change by trying to stay ahead of the stock market and adjusting to the business cycle. Once acquired, the habit enabled Baruch to view the economy from a perspective different than that of policy makers. He was converted from the outlook of a laissez-faire entrepreneur to being an advocate of government planning and regulation.

Eccles acquired the habit of habit change in his forays into the unsettled banking world of the 1920s. The habit prepared him for a leadership role in the New Deal era. Baruch and Eccles, Dr. Bailis shows, had quite different social backgrounds, and the evidence indicates that the habit of habit change became pervasive after 1870.

Dr. Bayor's essay, "A City Too Busy to Hate: Atlanta's Business Community and Civil Rights," is a case study of people accommodating and abetting change. Although these businessmen in a Southern city conform to segregationist ways, they recognize that they must change their behavior, if not their thinking, in order to preserve a stable business environment. Atlanta businessmen, like Professor Cochran's railroad leaders, carried out the aims and beliefs of American business society until the force of integration became irresistible, and the business leaders then helped to promulgate the new social objectives. Dr. Bayor found that, even though Atlanta businessmen would not initiate change, they helped to diffuse the change because accommodation to this change, they recognized, was the only way to reduce racial tension that was bad for business. The lesson seems to be that for reformers to diffuse ideas, such as integration, they must apply pressure on the business community by showing them that resistance to change is bad for business, and then businessmen will become allies in promoting change. The business community, one might add, having a firm stake in a socially acceptable outcome, will be powerful allies.

The fourth pair of essays, by Robert H. Walker and Michael Zuckerman, is an appropriate keystone to the Festschrift because they are an ideal illustration of how the social sciences and history complement each other. Dr. Walker's essay describes a simple structure and a common vocabulary with which to discuss reform. His anatomy consists of the uniform characteristics of social change. Dr. Zuckerman begins with origins of American business-social environment relations. He has insights into what is distinct about the relationship and why, in the United States, business's interaction with its environment is so different than it is in the rest of the world. This essay gives further support to Professor Cochran's idea that "the entrepreneur, the agent of change, continued to be differently conditioned than his European counterpart."[54]

Dr. Zuckerman's essay, "Fate, Flux, and Good Fellowship: An Early Virginia Design for the Dilemma of American Business," describes an early eighteenth-century Virginia planter who was, in Professor Cochran's terms, a farmer-businessman. This part-time farmer paid much more attention to business than to growing crops. A colonial entrepreneur, the planter developed a social environment that was counterpart to a business environment, which was much more uncertain than the undependable weather and fluctuating market. Because of extreme conditions of uncertainty, the planter created an extraordinary and uniquely American social life that was shallow by European standards.

In the face of recurring calamities in a business where privateers or Atlantic storms caused staggering losses, the planter, William Byrd, established a system of social relations that consisted of frantic rounds of visits followed by periods when he was host to scores of neighboring planters as well as to close and distant relatives. Byrd's "casual conviviality," Dr. Zuckerman believes, was the first step in establishing community in the colonies, and he contends the Byrd's social life was compatible with the extreme change in his business fortunes.

This relationship between the character of business affairs and of social structure, Dr. Zuckerman declares, was continued into the nineteenth century. As business organizations assumed a more definite shape, in the form of joint stock companies and incorporated businesses, Byrd's type of social life with its rounds of visiting was replaced by a more organized system of voluntary societies, such as lodges, country clubs, and benevolent fraternal organizations. In the twentieth century, Dr. Zuckerman thinks, the business-social structure relationship might mean that the increased security of the business environment will encourage a social structure that is more individualistic in nature than dependent on community.

Businessmen's attitudes described by Dr. Zuckerman have a strong cultural influence because, as Professor Cochran has found in his research, "the ideals of our business leaders become the ideal of the great majority of the people, though only a few were themselves endowed with talent for leadership."[55]

Dr. Walker in his essay, "The Anatomy of American Reform," is interested in the elements of the forces of reform that cause change in the social structure. He is writing about the uniform or social science character of these elements and uses the unique events of history to illustrate his model. Five forms of reform activity comprise the anatomy of American reform: modes, actors, forms, dynamics, and arguments. Dr. Walker asserts that his anatomy is a means of generalizing the notion of reform in American history, and he discusses reform by reference to a simple structure of concepts and a common vocabulary.

Dr. Walker's vocabulary for describing reform as one aspect of social change both distinguishes between and relates the five categories of reform activity. Modes, for example, are something more than goals; they are the essence of what a reform movement is striving to accomplish. If the mode can be identified, then something decisive can be said about the forms, dynamics, and arguments for reform. The actors are those individuals, groups, or institutions that direct the reform initiative.

The dynamics of reform activity, be it "random negative (unorganized protest)" or "structural negative (organized protest)," describes stages of reform in a way that a social scientist would easily understand. Historians, Dr. Walker complains, too often contrast ages of reform to periods of inactivity or eras of apathy, and they miss the point—that social change is a process consisting of identifiable phases. Dr. Walker's contribution to historical discourse is to describe the method of social change so that change can be understood as an ongoing process, as Professor Cochran has maintained, rather than a matter of great leaps from one historical period to the next.[56]

One might say that the questions Professor Cochran has been asking are, What makes the U.S. economy different from the rest of the world? What is the historical cause of the success of the United States in producing and distributing an enormous amount of wealth? His technique for discovering the answer to these questions has been the social sciences, and, using its critical tools, Professor Cochran has found that the pervasive forces were not wars or the captains of industry but the great number of entrepreneurs—organizers of production and agents of change.

This volume is not intended to sum up Professor Cochran's work, as though writing a concluding chapter to his career, but to demonstrate how useful Professor Cochran's approach has been to those who want to analyze the historical causes of social and economic change. The Festschrift is a timely suggestion for policy makers who want to know how the United States can maintain its competitive position in the world. One very helpful approach to the problem of technological lag and falling productivity is to place that problem in historical context, as Professor Cochran has consistently done.

NOTES

1. Thomas C. Cochran, *Frontiers of Change: Early Industrialism in America* (New York and Oxford: Oxford University Press, 1981).

2. Harold Issadore Sharlin, in collaboration with Tiby Sharlin, *Lord Kelvin: The Dynamic Victorian* (University Park: Pennsylvania State University Press, 1979), p. 29.

3. Thomas C. Cochran, "The History of a Business Society," in *The Uses of History* (Wilmington, Del.: Scholarly Resources, 1973), p. 113.

4. Thomas C. Cochran, *Business in America Life: A History* (New York: McGraw-Hill, 1972), pp. 1-6.

5. Cochran, *Uses of History*, pp. 100-101.

6. Cochran, *Business in American Life*, p. 1.

7. Cochran, *Uses of History*, p. 102.

8. Cochran, *Uses of History*, pp. 99-104

9. Charles E. Lindbloom, *Politics and Markets: The World's Political-Economic Systems* (New York: Basic Books, 1977), p. ix.

10. Ibid., p. 356.

11. A good *historically* based argument for this view is Jonathan R. T. Hughes, *The Governmental Habit: Economic Controls from Colonial Times to the Present* (New York: Basic Books, 1977).

12. Arthur H. Cole founded the Research Center for Entrepreneurial History at Harvard in 1948. Professor Cochran was one of the first members of that center.

13. Joseph A. Schumpeter, *The Theory of Economic Development*, new ed. (London: Oxford University Press, 1961), ch. 2. Reprinted 1974.

14. Ibid., p. 66.

15. Cochran, *Business in American Life*, p. 141.

16. Schumpeter, *Theory of Economic Development*, p. 66.

17. Thomas C. Cochran and Ruben Reina, *Entrepreneurship in Argentine Culture* (Philadelphia: University of Pennsylvania Press, 1963), p. 260.

18. Thomas C. Cochran, *American Business in the Twentieth Century* (Cambridge: Harvard University Press, 1972), p. 18.

19. Schumpeter, *Theory of Economic Development*, pp. 67-68.

20. Thomas C. Cochran, "The Entrepreneur in American Capital Formation," in *The Inner Revolution: Essays on the Social Sciences in History* (New York: Harper & Row, 1964), p. 107.

21. Cochran, *Business in American Life*, p. 73.

22. Thomas C. Cochran, "Entrepreneurial History," in *Inner Revolution*, p. 56.

23. Thomas C. Cochran, "A Systematic Approach to Change," in *Uses of History*, p. 36.

24. Ibid., pp. 34-35.

25. Thomas C. Cochran, *Railroad Leaders: The Business Mind in Action, 1845-1890* (Cambridge: Harvard University Press, 1953), p. 218.

26. Ibid., pp. 226-27.

27. Ibid., p. 228.

28. Cochran and Reina, *Entrepreneurship in Argentine Culture*, ch. 8.

29. Alfred D. Chandler, Jr., *Strategy and Structure* (Cambridge, Mass: MIT Press, 1962), pp. 24-29.

30. David S. Landes, *The Unbound Prometheus* (Cambridge: Cambridge University Press, 1972), pp. 66, 84.

31. Cochran, *Business in American Life*, p. 73.

32. Cochran, *Inner Revolution*, p. 179.

33. Thomas C. Cochran and William Miller, *The Age of Enterprise: A Social History of Industrial America*, rev. ed. (New York: Harper & Row, 1961), p. 2.

34. Cochran, *Business in American Life*, p. 2.

35. Cochran, "A Systematic Approach to Change," pp. 33-34.

36. Cochran, *Inner Revolution*, pp. 22-24.

37. For a description and background on the Norristown study, see Professor Cochran's foreword, editor's preface, and chapter 1 of Sidney Goldstein, ed., *The Norristown Study: An Experiment in Interdisciplinary Research Training* (Philadelphia: University of Pennsylvania Press, 1961).

38. Sharlin, *Lord Kelvin*, p. 29.

39. Cochran, "Did the Civil War Retard Industrialization?" in *Inner Revolution*, p. 39.

40. Ibid.

41. Thomas C. Cochran, "Historical Use of the Social Sciences," *Inner Revolution*, p. 28.

42. Simon Kuznets, *Growth, Population, and Income Distribution* (New York: Norton, 1979), pp. 8-10.

43. Cochran, *Inner Revolution*, pp. 46-47.

44. Ibid., pp. 45-46.

45. Ibid., p. 45.

46. Thomas C. Cochran, "The Social Sciences and the Problem of Historical Synthesis," in *The Varieties of History*, ed. Fritz Stern (New York: Vintage Books, 1973), pp. 348-59. Revised from Thomas C. Cochran "The Presidential Synthesis in American History," *American Historical Review* 53 (July 1948): 748-59.

47. Cochran, *Inner Revolution*, p. 2.

48. John Stuart Mill, as quoted in Sharlin, *Lord Kelvin*, p. 10.

49. See supra or Cochran, *Business in American Life*, p. 73.

50. Cochran, *American Business in the Twentieth Century*, p. 74.

51. Cochran, *Business in American Life*, p. 5.

52. Cochran, *Uses of History*, p. 45.

53. Cochran, *Inner Revolution*, p. 74.

54. Cochran, *Business in American Life*, p. 73.

55. Cochran and Miller, *Age of Enterprise*, p. 153.

56. Cochran, *Inner Revolution*, p. 28.

The National Parks: The Business of the Environment

JAMES J. FLINK

The concept of the democratic access to and the preservation of scenic and wilderness areas exemplified in our National Park System is one of America's more significant contributions to world civilization. Roderick Nash points out, "The establishment of Yellowstone Park on March 1, 1872, was the world's first instance of large-scale wilderness preservation in the public interest. Since then we have exported the national park idea around the world."[1] By the 1972 Yellowstone Centennial, the National Park System consisted of 289 units totaling almost 30 million acres of public land. About half this total acreage was accounted for by the 36 areas designated as national parks. Annually the National Park System was accommodating over 200 million visitors. The 1976 Bicentennial year of American independence was celebrated in part by 267,762,100 visits to 293 units of the National Park System representing "treasured historical aspects of our past, cultural aspects of our people, and natural aspects of our land."[2]

An apparent anomaly in our materialistic, exploitive, business-dominated society and culture, the National Park System is the most notable exception to John Muir's cynical 1910 assessment that in America "nothing dollarable is safe, however guarded."[3] For in a society historically oriented toward the wasteful exploitation of natural resources in response to the demands of industrial growth, the National Park System has both continued to expand and remained relatively inviolable, a source of national inspiration and pride. Recognizing this tradition, Ray Lyman Wilbur, Herbert Hoover's secretary of the interior, observed in 1931 that our national parks were one of the few things that future generations would thank us for.[4]

National park policy historically has stood in opposition to the conservationist "wise use" doctrine that has been exemplified in the management of our national forests by the Department of Agriculture. As Samuel P. Hays in particular has demonstrated, "Conservation, above all, was a scientific movement, and its role in history arises from the implications of science and technology in modern society." During the progressive era, conservationists not only pushed for the rational and efficient use of natural resources but "bitterly opposed those who sought to withdraw resources from commercial development." Archetypical conservationist Gifford Pinchot, for example, favored permitting lumbering and grazing in the national parks as well as the construction of the notorious Hetch Hetchy Dam in Yosemite to provide water for the city of San Francisco.[5] A. Hunter Dupree points out that "implicit in the conservation movement even during Roosevelt's administration was a split between those who urged managed use of natural resources and the lovers of the outdoors who wished to preserve nature unspoiled." Contrasting these "aesthetic conservationists" (or preservationists) to "practical conservationists" such as Pinchot, Dupree credits the former with gradually bringing about "an increased appreciation of parks and monuments." He observes, that "because of the dominance of the idea of conservation for use in the Forest Service and the Department of Agriculture, the nature lovers looked to the Department of the Interior" to implement their goal of "using the parks as outdoor living museums of nature."[6]

Conception of our national parks as "outdoor living museums of nature" by preservationists in turn has entailed a dilemma that historically has dominated debate over national park policy from their inception, for the parks have been dedicated to serve the apparently antithetical purposes of wilderness preservation and mass recreation. Although Yellowstone was "dedicated and set apart as a public park or pleasuring ground for the benefit and enjoyment of the people," Congress also intended that "rules and regulations . . . provide for the preservation, from injury or spoilation, of all timber, mineral deposits, natural curiosities, or wonders within said park, and their retention in their natural condition." The presidential order of August 25, 1916, establishing the National Park Service (NPS) to regulate the national parks and the national monuments, similarly included the directive "to conserve the scenery and the natural and historic objects and the wild life therein and to provide for the enjoyment of the same in such manner and by such means as will leave them unimpaired for future generations." Succeeding legislation and administrative policy statements affecting the National Park System have continued to mandate use consistent with preservation while the National Park Service underwent fundamental change. The purview of the National Park Service, for example, was widened by a 1933 presidential executive order to include national cemeteries, military parks, and the urban parks system of Washington, D.C. The Historic Sites Act of 1935 (expanded by the National Historic Preservation Act of 1966) deepened NPS involvement in historic, as opposed to wilderness, preservation. And the NPS was moved further into the field of mass public recreation by the Park, Parkway, and Recreation Study Act of 1936, which charged the service with administering national parkways, recreation areas, and seashores in cooperation with other governmental agencies, such as the Bureau of Reclamation. Recognizing the heterogeneity of the National Park System, on July 10, 1964, Secretary of the Interior Stewart L. Udall issued a long-overdue statement of management principles calling for different management concepts for the natural areas, the historical areas, and the recreational areas in the system. The Wilderness Act, passed on September 3, 1964, then further attempted to resolve the growing conflict between wilderness preservation and mass recreation by requiring the National Park Service to review, for inclusion in the National Wilderness System, all roadless park areas 5,000 acres or more in size and to make specific recommendations for wilderness areas within the national parks. The act further banned the internal-combustion engine from these designated wilderness areas, marking a turning point in public policy.[7]

Yellowstone and the other early parks were established neither to preserve wilderness nor to provide mass recreation. Rather, they were primarily congressional concessions to small groups of dedicated people whose main goal was protecting "natural wonders" and curiosities, such as geysers and hot springs, from commercial exploitation. The average citizen was apathetic about the parks because they were located in remote regions far from the major centers of population and because transportation to and through the parks was primitive and expensive. The vast majority of Americans also held an exploitive attitude toward natural resources. Indeed, the early parks were established only after considerable pressure by special interest groups and after Congress determined that the land was unsuitable for other uses. The report on Yellowstone by the House Committee on the Public Lands, for example, emphasized that the park would take "nothing from the value of the public domain" and "was no pecuniary loss to the government." In the words of Alfred Runte, "Yellowstone would not have become the first national park in the country if it had contained anything of solid economic value. . . . Almost without exception the National Park System became a means to preserve scenic refuges that very few developers or businessmen had wanted to exploit in the first place." Elsewhere Runte has pointed out that "in those instances when Congress was called upon to make a choice between parks and profits, almost without exception the encouragement of business took precedence over the protection of the environment."[8]

Even more important than the fact that business values and priorities have established the parameters within which the National Park System has developed from its origins is that our national parks have become increasingly profitable to the American business system. The Western railroads were the first businesses to seek and find profits in the development of the national parks. Then park development came to be primarily a function of the automobile revolution, which greatly increased access. Democratic access to the parks by automobile necessitated building improved roads within the parks and an interconnected system of improved highways to them and has been an important stimulus to the maturation of many tourist- and recreation-related industries, in addition to the increased business that travel to the parks has generated over the years for automobile manufacturers, oil companies, and ancillary industries. The stimulus to the American economy of over 267 million visits in 1976 alone to units of the National Park System is perhaps incalculable but nevertheless staggering to contemplate. Government statistics on participation in outdoor recreation for the period June 1976 to June 1977 reveal that 62 percent of the American population twelve years old and over participated in sightseeing at historic or national sites, 30 percent camped in developed and an additional 21 percent in undeveloped areas, and 28 percent hiked or backpacked. During the 1970s about 25 percent of all travel over one hundred miles from home by Americans was for purposes of outdoor recreation and/or sightseeing, activities in which the national parks played a central role.[9] An indication of the economic value of the national parks to surrounding communities is that in 1978 the park service issued some 218,000 fishing permits in Yellowstone, one for every ten visitors. "There are at least twelve states that have fewer total licensed anglers than that. . . . Fishing is an industry in Yellowstone. Anglers spend about $4 million annually in and near the park, so that a local economy depends in part on their trade."[10]

Contrary to Muir's contention, perhaps the best hope that the national parks remain safe from exploitation by the extractive industries and power interests is that they have become "dollarable" to so many other segments of the American business system. The thorny problem here, however, is that the profitability of the parks to the business system is positively related to a high level of use and to emphasis on mass recreation—tendencies that are increasingly viewed as incompatible with the preservation of fragile park ecosystems and the quality of "the park experience" for visitors.

Recognizing the truism that in a democratic society strong public support was essential to park development, the National Park Service from its inception until very recently encouraged a high level of use of park facilities with its policy, "Parks are for people," which, according to Edward Abbey, decoded to mean: "Parks are for people-in-automobiles."[11] The overriding concern of the NPS in the immediate post-World War II period was that the deterioration during the war of park visitor facilities—"washboard" roads, run-down campgrounds, and inadequate in-park food service and lodgings—discouraged a higher rate of park use by the motoring public. The Eisenhower administration responded with Mission 66, an ambitious ten-year program to rehabilitate, upgrade, and expand park facilities. With the phenomenal success of Mission 66—120 million park visits were recorded in 1966 rather than the target goal of 80 million—NPS concern abruptly shifted. By the 1972 Yellowstone centennial, preservationist organizations and the NPS were alarmed about an alleged "overuse" of the national parks that was widely held to be antithetical both to the preservation of wilderness and to the quality of the so-called park experience. The alleged deleterious impact of increased automobile traffic in the parks became a particular focus of attention. Plans began to be made and implemented for establishing "carrying capacities" for the parks; limiting access through entry quotas and reservation systems; cutting back on overnight camping facilities; moving visitor facilities into the surrounding national forests and gateway towns; and even banning access to

some areas by private passenger cars. Alarmed by these trends away from democratic access to the parks by automobile, the leading historian of the road and the
car, John B. Rae, said in 1971:

There would appear to be a heavy burden of proof on those who would restrict access by
car to scenic or recreational attractions. These areas are the heritage of all the people; on
what grounds are we to justify excluding the great majority of the people because the only
way they can get there is by automobile?[12]

***

The key to national park development has always been transportation technology and the needs of transportation interests. The early parks were in the main
the result of what Runte calls a "pragmatic alliance" between upper-class
preservationists and the Western railroads. Jay Cooke and Company, promoters
and financiers of the Northern Pacific Railroad extension project, were centrally
involved in winning congressional approval for Yellowstone. Southern Pacific
Railroad lobbyists campaigned for Yosemite, Sequoia, and General Grant, and
the Southern Pacific became the leading booster of West Coast national parks.
Grand Canyon was pushed by the Santa Fe Railroad. And Louis W. Hill of the
Great Northern enthusiastically supported the creation of Glacier National Park
as part of his railroad's "See America First" campaign. Western railroads spent
vast sums of money advertising the national parks and were also responsible for
inaugurating "proper" tourist facilities—the grand hotels at major visitor attractions. Runte concludes,

Every major Western railroad played a crucial role in the establishment, protection, and
improvement of national parks. Of course the managers of the lines were not being
altruistic or environmentally conscious; their aim was to promote tourism and thereby
increase profits....Tourism at that time, however encouraged, provided the national
parks with a solid economic justification for their existence. No argument was more vital
in a nation unwilling to accept scenic preservation at the cost of business achievement.[13]

Dependence upon railroad and horse and wagon transportation imposed stulti-
fying limitations on park development and was responsible for the establishment
of ecologically unsound development patterns that the automobile inherited and
minimally changed. Prior to the automobile revolution of the 1920s, extended
vacations away from home were the prerogative of a privileged upper class. The
average middle-class family could not afford railroad fares to a remote Western
park and a long stay at a luxury hotel. Stays in the parks had to be long because,
although the railroad transported one swiftly and in comfort to the park periph-
ery, travel through the park by horse-drawn coach over the few crude roads was
slow and arduous. Consequently, the grand hotels and other tourist facilities had
to be clustered not only within park boundaries but in close proximity to major

scenic attractions. Similarly, because the parks were visited by so few people, Congresss was loath to provide money for road building. Consequently, roads were built as cheaply as possible, most often following stream beds or connecting major scenic attractions along the easiest natural routes available. In addition, as John Ise describes early conditions in Yellowstone,

With hundreds of horses around, stabled near the hotels, it was inevitable that there should be a great deal of unpleasant litter and flies. As late as 1907 Secretary [of the Interior] Garfield reported that the hotels were good but around the barns and stables there were masses of manure, rubbish, waste material, and dump from the hotels, as there were also around the permanent camps. The "horse and buggy days" lacked a few points in sanitation.[14]

The point here is that the intense use of any form of transportation poses inevitable environmental problems.

Three transcontinental crossings by automobile in 1903 inaugurated informal touring by the average driver. And with the advent of the moderately priced car and improved roads in the 1920s, the automobile outing and the automobile vacation became national institutions. As Foster Rhea Dulles says in his history of American recreation, the automobile "greatly stimulated the whole outdoor movement, making camping possible for many people for whom the woods, mountains, and streams were formerly inaccessible."[15] The early impact of automobility on the national parks has been succinctly summarized by Robert Shankland in his biography of Steven T. Mather, first director of the National Park Service: "The auto reached swarming ubiquity fast—faster than people now remember. As the auto prospered so did the national parks."[16] Recognizing that park development was intimately linked to the growth of tourism, Mather energetically built a "pragmatic alliance" between the NPS and automobile interests throughout the country.

Automobiles were first admitted into Mount Ranier in 1908, General Grant in 1910, Crater Lake in 1911, Glacier in 1912, Yosemite and Sequoia in 1913, Mesa Verde in 1914, and Yellowstone in 1915. As early as 1916 more visitors entered Yosemite by automobile than by railroad, and the largest source of revenue for the newly formed National Park Service already was automobile admission fees—levied for paying for park roads and improvements. Mather, along with other prominent preservationists, welcomed the automobile into the parks because he recognized the potential political power of the automobile industry, automobile clubs, and the growing number of automobile tourists. A broad base of popular support was deemed essential to the parks both to obtain adequate congressional funding for development and maintenance and to thwart mounting pressure for the exploitation of park resources from commercial interests and other governmental agencies. The main opposition to opening the parks to the automobile came, significantly, not from the preservationists but from park concessionaires who operated horse-drawn stage lines. Their fears were

borne out when Mather ordered Yellowstone's stage lines motorized in 1917, a
scant two years after the automobile was admitted into that park. On the other
hand, automobilists were prominent in many early preservationist organizations,
an example being that the Save the Redwoods League originated at the Pacific
Auto Show of 1920.

Although railroad travel to the national parks continued to increase into the
1930s and coach-class fares from Chicago to points west were halved between
1921 and 1936, automobile travel for a family was cheaper as well as more
convenient and, consequently, by the late 1920s came to surpass in volume travel
to the parks by train. As Earl Pomeroy writes,

The automobile represented a new democratization of vacation travel. In the same years
when the average American had more time for trips away from home and more money to
spend on them, he could buy gasoline to carry his whole family from his own front door
for what he alone would have to pay to ride the train. The growing western highway
systems, growing in response to his demands, represented his expanding opportunity and
the opportunity of the sections that they fed.

He goes on to say, "What the motor cars and the motorists did to the outdoors
would be long debated, but there is little doubt that the age of the automobile was
the age in which the average American vacationer first found the West within his
reach." With this democratization of travel, "a mass market became more important to the tourist industry as a whole than the patronage of the elite. The great
profits in the Western tourist and vacation industry came not from serving squab
to the few but from selling gasoline, hamburger sandwiches, and postcards to the
many."[17]

Automobile travel into the national parks increased phenomenally with the
success of the good roads movement in the 1920s. The Federal Highway Act of
1921 provided fifty-fifty matching grants to the states for highway construction
that was financed at the state level by universal adoption of the gasoline tax by
1929. This resulted in an interconnected system of paved highways that made
even the more remote Western parks accessible to the average family. Moreover,
agitation by the National Parks Highway Association, formed in 1915, resulted
in a route that interconnected all national parks being laid out and signposted by
the early 1920s. This interpark route was not totally paved. Nevertheless, it
served as a psychological as well as a physical link among the national parks and
encouraged travel to them.

Until at least the mid-1930s, however, good roads ended at the boundaries of
the national parks. In 1915 Yellowstone was the only park with sufficient road
mileage to make driving worthwhile, and all park roads were not only unpaved
but were too narrow and had grades too steep for automobile traffic. Up to 1924 a
total of only $3.5 million had been spent on park roads, with the result that as late
as 1924 there were only 12 miles of paved road in the entire National Park
System, and Glacier and Mount McKinley still lacked through roads. Although

by 1924 Yosemite had 138 miles of rutted wagon road, all except 20 miles were private. With 356 miles of unpaved road for a land area larger than several of our Eastern states, Yellowstone still had the best road system of any national park.

The turning point came in 1923, when Congress appropriated $7.5 million for road building in the national parks between 1924 and 1927. However, altitude, a short working season, rocky terrain, and preservationist considerations made the cost of building new paved park roads extremely high—$20,000 to $60,000 a mile. Consequently, although some 360 miles of new park roads were planned, paving the bulk of either these or existing park roads was out of the question. So the appropriation was used primarily to reduce grades, straighten sharp curves, and widen existing wagon roads to handle automobile traffic more safely. The philosophy of park road building early adopted by the NPS was first laid down by Hiram Chittenden, the Army Corps of Engineers officer in charge of building many of Yellowstone's wagon roads:

As a general policy the extension of the [park road] system should be restricted to actual necessities. The park should be preserved in its natural state to the fullest degree possible.... and the great body of the park should be kept inaccessible except on foot or horseback. But a road once found necessary should be made as perfect as possible. So far as it may detract from scenery it is far less objectionable as a well-built work than if left in a rough or incomplete state.[18]

Translated into policy, this meant a limitation to one well-built, low-speed, scenic through road per park—an NPS policy that remains in effect to this day.

Roads were first made adequate to the demands of automobile traffic in our national parks as a byproduct of increased governmental spending to stimulate the economy during the Great Depression of the 1930s. Although the number of park visitors remained about the same as in 1929, for example, park appropriations were nearly doubled in 1931; and between January 31, 1931, and July 21, 1932, Congress appropriated over $13 million specifically for road building and improvement in the national parks and monuments. Where the Hoover administration measured, the Roosevelt administration poured funds, inaugurating what has been called "the golden age of national park development." According to William Everhart, "In the seven hectic years from 1933 to 1940, the Park Service received $220 million for projects from a variety of emergency relief agencies."[19] A major use of these funds was a massive program of rebuilding and paving park roads, as well as the addition of several impressive new scenic through roads, including the Zion-Mount Carmel road and tunnel, Wawona tunnel and road in Yosemite, the Cape Royal road in Grand Canyon, the Paradise Valley and Yakima Park Highway in Mount Ranier, the Sylvan Pass road in Yellowstone, and the Going-to-the-Sun road in Glacier.

Further development of park roads was abruptly curtailed by the outbreak of World War II, which saw the National Park Service's operating budget reduced from $21 million in 1940 to a low of only $5 million in 1943. But wartime rationing of gasoline and tires and a ban on passenger car production for the civilian market also meant so drastic a decline in park use that most parks might as well have been closed for the duration of the war. Although the war's end brought a record 22 million visitors to the parks in 1946, NPS budgets remained stringent through the Korean War. The result was that in 1949 it was estimated that some $321 million was needed to rehabilitate park facilities, whereas the NPS budget was only $14 million. Everhart points out that "by 1954 the parks were absorbing 54 million visitors a year, with a level of staff and the run-down facilities [including park roads] designed for the 17 million visitors in 1940."[20]

A significant point is that as late as the mid-1950s literally no one was concerned about "overuse" of the national parks. Nor was there evidence that the impact of the road and the car had been deleterious. In fact, road building in the parks still lagged significantly behind the increase in automobile traffic in the parks and only moderately exceeded the increase in park acreage. From 1924 to 1947, for example, $107 million was spent on national park roads, and total park road mileage was increased about five times—from 1,060 to 5,387 miles. However, during this same period total park acreage almost tripled—from 13,230 to 33,720 square miles. On the other hand, the number of automobiles entering the parks skyrocketed from 330,000 in 1924 to over 7 million in 1947, an increase of twenty-one fold. Thus the impact of the automobile on road building in the parks was incremental rather than dramatic. As late as 1961, John Ise, the eminent historian of the national parks, could declare with little fear of contradiction:

In an hour's walk from the most congested area of Yellowstone, one can lose himself in a wild forest where there is little scent of man. The lover of nature who does not like to drive his car over the glorious Going-to-the-Sun Highway in Glacier can walk or ride horseback across the divide—horseback if he can get a horse. He has about every freedom that he had before the road was built.[21]

Ise's comment is indeed typical of those found in the early 1960s in the *National Parks Magazine*, journal of the National Parks Association, the leading preservationist critic of the National Park Service since 1919.

In the mid-1950's preservationists viewed inadequate appropriations and deteriorating facilities as the main problems of the National Park System. Therefore, they enthusiastically supported Mission 66, which brought park facilities up to standards by 1966 at a cost to the taxpayers of over one billion dollars. As a consequence, by the mid-1960s the preservationists were attributing the problems of the national parks not to poverty but to affluence. Mission 66 had succeeded, now said the preservationists, in encouraging too many people demanding too many conveniences to spend too much time in our national parks. Still, as late as 1965, the annual report of the National Parks Association claimed that "the difficult dilemma of protection as against visitation has been solved in principle; practical application should not be unduly difficult as time goes on," and an editorial in the *National Parks Magazine* that year went so far as to find "no contradiction between wilderness protection and mass recreation if the double objective is approached by comprehensive regional planning." In 1966 *National Parks Magazine* still thought that the main threat to the parks came not from people in automobiles but from an expanding population: "Although much publicity has been given to overdevelopment, the biggest threat to our wilderness areas, national parks, and scenic splendors is not four-lane highways or power projects or housing developments. They are only symptoms of the real pressure on our irreplaceable natural resources: the pressure of people." After this, however, antiautomobile sentiment crystalized rapidly into official National Parks Association policy. In a diametric reversal of its 1966 statements, the association claimed in early 1968, "The great problem in the national parks is not people, and perhaps not even shelter, but the private automobile." Beyond protecting the wilderness against the automobile, the association now claimed that it had become "a question of protecting the people against the [automobile] traffic."[22] Similarly, the Conservation Foundation report of 1972 alleged,

Automobiles are inconsistent with the preservation mission, with what is called "the park experience" and with even the most rudimentary ethic. It is not now feasible to recommend that private automobiles be banned from every unit of the National Park System, but that would be our choice. We do recommend this: first, an immediate moratorium on road building, parking lots, and other auto-oriented improvements; second, appointment by the secretary of the interior of a special commission to study the entire question of private automobiles in the parks and alternative methods of intrapark transportation.[23]

***

This abrupt change in preservationist attitudes was part of a broader reaction against the road and the car in the late 1960s and early 1970s. Concern about the automobile in the parks coincided with widespread acceptance of what can best be called the Yosemite fallacy. On June 24, 1966, the *Wall Street Journal* published a front-page story titled, "Ah Wilderness; Severe Overcrowding Brings Ills of the City to Scenic Yosemite." The article claimed that on an average summer day the Yosemite Valley had a population density per square mile three times greater than Los Angeles County. It described conditions in Yosemite as follows:

The damp night air, heavy with a pall of eyewatering smoke, is cut by the blare of transistor radios, the clatter of pots and pans, the roar of a motorcycle, and the squeals of teenagers. Except for hundreds of shiny aluminum trailers and multicolored tents squeezed into camping areas, this might be any city after dark.

In October 1967 a writer in *National Parks Magazine* reported, "Apparently stimulated by this story, a number of national magazines and newspapers have run articles about overuse of the national parks until now it is knowingly referred to by almost anyone you talk to. It has even been on TV." Yosemite is one of the few national parks an easy drive from two major population centers, the San Francisco Bay area and Los Angeles. And the writer noted that the Yosemite situation was otherwise unique: In no other park were nearly as many as 1.7 million automobile tourists being annually accommodated in an area only seven miles long by two miles wide that was also particularly pollution prone because it was bounded by sheer granite walls. The writer even admitted, "Such severe problems can be avoided in other parks by building more facilities." Nevertheless, in a perverse twist of reasoning he concluded, "Perhaps it is fortunate that this opportunity is not available in Yosemite, as it is forcing attention on the problem *before it occurs in all of our most famous wilderness parks*"(emphasis added).[24]

Facile overgeneralization by the media and preservationists thus built the case that Yosemite was a harbinger of impending disaster for Yellowstone and Grand Teton—a land area that was larger than the states of Rhode Island and Delaware combined, remote from population centers, and easily accommodated 2 million visitors a year. No firm evidence supported the allegations. They were investigated by Robert Cahn, for example, who reported his findings in a series of sixteen articles for the *Christian Science Monitor*, "Will Success Spoil the National Parks?" that won a Pulitzer Prize for reporting in 1969. After six months of research and 20,000 miles of travel, Cahn found that there was overcrowding in the national parks, but "only during the peak periods of use," and he concluded that "on the basis of my observations, the National Park System appears to be in relatively good physical condition. No disaster situation is evident." Similarly, the blue-ribbon National Parks Centennial Commission concluded in 1972 that, after two generations of coexistence with mass personal automobility, "the properties entrusted to the [National Park] Service are generally in far better condition today than at the time they were taken into the [National Park] System."[25]

Hysteria over alleged deterioration of the parks in the late 1960s resulted in large part from the almost complete absence of a historical perspective on park problems. The conditions complained about in Yosemite by the *Wall Street Journal* in 1966, for example, were not, as the article implied, of recent origin. The same complaints had been made as early as 1937 by Lewis Gannett:

The gleaming granite walls of the canyon and the tremendous water-leaps were all that we had dreamed; but the floor of Yosemite is an amusement park, as crowded a city as New York's Central Park, and only twice as large. There, if you come at dusk as we did, you see crowds waiting, behind Hollywood Kleig lights, to see the bears eat hotel garbage as if on a spotlit stage. From a peak above the tent cities each night a campfire is shoved over the cliff to make a gaudy "fire-fall," announced by shouts that desecrate the valley as if a loudspeaker were there proclaiming the virtues of some vile toothpaste. And in the tents portable radio sets murmur Los Angeles jazz.

Nothing in America is less wild that the floor of Yosemite Valley. Once it was a wild garden; now it is a dead museum. There is, indeed, a little museum garden, intelligently maintained by the park naturalists; but they have to bring in the wild flowers from far corners of the park. Campers and the herd of tame deer long ago trampled and browsed all the original garden floor into a semblance of a city square. When you "camp" in a space six miles long and a mile wide, with several thousand other "campers" in tents set up so close to one another that the guy-ropes cross, you do not camp at all.[26]

The grandeur of its scenery notwithstanding, Yosemite has not been a wilderness park in reality for over a generation, and its valley no longer has much of a "natural" ecosystem to preserve. In an ultimately rejected master plan, for example, the objectives of resource management in Yosemite focused not on preservation but on

restoring altered systems as nearly as possible to the conditions they would be in today had ecological processes not been disturbed and, when practical, by reintroducing species which have been eliminated from the natural systems. In heavy-use areas, such as Yosemite Valley, additional management programs will be utilized to simulate natural processes and to restore natural settings and vistas.

Similar to the San Diego Zoo or Lion Country Safari, Yosemite would allow visitors the opportunity "to view and enjoy wildlife in an atmosphere of minimal artificiality." The attempt to "restore Yosemite Valley's natural appearance to the greatest extent possible" ironically would involve the burning and selective cutting of "former meadows.... partially obscured by trees" because the open meadows that so impressed early visitors were in fact due not to nature but to the continual burning back of the forest by the Indians. Similarly, stocking fish in the high lakes (begun in 1877) would be discontinued despite its recreational value because the lakes were initially devoid of fish. However, exotic trout introduced into the lower watercourses would not be eliminated because "the native race of rainbow trout is no longer in existence." And although Yosemite was once literally ruled by *Ursus horibilis*, the NPS recognizes that "the high level of visitor use would make reintroduction of the grizzly bear inadvisable"—an especially sensible decision because the last known sighting of a California "golden" grizzly occurred in 1922.[27]

The bulk of physical damage that the national parks has sustained was inflicted before the National Park Service was formed; and since 1916 the bulk of physical damage to the parks is attributable to natural disasters and park service mismanagement. Before the rangers and the people in automobiles came to the parks, large herds of sheep and cattle grazed freely in Yosemite Valley; logging operations and market hunting were carried on in Yellowstone; and Mesa Verde's archaeological treasures were being decimated by vandals and souvenir seekers. Park service pest and predator control programs led to explosions of park ungulate populations; the ungulates, in turn, ravaged park flora. Yellowstone's history, for example, has seen park service destruction of over 1,200 bears and, prior to the winter of 1934-35, of 121 cougars, 131 wolves, and 4,352 coyotes. As a consequence, the Yellowstone elk herd increased to the point that the elk had entirely destroyed many of the park's aspen groves by the 1960s, resulting in another program to kill off the park's surplus elk. Forest fires set by careless campers and hikers generally have been especially destructive in the parks because park forests are overly protected against accumulations of underbrush being normally burned off by small lightning-caused fires. Floods and droughts have also taken their toll—often aided and abetted by federally financed Army Corps of Engineers and Bureau of Reclamation projects that impinge on park ecosystems, the current destruction of the Everglades being a prime example. And Yellowstone's irreplaceable thermal features were changed profoundly by the earthquake that began a few minutes before midnight on August 17, 1959. The quake made Old Faithful far less faithful, lowered the temperature that gave Morning Glory pool its unique color, created a new lake outside the park, and came close to permanently damming off the lower Madison River—ironically prevented by the Army Corps of Engineers promptly blasting open the river's channel with explosives.[28]

Compared with this complex of forces, the impact of people in automobiles on park ecosystems has been not only moderate but in several respects beneficial. Although the automobile revolution tremendously increased the number of visitors to the parks, it also drastically reduced the average length of the park visit from several weeks in the railroad and wagon era to only thirty-one hours in Yellowstone by the early 1970s. The vast majority of automobile tourists have little impact on the park ecosystem because they are content to view wildlife and scenic attractions in close proximity to their cars and spend almost all of their time in the park driving, stopping at the few major visitor centers, or chatting with the people in the next campsite. Indeed, Paul Shullery, a former Yellowstone ranger, has observed,

Hikers, who generally regard themselves as the most environmentally holy, dig trail ruts and cause erosion. It can be argued that a single hiker traveling on foot through a park's back country does far more damage to the natural systems than does the average car - and road-bound automobilist. The goal of complete primitiveness is unattainable as long as the park service honors that half of its mandate requiring it to make the parks available for human enjoyment.[29]

The speed and flexibility of the automobile permitted the development outside park boundaries in the gateway towns of tourist facilities that otherwise, even given a far lower number of park visitors, undoubtedly would have continued to proliferate near major scenic attractions within the parks. Had mass personal automobility not developed in the United States, it also seems doubtful that transportation within the parks would forever have relied on the horse and wagon traveling over primitive roads. Street railways were common in cities, and it seems probable that sooner or later major visitor attractions in the early parks would have been interconnected by a system of fixed rails and overhead wires, incurring at least as much damage to park ecosystems as park road systems have.

Democratic access by automobile, furthermore, was and remains the main reason for strong public support for the acquisition of park lands and for the protection of park resources from exploitation. That the infamous Hetch Hetchy Dam and Reservoir, built in Yosemite in 1913 to provide water for San Francisco, remains the only such structure in the parks is no accident. Schemes to build a series of dams on the Yellowstone River in the 1930s and in Grand Canyon on the Colorado River in the 1960s failed for one significant reason: countless letters to congressmen from irate constituents who recognized the value of preserving the parks because they had visited them. This is a particularly cogent point because the current mania for development of energy resources is already having a deleterious impact on park environments.

***

Viewed from this perspective, the problem is that access to our national parks has not been democratic enough. A 1968 survey, for example, showed visitors to our national parks to be almost exclusively white and middle class. As Everhart says,

No one would seriously contest that visiting parks and historic sites is an activity directly proportional to income. National Parks are essentially a middle-class experience. They are hardly within the scope of families hard-pressed for bus fare to travel to the local zoo. The culturally disadvantaged are not a significant part of the statistics of national park travel, and black families are seldom encountered in the campgrounds.[30]

This is an understatement: The typical working-class family rarely utilized the national parks until at least the late 1950s. As late as 1950 41 percent of all American families still did not own automobiles, as compared with only 17 percent of families being without a car by 1970. And family ownership of cars is significantly lower in big cities, with four families out of ten being without cars in New York City and about half of the population of the San Francisco Bay Area being entirely dependent on mass transit. For almost all urban working-class families, personal automobility combined with sufficient income and the leisure time to visit a remote national park became a reality within only the last two decades, and, contrary to cultural myth, "the park experience" remains largely the prerogative of the privileged. The extent to which this is true was revealed in testimony given in the Senate on June 8, 1977, before the Subcommittee on Parks and Recreation of the Committee on Energy and Natural Resources. Robert L. Herbst, assistant secretary for fish and wildlife and parks, Department of the Interior, pointed out, "Approximately 75 percent of all national park visitors are members of the 15 percent upper-income segment of the population (35 million upper-middle-income Americans account for 170 to 180 million park visits.) The remaining 180 million Americans, with lower economic status, make up the remaining 85 to 90 million park visits."[31]

One can only conjecture the extent to which upper- and middle-class preservationists by the mid-1960s were alarmed perhaps not so much by the increased number of people using the parks as by the fact that the parks were increasingly being used by people whose social values and life styles they found objectionable. Increased use by middle-class, tent-camping, fly-fishing professors might be tolerable. But could wilderness withstand a horde of Archie Bunkers equipped with four-wheel-drive campers, trail bikes, and spinning tackle? In a well-researched, as yet unpublished paper on off-the-road recreational vehicles, William Rhodes suggests the dimensions of this class conflict over wilderness use:

Surveys of snowmobile users, for example, revealed that the average snowmobile owner is a rural dwelling, married man, forty-two years of age with two children, [or] a blue-collar worker who has not attended college, and who earns in the neighborhood of $10,000 a year. Environmentalists and skiers on the other hand tend to be the educated upper-middle class.

Rhodes cites a letter to the editor of *Ski* magazine that was written in response to a story on snowmobiling that included a picture of a stout father of a seven-child snowmobiling family:

The article on snowmobiling was fascinating reading. I was particularly enthralled by the photo of Bill Ward, of Steep Falls, Me., and his delightful family. Can it be more than an obscene coincidence that these same shallow types who overload their bodies with fat and double chins are at the same time violators of Zero Population Growth and totally uncaring about what ecological disasters they commit with their bloody snowmobiles?

Just study that photograph! One need not be especially sensitive to feel waves of revulsion that fellow Americans (or humans) can be such intellectual pygmies that they get their jollies by ravaging the final limits of our frontiers, that they disturb wildlife, add to already unacceptable levels of noise and air pollution, and make general nuisances of themselves with their puerile goings-on.[32]

In addition to these so-called shallow types, by the mid-1960s the national parks had also become havens for a variety of counterculture groups. Everhart, for example, notes,

A number of subcultures have made up the customary pattern of park visitors: families, always the largest single unit, along with campers, tour groups, backpackers, retired couples. To these have been added in recent years a new subgroup, variously identified as "flower children," "long hairs," or "earth people," "bikers of the motorcycle brotherhood," and the political "revolutionaries." On the first travel holiday weekend of the first year of the new decade, representatives of these countercultures triggered the first civil riot within a national park.

The reference is to the July 3, 1970, bloody encounter between several hundred young people and park rangers at Stoneman's Meadow in Yosemite.[33] With the influx of these counterculture groups, narcotics, thefts, and assaults became part of "the park experience." And middle-class families who had looked to the parks as a refuge from the ills of an urban-industrial society began to feel threatened by their neighbors in the campgrounds.

Ignoring the importance of class and subcultural conflicts over wilderness use, the environmental historian Roderick Nash claims:

For the devotee of wilderness. . .a campground full of Boy Scouts, or even of people like himself, is just as destructive of the essence of wilderness as a highway. Any definition of wilderness implies an absence of civilization, and wilderness values are so fragile that even appropriate kinds of recreational use detract from and, in sufficient quantity, destroy wilderness.

On the assumption that "wilderness is. . .a 'game' that, by definition, cannot be played at any one time and place by more than a few people," Nash argues for limiting access through quotas based upon "psychological carrying capacity. . .the effect of other people's presence on the experience of a visitor to the wilderness."[34]

To use quotas based on "psychological carrying capacity" as opposed to physical and/or biological carrying capacity may be appropriate in primitive areas or some specially designated wilderness subareas within the national parks—areas that in any event are accessible primarily to the young, the vigorous, and the adventuresome. But to equate "the park experience" with a wilderness experience and thus to impose "solitude" as a cardinal goal on the mass of park visitors who do not seek it would be unconscionable; and to ration access to the overwhelming majority of park visitor attractions on debatable psychological grounds would be absurd. How viewing the grandeur of the Grand Canyon or an eruption of Old Faithful is diminished by the number of viewers simultaneously sharing the experience, for example, is difficult to understand. Why recreational activities compatible with physical and/or biological carrying capacity should be prohibited in the parks is equally difficult to understand, as is the idea that public campgrounds used mainly by families in recreational vehicles should somehow meet the expectations of backpackers.

Research has revealed significant differences in the social meaning of camping for wilderness campers and users of developed public campgrounds. Whereas wilderness campers seek the challenge of outdoor living in solitude, camping in developed public campgrounds is valued as a group activity, with the family as the basic social unit, and sociability rather than outdoor resources provides the main motivation for camping. Public campground users also reveal "a desire. . .to add urban comforts to the camp site" and see camping as "most desirable if it is not too different from the mode of social life to which the individuals are accustomed to in their domestic environment." As a consequence,

users of public campgrounds exclusively restrict their camping to this type, while the same holds true for wilderness campers. Of the combined totals of three surveys conducted during 1960-61 by the Census Bureau, 65 percent of all campers camped in developed areas only, 33 percent camped in undeveloped areas only, and only 2 percent camped in both.[35]

Traditional views of camping have become increasingly outmoded by the realities of public campgrounds. "Many campgrounds, once primitive and small, are now large and intensively developed with water systems, flush toilets, paved roads, increased supervision, and special facilities for trailers that now house nearly half of all campers," Clark, Hendee, and Campbell point out in a recent study of modern camping culture. "Campers are no longer required to forfeit many comforts of the urban environment to enjoy outdoor recreation. Equally important, the range of available camping behaviors, once limited by primitive conditions, has increased." The pattern has been one of the "invasion and succession" by the masses of naturally attractive locations initially accessible only to wilderness campers. "Consequently, a new camping style emerged with associated behavioral expectations less dependent on direct environmental contact, more compatible with highly developed structures, and increasingly social conditions."[36] Putting it another way, in his indispensible study of auto camping from 1910 to 1945, Warren J. Belasco observes:

It is an irony of modern travel that those who flee "off the beaten path" often beat a path for those they flee. Students of mass tourism have observed that, in the evolution of a popular attraction, the initial "discovery" is invariably made by nonconformist "drifters" who are deliberately seeking to escape crowded, overly institutionalized vacation places. In a consumption-based economy, however, the ability to purchase contrast cannot usually be confined to a small elite. But democratization inevitably changes the view. With numbers comes a specialized tourist infrastructure to control, service, and exploit the increased flow.[37]

Despite the development of such a modern campground institutional infrastructure and correspondingly supportive attitudes among campground users, "Traditional views of camping form the basis for most campground rules and regulations, and constitute managers' expectations of appropriate campground behavior." Clark, Hendee, and Campbell demonstrate, for example, that campground users have a far lower level of expectation regarding the "wilderness" aspects of camping than do campground managers: "Although recreationists seem to subscribe to the traditional goals associated with camping such as contact with the environment and isolation, they apparently feel that they can pursue such values in highly developed campgrounds."[38]

So too have recent surveys of users of our national parks, in sharp contrast to preservationist demands, demonstrated an almost complete lack of public support for cutbacks on the visitor facilities, operated by franchised concessionaires within the parks, much less the imposition of access quotas. A recent "scientifically controlled exit interview at each of four national parks—Yellowstone, Yosemite, Glacier, and Grand Canyon" revealed, for example, that a very substantial majority, 87 percent, of all park visitors were opposed to the removal of *all* campgrounds from National Parks, with only 7.1 percent favoring such removal. When it was proposed that only *some* campgrounds be removed, negative response remained high, 75.8 percent, with support for this idea less than 15 percent. . . . A significant majority of park visitors interviewed also indicated opposition to having *all or some* hotel and lodge-type facilities removed from the parks surveyed. A total of 75.3 percent opposed removal of all such facilities, with 15.1 percent in favor; 62.7 percent opposed removal of even some hotel-lodge facilities, with 23.4 percent in favor.[39]

Similarly, after two abortive attempts to come up with a master plan for beleaguered Yosemite by traditional NPS methods, worksheets were distributed in 1975 to solicit public opinion. Significantly, although workbook opinions overwhelmingly do not support expansion of current facilities, they equally overwhelmingly do not support an all-wilderness concept for Yosemite, with one proposal to ban all mechanized transport in the park receiving only 4 percent support.

Visitors from outside California [who account for only 20 percent of the visits to Yosemite] support a more pristine plan for Yosemite than do visitors from within the state [who account for 80 percent of visits]. Almost uniformly, out-of-state visitors were more staunch advocates of automobile restrictions and curtailments of present commercial activity.[40]

The views of users make eminent good sense. "At Yellowstone, for example, a visitor must travel a 140-mile loop to view the park's principal natural features," the Stanford Research Institute reports. "Without overnight facilities inside the park, each visitor would have to complete the loop between sunup and sundown, substantially diminishing the park experience and congesting the park entrances at sunup and sundown hours." Similarly, "A 1973 park service evaluation of moving what were termed 'nonessential' facilities out of Yosemite was projected at a cost of between $110 and $113 million in 1973 dollars—close to twice the $65.9 million in 1976 planning/construction/reconstruction dollars requested for the entire [National Park] System."[41]

Park users as well as park concessioners (who annually gross about one dollar per visitor to the natural parks) won a major victory over preservationists in November 1979, when the National Park Service, after ten years of bitter controversy, announced its final master plan for Yosemite. Park headquarters and personnel facilities as well as several unnecessary concessions would be removed from Yosemite Valley into outlying areas of the park, and overnight hotel accommodations would be reduced by about 10 percent. However, further restrictions on access to Yosemite Valley by automobile were abandoned as too expensive, and the campgrounds were permitted to remain. The Los Angeles *Times* reported that the master plan was

received with joy at the headquarters of the Yosemite Park and Curry Co. While Ed Hardy, president of the company, declined to comment pending further analysis, the plan appeared to free the company from many of the burdens that once threatened its profitability. A subsidiary of MCA Corp., the park company long has been an opponent of conservationists' desires to return the valley to its pristine level, arguing that modern visitors require modern, comfortable services.[42]

A major question for the future is the extent to which National Park Service policy will continue to be responsive to user opinion when it conflicts with the demands of preservationist interests. Clark, Hendee, and Campbell wisely point out that the proponents of a traditionalist outdoor ethic

form a powerful political force influencing use of resources, the focus of recreational policy, and the appropriate types of use and norms for outdoor recreation areas. These interests continually interact with recreation resource managers and, through mutual reinforcement, they come to assume that their own views and definitions of appropriate behavior are commonly held by the rest of society. If not assuming the universality of their views, a moralistic stance justifies the resource manager's position....As "moral entrepreneurs" there are persons who desire to improve all men, believing that their expectations are most appropriate for others. Whether or not such a view is legitimate in formulating policy is open for debate; but we would argue that as a minimum, managers should recognize how users really feel.[43]

***

Mounting preservationist fears in the early 1970s were that the National Park System had about reached its limits of potential development and that mass recreation was tending to replace nature appreciation as the main use of the parks with the rapid exhaustion of available public recreation land in close proximity to major population centers. In 1969 Secretary of the Interior Walter Hickel estimated that "it is in the urban areas that almost 80 percent of the new recreation needs are located," and he estimated that it would require "in excess of $25 billion above existing expenditure levels to give urban dwellers the same amount of nearby recreation opportunity by 1975 that was available on the average nationwide in 1965." Similarly, by 1975 proposals to create new national parks in Alaska, generated by the Department of Interior in compliance with the 1971 Alaska Claims Settlement Act, remained in limbo; and, despite the Nixon administration's stated goal to "Bring Parks to the People," Congress still had not provided funding for nineteen approved additions to the National Park System. "A May 3, 1973, memorandum from higher-ups requested establishment of a deadline year for rounding out the National Park System," reported the January 1975 issue of *National Parks and Conservation Magazine*. "The distressing signs of a new policy trend are rapidly emerging....Indeed, the [National Park] Service has taken all too seriously the spirit of this recent comment attributed to a high-ranking Interior Department official: 'It's time to close the door in the National Park System.'" To combat these trends, the National Parks Association claimed,

The great wilderness parks must be served by rail and bus transportation—the cheapest and most energy-efficient mode of transportation available—if national parks are going to continue to be enjoyed by people from distant metropolitan areas. The new urban regional parks will also need vastly improved mass transit access systems to prevent traffic congestion and allow urban residents equal access to recreation, regardless of automobile ownership.[44]

The theme that the national parks were overcrowded was thus being rapidly abandoned by preservationists as the main threats to the parks reverted to the familiar historic ones of lack of appropriations and the exploitation of wilderness to provide the energy resources to sustain economic growth. The need now was for the popular support for the parks that democratic access engendered—but not democratic access by automobile. For a strange combination of runaway inflation, deepening recession, and skyrocketing gasoline prices was each year making enjoyment of "the park experience" more difficult for most middle-class, automobile-owning families. The number of visitors to the more remote national parks, consequently, leveled off from 1971 through 1974, and the petty entrepreneurs in gateway towns became vocal about the resulting loss of tourist dollars. Within the parks, overnight stays in NPS-operated campgrounds fell dramatically from a high of 9,411,100 in 1968 and 9,023,800 in 1970 to only 7,934,300 in 1971. Campground use began to approach the late-1960s levels only in 1976, when 9,267,300 overnight stays were recorded. With dollar-a-gallon and higher-priced gasoline imminent, middle-class preservationists came to conclude that continuing access to the national parks for themselves, much less for the urban masses, depended upon an alternative to the road and the car. As in the railroad and automobile eras of park development, these interests of the preservationists at present coincide with those of the automobile manufacturers, who hope to develop into total transportation companies by the turn of the twenty-first century and will undoubtedly welcome lucrative government contracts for building modular park mass-transit systems.

Ironically, semblances of the balanced park transportation systems that policy makers now seek to restore existed in the parks until very recently. Despite the inroads of the automobile, the railroads managed to hang on, providing alternative transportation to the parks until the 1960s, when one by one they discontinued service. And as long as the trains ran to the parks, the yellow park tour buses were a familiar sight on park roads. By the mid-1960s, however, railway service to the parks and the tour buses had fallen victim to massive indirect governmental subsidization of highway transportation through the Interstate Highway Act of 1956 and its nondivertible Highway Trust Fund. Lobbied through Congress by a diverse group of highway interests, collectively dubbed the "Road Gang" by Helen Leavitt,[45] the Interstate Highway Act, much more than the parallel Mission 66 program, was responsible for increasing automobile traffic in the national parks to levels the preservationists found intolerable. Nevertheless, as Alfred Runte has pointed out, the Western national parks remain linked about a day's travel apart by an interconnected system of railroad tracks, ready to be utilized as the need arises.[46] Visitation to the parks, however, remains largely a summer business, while the profitable running of an interpark railroad necessitates year-round passenger traffic. And with the cost of rail transportation currently estimated at fifty to seventy-five dollars per person per day, access to the parks by automobile until very recently has remained far cheaper as well as much more convenient for families.

Although over 90 percent of visitors to the national parks still arrive in private passenger cars, that in the foreseeable future the national parks will come to rely more on rail and bus transportation than on the private passenger car is inevitable— for the age of the automobile is ending with escalating oil prices and the concurrent interest of capitalists and the government in innovating new transportation technology. Yosemite's unique problems began to be resolved with the reintroduction of shuttlebus service in 1967, elimination of the nightly firefall, halving the number of public campsites from 2,600 to 1,139, the elimination of overflow camping, and imposition of a one-week camping limit. By 1972 a fleet of specially built, propane-burning minitrains and double-decker shuttlebuses provided free service in Yosemite and had won public acceptance. Private passenger cars were being used primarily to get to and from the park. George B. Hartzog, Jr., director of the National Park Service, pleased by the results, was engaging in advanced planning for a total visitor transportation system that would eliminate the automobile entirely from the park, and he viewed "Yosemite's transportation program as the first of many similar actions that will be taken in other parks to diminish traffic congestion, pollutant effects, and noise caused by increasing numbers of motor vehicles—factors that frustrate visitor enjoyment."[47] Recognizing that the transportation problems of the parks were complex and differed greatly—especially as between the large parks and the small ones— the National Parks Centennial Commission, however, could find no definitive solution and ended up merely recommending "that separate transportation studies be made and policy statements issued for each park." It further urged the National Park Service "to be innovative and take advantage of any technological improvements in matters of transportation."[48]

Limited progress in implementing the commission's 1972 recommendations is evident. Studies identifying the transportation facilities and services for twelve units of the National Park System either had been completed or were in process by 1977 at an approximate cost of $905,000, with additional studies for twenty-one units programmed through 1979 at an estimated cost of $1.24 million. These studies are parts of general management studies or special transportation studies, however, and the only full-scale regional transportation study in process is one for the Yellowstone-Grand Teton region. More impressive than the studies in progress, in-park visitor transportation services sponsored by the National Park Service have been inaugurated at an annual cost of $3.4 million in nineteen parks—including Everglades, Mesa Verde, Point Reyes, Grand Canyon, Mount McKinley, and Yosemite—in addition to limited visitor transportation services provided in twenty-nine parks solely by private concessioners. Federal legislation passed in 1979 provides $6 million more over three years for specific demonstration projects to improve access by public transportation to Cape Cod National Seashore, Cuyahoga Valley National Recreational Area, Fire Island National Seashore, Gateway National Recreation Area, Glacier, Golden Gate National Recreation Area, Indiana Dunes National Lakeshore, Mount Rushmore National Memorial, and Yellowstone, with a view toward facilitating recreational access to new urban parks—especially Gateway and Golden Gate—by the urban poor, senior citizens, the handicapped, and others who lack personal automobility.[49]

Initial conclusions from the regional transportation study of the Greater Yellowstone Region, presented as testimony in 1979 congressional hearings on park transportation, illustrate the formidable problems involved in planning alternative park transportation systems for the future. Although the investigators conclude that "the end of mass reliance on the private automobile is imminent," they also acknowledge that the more exotic forms of mass conveyance, such as tramways, automated people movers, and similar systems ". . . are very expensive to install and operate. These are not considered feasible solutions in most instances." Important considerations are that "much of the transportation planning and hardware development which has come out of the search for solutions to urban traffic problems is not easily adaptable to the unique problems and situations encountered in wildland resource areas without substantial modification" and that "wildland recreational area transportation requirements may fluctuate seasonally while most alternatives to the private automobile in typical situations require stable year-round volumes to be economically justifiable, or else very high profits." Consequently, alternatives that can operate on existing park road systems—that is, motor vehicles—seem most desirable, and "the most heavily used recreational sites are the most appropriate areas to consider the switch to total or limited reliance on mass conveyance."[50]

Particularly notable is the recognition that the cooperation of key segments of the American business system with government is central to solving park transportation problems and hence toward preserving our national park heritage. The National Park Service must "work closely with Amtrak, the railroads, bus companies and [the] lodging industry to link up mass conveyance networks which are attractive, profitable, enjoyable, and reasonably priced," and transportation planning for the parks must be viewed in part as "a new opportunity to expand the private tourist industry by providing sound business opportunities at appropriate locations, such as gateway communities outside the parks." At an even more fundamental level, in addition to necessitating massive technological innovation in the automobile industry, "the development of transportation technology and hardware for mass conveyance systems is extensive and involves many of the large diversified aerospace firms such as Ling-TempCo Vought, Boeing Aircraft, General Dynamics, and Lockheed Aircraft."[51]

An additional stimulus to this developing market for new park transportation systems is the imminent promise, contrary to preservationist fears of a few years ago, for great expansion of the National Park System. Legislation passed in 1976 (Public Law 94-458) provides that the secretary of the interior must recommend at the beginning of each fiscal year at least twelve potential new park areas in order of their priority. Then, on November 10, 1978, President Carter signed into law the omnibus National Parks and Recreation Act (Public Law 95-625). Sponsored by Representative Phillip Burton (D-Calif.), this legislation was the most ambitious parks bill in American history, and it passed in the House of Representatives by the overwhelming margin of 341 to 61. Capital wags referred to the bill as the "park barrel" and the "Christmas tree bill," for it contained something for everyone. Tremendous expansion of the National Park System was the bill's keynote: It created 11 new units, provided for the study of 9 more for inclusion, and added land and/or facilities to some 131 existing units. Preservationists were enthralled that the bill added Mineral King to Sequoia National Park, thus thwarting the Disney Corporation's plans for commercial development of the area as a ski resort. The bill tripled our national wild and scenic rivers by adding eight new rivers to the system and by authorizing seventeen other segments of rivers in fourteen states for study, thereby temporarily protecting them from alteration by damming or channelization; and it doubled the National Wilderness Preservation System by adding 1.8 million acres and specifying another 120,000 acres as possible additions in eight national parks. Counterbalancing these strong wilderness preservation commitments, the bill authorized spending $725 million over a five-year period for a new urban park and recreation recovery program to provide for the mass recreation needs of our cities. It also authorized the purchase of privately owned concession facilities in Yellowstone as a first step toward a general upgrading of tourist facilities in the National Park System.

Expanding demand for "the park experience" combined with general recognition of the need to innovate park transportation systems for the future that will continue to permit wilderness preservation to be reconciled with democratic access promises another golden era of national park development. A market clearly has been created that promises enormous potential profits to recreation-tourist- and transportation-related industries and that can serve as the basis for a new pragmatic alliance among key business interests, governmental bureaucracies, politicians, preservationists, and the general public. Thomas C. Cochran once astutely observed that massive capital investment to accommodate American society to the automobile was the main source of the business boom of the 1920s,[52] and, existing evidence warrants the forecast that massive capital investment to develop more balanced, alternative transportation systems will be a mainstay of the American economy in the foreseeable future.[53] Viewed from this perspective, the imminent end of mass access to the national parks by automobile is neither the boon to wilderness preservation claimed by misinformed preservationists nor the disaster for democracy perceived by Professor Rae but simply part of a general and very complex challenge to American capitalism to respond with appropriate technological and social structural innovation to changing markets. It remains to be seen, as Professor Cochran recently has suggested holds true in general for American historical development,[54] whether appropriate technological innovation and social structural changes will occur in response to this developing market for new transportation systems in our national parks. But it appears certain that our national parks have weathered the automobile revolution to emerge in excellent condition and that the prospects are bright for the continuing compatibility of parks, people, and profits.

NOTES

1. Roderick Nash, "The American Invention of National Parks," *American Quarterly* 22 (Fall 1970):726.

2. U.S. National Park Service, *Public Use of the National Park System* (Washington, D.C.: Government Printing Office, 1977), p. 1.

3. John Muir, "The Hetch Hetchy Valley: A National Question," *American Forestry* 16 (May 1910): 263.

4. *Report, Secretary of the Interior*, 1931, p. 36, cited in John Ise, *Our National Park Policy: A Critical History* (Baltimore: John Hopkins University Press, 1961), pp. 4-5.

5. Samuel P. Hays, *Conservation and the Gospel of Efficiency* (Cambridge: Harvard University Press, 1959), pp. 2-3.

6. A. Hunter Dupree, *Science in the Federal Government* (Cambridge: Harvard University Press, Belknap Press, 1957), p. 252.

7. The most useful single source on the history of our national parks and the National Park Service remains Ise, *Our National Park Policy*.

8. Alfred Runte, "Yellowstone: It's Useless, So Why Not a Park?" *National Parks and Conservation Magazine* 46 (March 1972): 5, and idem, "The National Park Idea," *Journal of Forest History* 21 (April 1977): 66.

9. *Statistical Abstract of the United States*, 95 annual ed. (Washington, D.C.: Government Printing Office, 1978), pp. 241, 250.

10. Paul Schullery, "A Reasonable Illusion," *Rod and Reel* 5 (November-December 1979): 51.

11. Cited in William C. Everhart, *The National Park Service* (New York: Praeger, 1972), p. 93.

12. John B. Rae, *The Road and the Car in American Life* (Cambridge, Mass.: MIT Press, 1971), p. 143.

13. Alfred Runte, "Pragmatic Alliance: Western Railroads and the National Parks," *National Parks and Conservation Magazine* 48 (April 1974): 14.

14. Ise, *Our National Park Policy*, p. 30.

15. Foster Rhea Dulles, *A History of Recreation: America Learns to Play* (New York: Appleton-Century-Crofts, 1965), p. 319.

16. Robert Shankland, *Steve Mather of the National Parks* (New York: Knopf, 1954), pp. 146-47.

17. Earl Pomeroy, *In Search of the Golden West* (New York: Knopf, 1957), pp. 113, 130, 149.

18. Quoted in Shankland, *Steve Mather of the National Parks*, p. 152.

19. Everhart, *National Park Service*, p. 32.

20. Ibid., p. 35.

21. Ise, *Our National Park Policy*, p. 656.

22. "Report of the President and General Counsel, Anthony Wayne Smith, to the General Membership of the National Parks Association," *National Parks Magazine* 39 (May 1965): i; Anthony Wayne Smith, "Wilderness in the Parks," *National Parks Magazine* 39 (October 1965): 2; William H. Draper, Jr., "Parks—Or More People?" *National Parks Magazine* 42 (March 1968): 2.

23. Reprinted in U.S., Congress, Senate, Committee on Energy and Natural Resources, Subcommittee on Parks and Recreation, *Transportation Access to the National Park System, Hearing*, 95th Cong., 1st sess., June 8, 1977 (Washington, D.C.: Government Printing Office, 1977).

24. Warren A. Johnson, "Over-Use of the National Parks," *National Parks Magazine* 41 (October 1967): 4-7.

25. *Preserving a Heritage: Final Report to the President and Congress of the National Parks Centennial Commission* (Washington, D.C.: Government Printing Office, 1973), p. 99.

26. Lewis Gannett, *Sweet Land* (Garden City, N.Y.: Sun Dial, 1937), pp. 160-61.

27. National Park Service, "Yosemite National Park Master Plan" (Preliminary draft, August 12, 1974), pp. 2-3, 37.

28. See especially Ise, *Our National Park Policy*, for instances of early abuse of the parks, NPS mismanagement, and natural disasters.

29. Schullery, "A Reasonable Illusion," p. 54.

30. Everhart, *National Park Service*, p. 234.

31. U.S., Congress, Senate, *Transportation Access to the National Park System*, p. 27.

32. William Rhodes, "The Technological Development and Environmental Impact of Off-Road Recreational Vehicles" (Unpublished paper).

33. Everhart, *National Park Service*, p. 223.

34. Roderick Nash, *Wilderness and the American Mind*, rev. ed. (New Haven: Yale University Press, 1973), pp. 263-73.

35. K. Peter Etzkom, "Leisure and Camping: The Social Meaning of a Form of Public Recreation," *Sociology and Social Research* 49 (October 1964): 76-89.

36. Roger N. Clark; John C. Hendee; and Frederick L. Campbell, "Values, Behavior, and Conflict in Modern Camping Culture," *Journal of Leisure Research* 3 (Summer 1971): 144-45.

37. Warren J. Belasco, *Americans on the Road: From Autocamp to Motel, 1910-1945* (Cambridge, Mass.: MIT Press, 1979), p. 71.

38. Clark; Hendee; and Campbell, "Values, Behavior, and Conflict in Modern Camping Culture," p. 156.

39. U.S., Congress, Senate, Committee on Interior and Insular Affairs, Subcommittee on Parks and Recreation, *National Park Service Concessions Oversight, Hearing*, 94th Cong., 2nd sess., March 10, 1976 (Washington, D.C.: Government Printing Office, 1976), p. 247.

40. Robert A. Jones, "Vision of Yosemite's Future Emerges," Los Angeles *Times*, July 20, 1976.

41. U.S., Congress, Senate, *National Park Service Concessions Oversight*, p. 248.

42. Robert A. Jones, "Reactions to Yosemite Decisions Range from Relief to Dismay," Los Angeles *Times*, November 30, 1979.

43. Clark; Hendee; and Campbell, "Values, Behavior, and Conflict in Modern Camping Culture," p. 157.

44. "Closing the Door on Our National Parks," *National Parks and Conservation Magazine* 49 (January 1975): 23-24.

45. Helen Leavitt, *Superhighway—Super Hoax* (Garden City, N.Y.: Doubleday, 1970).

46. Alfred Runte, "Blueprint for Comfort: A National Park to Park Railway," *National Parks and Conservation Magazine* 50 (November 1976): 8-10.

47. George B. Hartzog, Jr., "Clearing the Roads—and the Air—in Yosemite Valley," *National Parks and Conservation Magazine* 46 (August 1972): 14-17.

48. *Preserving a Heritage*, p. 129.

49. U.S., Congress, Senate, *Transportation Access to the National Park System*, pp. 31-35, 65-67.

50. Ibid., pp. 138-41.

51. Ibid.

52. Thomas C. Cochran, *The American Business System: A Historical Perspective 1900-1955* (Cambridge: Harvard University Press, 1957), p. 44.

53. James J. Flink, *The Car Culture* (Cambridge, Mass.: MIT Press, 1975), pp. 191-233. For the usefulness of history to forecasting and as a guide to public policy decisions, see Thomas C. Cochran, *The Uses of History* (Wilmington, Del.: Scholarly Resources, 1973).

54. Thomas C. Cochran, *Two Hundred Years of American Business* (New York: Basic Books, 1977).

The Government as Manager: Emergency Fleet Shipbuilding, 1917-1919

BERNARD MERGEN

"Characterization of the twentieth century as one of managerial enterprise, labor bureaucracy, or dictatorship have one element in common: The emerging system had to operate through hierarchical administration."[1] Thomas Cochran's observation on the rise of big management, big labor, and big government has been confirmed by innumerable studies of business, trade unions, and the civil service. In most cases business executives reorganized their companies in response to changing technology, products, and markets. As industries grew, the recruitment, training, and productivity of workers became problems for which managers developed a variety of solutions. In the steel industry, for example, mechanization reduced the percentage of skilled workers in the mills. Since these workers were likely to be organized and well paid, their replacement by unskilled, unorganized workers helped to lower costs and increase profits. Maintaining a surplus of labor by encouraging immigration, the steel companies lengthened the work day and lowered wages, compensating for these actions with a limited amount of paternalism such as company-built hospitals, schools, and houses.[2]

Labor responded to changing business environments by developing its own hierarchy of specialists in organizing and contract negotiating and by strengthening the control of the national unions over the locals. Government, not motivated by the desire for profits, made efficiency an end in itself, reasoning that service to the nation's citizens was its primary function and that dollar savings would follow naturally from a job well done. The federal government's experience as either employer or manager of labor was limited. In its legislation for railroad workers the government had begun to develop a labor policy. These acts pro-

I would like to thank the Smithsonian Institution for a postdoctoral fellowship and George Washington University for a sabbatical leave that allowed me to pursue research for this essay.

vided for mediation and arbitration of disputes between operating employees on the railroads and their employers. The Adamson Act of 1916 established an eight-hour day. Nothing, however, could have prepared the government for labor relations of the magnitude created by the war. When the United States entered the World War in 1917, the federal government employed 438,500 persons; within a year it would have that many working under government contracts in shipyards alone. Relationships among workers, managers, and the federal government, which had been ignored in the doldrums of prewar commerce, became the subject of intense scrutiny in the winds of war. The extreme self-consciousness of the men who worked for the Emergency Fleet Corporation is evident in the records of that organization. This chapter examines the development of personnel management in the shipyards; the establishment of boards, committees, and departments to deal with workers; and the attitudes of some of the men who served the government for two hectic years.

Shipbuilding in the United States has a long and distinguished history, but in the twentieth century it became an industry crippled by the lack of a national maritime policy and at a competitive disadvantage in the cost of material and labor with Great Britain and Germany. For ten years prior to World War I, Congress debated several plans for reviving the American merchant marine, ranging from subsidies to outright government ownership, but failed to pass any legislation to encourage shipbuilding. Shipyard owners and managers were themselves divided on the causes and cures of the decline in American shipbuilding. In 1900 the members of the Society of Naval Architects and Marine Engineers heard a report on costs in shipbuilding which concluded that "the tariff on steel plates and shapes makes it possible for us to find the British shipbuilder working into his ships American steel from Pittsburgh at a less cost to him than the English material, and at less cost than is charged the American shipbuilder for the same material in Pittsburgh." Wages, too, were higher in the United States, but the author hoped that, "as we gain experience and adopt new methods, especially in regard to the management of that important factor, labor, this difference may ultimately disappear." The report engendered a lively discussion, especially on the habits of the workers. On the East Coast, one member reported, "Some of the men who belonged to the riveting gangs made very large wages and would work about three days in the week, and during those three days they would make the equivalent of an ordinary week's work. Then they would simply quit work and drink, or something of the sort, for the rest of the week, and show up again at the beginning of the following week and do another three or four days' work, so that per head they got actually less work from the man than they would have got if they paid him lower wages." Charles H. Cramp, of the William Cramp & Sons Ship & Engine Building Company of Philadelphia, complained that men in his yard were getting double time for working Saturdays and Sundays, and then staying out on Mondays and Tuesdays.[3]

The managers disagreed on the solution to problems of worker malingering. Some favored piece work, others stricter supervision, while a few hoped to reduce the total work force through "mechanical handling of material." One executive shrewdly observed,

Where large bodies of men are employed, as in shipyards, and where personal supervision is difficult, a large amount of what we call loafing goes on in spite of all devices to stop it. I do not say that our American workmen are more skilled in loafing than others, although it requires considerable skill to be a successful loafer.[4]

The physical layout of shipyards is an important factor in establishing the pace and routine of work. Most shipyards are linear, stretching along a waterfront for a mile or more and occupying as much as 250 acres of land. The huge buildings housing the mold loft, machine shops, and fabrication shops; the acres of steel storage along railroad tracks; and the towering cranes by the shipways and outfitting basins, provide a setting in which workers can play, out of sight of supervisors and foremen. Delays in getting material or equipment to the appropriate crews inevitably occur. During these delays workers smoke, talk, read papers, and play tricks on one another.[5]

Still another factor in the behavior of workers was the kind of construction on which they were engaged.

A shipyard that is employed in building government work as well as merchant work, gets the men into habits of extreme carefulness, and the men who are changed from the government work onto the merchant work retain to a large extent this carefulness which the government inspectors require. Now for ships built for the merchant marine and the general run of tramp steamers, we know that such carefulness is not required.[6]

The answer to this problem was clear. Yards should specialize in certain kinds of construction. If enough contracts for ships could be secured, ships could be manufactured instead of built. Shipbuilding could be standardized as well. The guns of August 1914 provided the opportunity for American shipbuilders to prove their contention that they could build ships as cheaply as Europeans if they could apply the methods of prefabrication and standardization.

Significantly, many of the ideas for prefabrication and standardization originated with men who came to shipbuilding from other steel construction industries. Henry G. Morse planned the yard of New York Shipbuilding Corporation in Camden, New Jersey, in 1899, based on his experience in bridge building. In 1912 a sudden demand for oil tankers prompted an engineer to design vertical cylindrical tanks that could be built and tested ashore, then installed on ships. Within a few years, Chester Shipbuilding Company was manufacturing just four basic types of tankers and freighters.[7] On the Great Lakes, shipbuilders responded to the need for vessels that could carry large cargoes, yet negotiate the lake canal system, by designing a flat-bottomed bulk carrier. Even ships of different size were as much as one-half to two-thirds alike amidships, allowing both plates and shapes to be ordered from a small number of molds. Since the entire bottom of a ship was completed before the sides and their framing were commenced, a firm platform from which to work was provided, and construction was quicker and more economical.[8]

By 1916 American shipbuilding was an industry in transition. Technologically, pneumatic tools, riveting, and larger cranes made prefabrication possible, but generally workers constructed steel ships in the same manner as wooden ones. A full-scale template was made in the mold loft, and steel frames made from them. A framework was then erected with rivet holes punched, and the plating, decks, and bulkheads partially laid. Additional templates were then made directly on the ship from the surrounding plates for the plates that were to fit between them.[9] Shipyards employed a wide variety of craftsmen—blacksmiths, boilermakers, carpenters, electricians, machinists, painters, pipefitters, riveters, structural iron workers, sheetmetal workers, and welders—whose work was similar to that done outside shipyards, and other crafts—ship fitters, template makers, chippers, caulkers, shipwrights, and loftsmen—whose skills were more specialized. Shipyard workers were also divided into a bewildering number of departments and classes. A few retained membership in one of the craft unions of the American Federation of Labor, but most were unorganized, and the owners and managers intended to keep it that way. It was this changing and volatile situation that the government entered on September 7, 1916, with the passage of the Shipping Act.

The act was designed to do several things. First, it created the U.S. Shipping Board, composed of five commissioners appointed by the president with the approval of the Senate. These commissioners were given power to regulate water-borne commerce in a manner similar to the regulation of the railroads by the Interstate Commerce Commission. A second responsibility of the board was acquisition of vessels by construction, purchase, or lease. This vague authority was limited only by restrictions that forbade the purchase or charter of ships under the registry of nations then engaged in war. Most importantly, the board was authorized to create one or more corporations for the purchase, construction, equipment, and maintenance of merchant vessels.[10] To head the USSB, President Wilson turned to a California lawyer who had been active in the state movement for nonpartisan election of judges, William Denman. On January 17, 1917, the Senate confirmed Denman's appointment, and the board was formally organized on January 30.[11]

Denman and the other board members were apparently convinced that a fleet of wooden ships could be built more quickly and efficiently than steel vessels. This position was the result of three factors. First, undoubtedly, was Denman's unfamiliarity with the shipbuilding industry, an ignorance shared by most of Wilson's advisors. A recent study of the War Industries Board points out the Advisory Council of National Defense also recommended that the wooden ship program be pressed forward in advance of all else because of the scarcity of raw materials for steel construction.[12] The problem was less scarcity than price. Secretary of the Navy Josephus Daniels forced Bethlehem and other steel companies to lower their prices, and Denman threatened to appeal to the president to empower the Trade Commission to fix prices.[13] Still, the general state of unpreparedness in the steel industry and the lack of a clear priority for the distribution of raw material was a second reason for the board's decision to favor wooden ships. A third reason lies in the relation of the USSB to its subsidiary, the Emergency Fleet Corporation.

The EFC was created on April 16, 1917, with General George Goethals as general manager. The choice of Goethals was natural, since the precedent for the EFC was the Panama Railway Company. The authority of the general manager of the EFC in relation to the chairman of the USSB was not clearly defined. Goethals wanted steel ships. Moreover, according to W. C. Mattox, who served as head of the Publications Section of the EFC, Goethals wanted to build a permanent merchant marine, not just a wartime emergency fleet. Finally, Denman was concerned about cost, and Goethals was not.[14] Through June 1917 the EFC operated in confusing and often contradictory ways. A metallurgical engineer from the Penobscott Chemical Fibre Company was appointed agent for the EFC with authority to make contracts with shipyards. One of his agents apparently told several firms to begin construction of shipways without contracts. When informed of this, Goethals immediately stopped all projects and asked Joseph P. Cotton, who was soon to serve as U.S. food administrator and later as under secretary of state, for legal advice. On July 25, Cotton submitted a twelve-page report entitled, "Fabricated Steel Ship Project."

Several interesting points emerge from Cotton's report, the most important being that Goethals's chief interest in the emergency fleet was technological. His experience on the Panama Canal had familiarized him with the ability of bridge builders to prefabricate large steel structures. During May, Goethals met with the vice president of the Submarine Boat Corporation of Newark Bay, New Jersey, which had already built 550 submarine chasers for the British Admirality, fabricating the ships at the company's Bayonne yard and assembling them in Montreal. He also met with W. A. Harriman and G. J. Baldwin. Harriman had become interested in fabricated ships after working at the Chester yard, and Baldwin was senior vice president of American International Corporation, an organization that controlled New York Shipbuilding Corporation and was affiliated with the engineering consulting firm of Stone & Webster. "Realizing the need for speed and the danger of crossing wires," Cotton wrote, "General Goethals got these three organizations working together. The work of Mr. Sutphen's organization, in cooperation with Mr. Worden of the Lackawanna Bridge Company, was largely the organization of the trade. The largest single mill concern was the American Bridge Company, which had prior understandings with Mr. Harriman. That concern, therefore, was left out of Mr. Sutphen's work."[15]

By July 11, three companies had been formed and the sites for the yards selected. Daniel Willard, new head of the War Industries Board, promised Goethals fast freight service from Pittsburgh and Chicago mills to the assembling plants, provided there was no car detention at the plants or mills. Three new shipyards were designed around railroad and storage yards to facilitate unloading. The first contract contained a lump-sum bid by each of the companies on the cost of constructing both the yards and ships. In addition, American International and Submarine Boat insisted on a sum free of war taxes and guaranteed increases to cover the rising cost of labor. Cotton pointed out "that such a provision meant that the contractors took substantially no financial risk at all," and his law committee refused to accept this contract. A second contract, making the contractors government agents who should take no financial risk but furnish an organization to take charge of the work, was drawn up on July 6. Although the government retained the right to stop work at any time, the contractors got an option to continue ownership after the war or to sell to the government. Baldwin, particularly, believed that the government would nationalize shipbuilding after the war. With the general nature of the contract settled, Goethals informed the president and Denman. The latter objected to the contracts, which not only obviated his wooden ship program but challenged his authority as chairman of USSB. A public controversy led to the resignation of Goethals and Denman and delayed the signing of the contracts with American International, Submarine Boat, and Merchant Shipbuilding Corporation until September.[16]

President Wilson was ready with replacements for Goethals and Denman. Rear Admiral Washington Lee Capps replaced the former, and Edward N. Hurley was confirmed by the Senate as chairman of the USSB on July 25, 1917. Hurley was a fifty-three-year-old self-made millionaire from Chicago who had worked his way from railroad fireman to manufacturer of pneumatic tools and electrical appliances. In six years he had created Standard Pneumatic Tool Company and sold it for $1.25 million in 1902. He met Wilson in 1910 and had supported him for governor of New Jersey and for president. From 1915 through 1917, Hurley served on the Federal Trade Commission. He was an excellent choice to head the USSB for several reasons. He seems to have combined a good organizational sense with a flair for public relations. His lack of knowledge of shipbuilding was more than compensated by his experience in pneumatic tools, which had become crucial in steel shipbuilding. He was undoubtedly more acceptable to the business community then Denman, and his Chicago connections helped him recruit administrators from the steel and Great Lakes shipbuilding industries.[17]

One of the key assistants selected by Hurley was Charles Piez, a graduate of the School of Mines at Columbia University and president of Link-Belt Company. Piez made informal surveys of shipbuilding and steel at Hurley's request thoughout the summer and fall. In the meantime, Harley acted swiftly to revise the EFC bylaws, making himself president with full power to hire and fire. He also requisitioned all steel ships over 2,500 deadweight tons under construction in American shipyards. When Capps moved too slowly to clear up legal and construction details, Hurley replaced him with Piez. Hurley struggled to create regional offices to oversee individual yards and to establish an administrative structure that would perform specific tasks. Ten district offices were created to provide field inspection and supervision. The Great Lakes office was headed by

Henry L. Penton, an engineer who had worked at Chicago Ship Building Company and had been a partner in a naval architectural firm in Cleveland. Penton and his staff apparently did a conscientious job, since executives of American Ship Building complained to Hurley that the inspectors were too exacting.[18] The sensitive role of the regional inspectors is confirmed by Mattox in his book, *Building the Emergency Fleet*: "Inspectors in the field, therefore, had to play a responsible part in the great game."[19]

The game metaphor was a favorite with EFC spokesmen. With his assistants searching for solutions to the problems of ship design and procurement of raw materials, Hurley focused his attention on another pressing need—manpower. His approach turned labor recruiting into a national game. Robert D. Heinl, a newspaperman with experience at *Leslie's Weekly*, *Good Housekeeping*, and the U.S. Chamber of Commerce, was made head of publications. His section produced posters, pamphlets, magazine advertisements, and slogans, such as, "The Man of the Hour Is the Shipbuilder." Every man who volunteered to work in a shipyard received a certificate of enrollment acknowledging his patriotism and a bronze button. Julius S. Holl, a Chicago advertising man, recruited the nation's best poster artists, including Jonas Lie, Hibbard V. B. Kline, James Montgomery Flagg, Adolph Treidler, and Joseph Pennell. The themes of these posters developed both the dramatic and the competitive aspects of the shipbuilding campaign. Jonas Lie contributed a poster in two panels, the top half depicting soldiers in a bayonet charge, the bottom a forest of giant cranes and scaffolding around a ship, and between them the caption: "Nothing stops these men—Let nothing stop you." Kline's poster, "Teamwork Wins," showing a riveter and a holder-on joining plates, caught some of the analogy of athletic team spirit. Another poster portrayed a cheering worker climbing a flagpole with the caption, "Hip-hip, another ship—another victory."[20] The pervasiveness of the analogy between work and play is so complete in the EFC propaganda campaign that it strongly suggests a basic change in popular attitudes toward work. War production, with its emphasis on speed and innovation, undoubtedly encouraged these changes. Moreover, high wages, full employment, and government regulation of hours and working conditions gave workers an unprecedented measure of security and leisure. In these circumstances, a worker could look beyond the shop for the psychological and emotional rewards promised by the motion pictures and popular magazines.

All the yards published newspapers to build morale and team spirit. Both work-related and purely recreational contests between workers in a yard and between yards was encouraged. The *Emergency Fleet News* of April 15, 1918, announced in its front-page headlines that the "New National Game of Riveting Promises Novel and Patriotic Sport." A board was created to award flags and medals to yards and individuals for best performance each month. The champion yard received a blue flag, and second and third place yards received white and red banners. This kind of activity seems to have been of special interest to Charles Schwab of Bethlehem Steel, who became director general of the EFC in April 1918. Commenting on the awards, Schwab noted,

The public always responds to the human interest that is contained in a contest. There is a romantic angle to this great national effort to build up a merchant marine, and, placed on a competitive basis in which the East shall compete against the West, the South against the North, and all, including the Great Lakes, against each other, I believe we can work up a great national game that will redound to the benefit of the nation.[21]

By December orders had been placed for winter uniforms for shipbuilding workers, and in January 1919 Hurley announced that he had furnished a toy manufacturer with plans and blueprints for some of the ships built by the EFC in the hope that the toys would popularize the idea of an American merchant marine. "It is none too early," Hurley wrote to the toy maker,

to begin waking Americans to the importance of ships, putting ships and the sea into their daily thought and work, and making ships appeal to the imagination of everybody in the country. We want to reach the children as well as the grown-ups, and, in this connection, knowing how closely toys follow popular interest and what an educative value they have, it has been in my mind to have this great new national interest before the men who invent and design your goods.

A merchant marine game, played on a map of the world, was designed to give "players a familiarity with the greater game that is to be played by the American Merchant Marine of the future."[22]

Hurley knew, of course, that the manpower shortage and related problems of training and housing would not be solved by appeals to patriotism or a public relations campaign, no matter how clever. In September 1917 he created an Industrial Service Department within the Division of Construction. There were already almost 100,000 men engaged in plant and ship construction, and the best estimates were that another 300,000 would be needed. With labor turnover running as high as 300 percent, almost a million men would have to be recruited, trained, and housed in the year ahead. To direct this important department, Hurley turned to Meyer Bloomfield. Bloomfield, who has been called the father of personnel management, was born in Bucharest in 1878, arrived in New York City in 1882, and graduated from City College in 1899. He moved to Boston and studied at Harvard, where he received another bachelor's degree in 1901 and a law degree in 1905. He also became active in social work and served as director of Civic Service House until 1910. During this time Bloomfield became an authority on vocational guidance, publishing *The Vocational Guidance of Youth* in 1911, and helping to organize the National Vocational Guidance Association in 1913. It was a relatively short step from counseling students on careers to managing employees in large industries. As Bloomfield conceived it, employment managers would help employers formulate a philosophy of management and then interpret that philosophy to the workers. At the same time, they would analyze job conditions in order to improve training and reduce dissatisfaction. The employment manager would use psychological tests and keep detailed records on each employee in order to understand individual differences. The manager would also promote good feeling through the use of company newspapers, recreational facilities, and other welfare activities. Employment management was "essentially an intelligent merchandising of men."[23]

Bloomfield's new profession combined ideas from social welfare, scientific management, applied psychology, and vocational guidance. His association with A. Lincoln Filene, Henry Moskowitz, and Louis D. Brandeis during the garment strike of 1910 had obviously helped shape his approach to industrial relations. Basically Bloomfield believed in enlightened employers dealing fairly with their workers. Labor relations at National Cash Register, Filene's Department Store, and the Clothcraft Shops of Joseph and Feiss Company provided examples of scientific management applied to personnel work, but they were admittedly exceptions to the general conditions of employer-employee relations. Bloomfield began to promote the cause of employment management nationally in 1915, teaching courses that year at both the University of California and Boston University. The September *Annals of the American Academy of Political and Social Science* contained his essay, "The New Profession of Handling Men," and the following year he began teaching at Columbia University. Bloomfield seems to have hoped to create a third force to stand between employers and employees. This force would speak with the authority of academic psychology, for Bloomfield drew heavily on the work of E. L. Thorndike, Walter Dill Scott, and Hugo Munsterberg. Bloomfield knew that service departments would not solve all labor problems quickly and easily. He warned businessmen that Professor Thorndike had shown "that the application of science to the problem of handling men involved long and painstaking, not to say exceedingly laborious, investigation."[24] Although the wartime shipbuilding program provided Bloomfield an opportunity to put into practice on an enormous scale what he had been preaching for two years, there was simply not enough time to treat each employee as an individual. The gap between theory and practice was immediately apparent and became the subject of two important conferences in the fall of 1917.

The New England Shipbuilding Conference took place in Boston on October 1 and 2. The principal topic was the recruitment and training of labor. Admiral F. T. Bowles, former president of the Bethlehem Fore River Shipyard and assistant general manager of the EFC, appealed to the patriotism of the participants and then turned the meeting over to Bloomfield with the words, "In order to show that the Fleet Corporation appreciated the enormous task that is before you, we have undertaken to organize an industrial service department, whose business shall be to help you in these tasks."[25] With that simple sentence, much of the initiative in labor-management relations passed from private to public control. Bloomfield introduced a representative from the U.S. Employment Bureau of the Department of Labor who urged the shipyards to hire exclusively through the bureau in order to avoid competitive bidding for workers. This problem, called "scamping," would remain a major obstacle to employment stability throughout the war, even though the conference adopted a resolution that "the employment department of each yard see to it that men from other yards doing government work are not employed without clearance papers from the local, federal, or state employment bureau at the point where they last worked." Recognizing that a major source of labor turnover was variation in wages, hours, and working conditions, the conference further adopted a resolution calling for standardization of the wage scale and hours of labor, "taking into account conditions in different districts." The establishment of zone standards would become a controversial issue, with the government imposing its solution on unwilling owners and workers in some cases. Uniform wages was a response not only to scamping but to changes in shipbuilding technology and in attitudes toward work.

As ship construction was simplified and skilled workmen were replaced by less skilled specialists, the old system of piece rates and bonuses for increased productivity was upset. This change, plus the fact that piece workers in the new, better-equipped, and better-managed yards could earn more than those in the same craft in the older yards, created rivalries that the government had hoped to prevent though standardization of piece rates as well as hourly rates of pay. Moreover, standardization of both piece and hourly rates reduced the financial incentive to increase output and relied instead on appeals to patriotism and pride of workmanship, appeals that were stronger to skilled craftsmen than to the new men receiving four to six weeks of instruction in a specialized task. The New England Shipbuilding Conference spent considerable time on the problem of training inexperienced men for shipyard work, but the only specific recommendation was that "each yard agree to install a definite program of shop instruction in its own yard and cooperate with industrial schools and such other educational agencies as may be found available in each locality."[26] This was really no solution, however, since few of the established yards had any experience in formalized instruction and the new yards were already straining the capacity of local educational institutions with the influx of families with children.

With recruitment and training procedures underway, and with the adjustment of labor disputes delegated to the Shipbuilding Labor Adjustment Board, the Industrial Service Section was free to concentrate on problems of morale, living conditions, and the causes of labor turnover. These were the subjects of the second and larger meeting in Washington, D.C. The sixty-three men who gathered in the Municipal Building on a cool November morning were only a small company of the army of civilians marching into the city that year. The Shipyard Employment Managers' Conference they were attending went unreported by the city's newspapers, but the policies they formulated helped to shape the profession of employment management, and their subsequent actions influenced the character of labor relations in shipbuilding for the next twenty years. Like the New England Shipbuilding Conference, the Washington meeting provides a glimpse into the attitudes of the managers toward the employees. Mark Jones, of the Edison Company, described how the company newspaper was intended to communicate the company's policies and build loyalty but said,

We so far have confined it to reporting activities of the workers in the plant rather than as educational, so that it will come to be an institution with them. We try to print their pictures. We find all these points of contact have a great bearing on the men's feeling toward the institution.[27]

The conference also heard reports on worker housing.

Joseph Larkin of Bethlehem's Fore River shipyard discussed problems of recruiting, supporting, for the most part, the spirit of the New England Shipbuilding Conference that the shipyards should work through state and federal employment offices, but noting that workers themselves were the real problem since "there are a lot of traditional things done in shipyards for years that perhaps will need no little housecleaning." The inference is clear; employment offices should not insist on previous experience, since experienced workers were likely to resist technological and managerial innovation. Larkin was especially proud of a recruiting booth that Bethlehem had put up at a county fair. "We displayed models of ships, we had a bird's-eye view of the plant and the things which we thought would be attractive. We had all sorts of literature in the tent, and as far as I understand, there was constantly a crowd of people around there becoming interested in shipbuilding."[28] Although there is no indication of the kinds of workers recruited in this way, it follows the pattern of Newport News Shipbuilding and Dry Dock Company, which had been drawing its labor force from villages and farms in Virginia and North Carolina since the 1880s. By employing men unfamiliar with shipbuilding, these companies hoped to break the grip of the craftsmen who traditionally had set the pace and style of shipyard work.

The Shipyard Employment Manager's Conference concluded with a reaffirmation of the New England meeting and the passage of nine additional resolutions. These called for the transfer of all ship mechanics and other mechanics likely to be of service in shipbuilding from the Army to the shipyards, the exemption of all shipyard workers from the draft, and the transfer of craftsmen from other industries to shipbuilding. Further, the conference recommended the establishment of a national housing commission with sufficient funds to bring immediate relief to industries doing government work that were affected by the housing problem and that an immediate appeal be made to the patriotism of citizens in towns and cities where war work was being done to open their homes to workers in need of lodging. Finally, the delegates endorsed government-sponsored training programs, use and expansion of federal employment offices, daylight savings time, and a program of "patriotic propaganda" under the auspices of the Council of National Defense.[29]

By December 1, 1917, when the USSB published its first annual report, the wartime shipbuilding program was finally underway. Over 1,118 ships in 116 shipyards were under construction. New yards were being built in Pennsylvania and New Jersey. A staff of more than 1,000 persons was supervising "the greatest construction task ever attempted by a single institution."[30] Yet the United

States had been at war for almost nine months, and there was still little to show in the form of ships on the sea. Although no one knew it, the EFC had less than a year to complete its ambitious projects. As 1918 began, there were signs of trouble everywhere. In late February and early March, the EFC began to receive answers to its survey of labor conditions and housing needs. A fifty-eight-part questionnaire covered such matters as proportion of foreign-born employees, causes of labor turnover, kinds and location of housing available, transportation facilities, and welfare services available. From Maine to the Gulf Coast, from Los Angeles to Seattle, and on the Great Lakes, too, conditions were appalling. Labor turnover ran from 688 percent yearly at Pusey and Jones in Wilmington, Delaware, to 60 percent at Fore River. Most yards had at least thirty percent foreign-born employees, with American Shipbuilding Company in Lorrain, Ohio, reporting 70 percent, mainly Hungarians, Poles, and Germans. Although this was a smaller percentage than in steel, it was considered a major problem by the EFC managers. On the East Coast Italian and Russian immigrants predominated in the shipyards. Housing was needed everywhere, although in some of the smaller communities, such as Bath, Maine, most of the workers lived within walking distance of the yard. For recreation, most companies mentioned motion picture theaters and company-sponsored boxing matches, talent shows, and ball teams.[31]

The housing and labor survey suggests some of the problems faced by the Industrial Service Section. The most striking feature of the section's activities was its breadth. No problem seems to have been too small for EFC employment managers to handle, and all problems were seen as interrelated. Letters from deserted wives trying to track down their wayward husbands were answered promptly, sometimes at considerable length. When a bride in Nebraska wrote to ask if she could be trained with her husband to become a ship's carpenter, she was praised for her "noble spirit of patriotism" but told that "the industrial forces of the government have not been so strained that it has become necessary to call upon our high-spirited women for assistance in the various trades and occupations coming under the supervision of this corporation."[32] Women were in fact entering shipyards in clerical positions. Hog Island employed 436 in February 1918, and New York Ship, Cramps, Sun, and Merchants hired another 175.[33] The hiring of women as production workers had been discussed at the New England Shipbuilding Conference, but no action was taken to implement the suggestion. When women began working on assembly lines in ordnance departments, Clara M. Tead was hired as supervisor of the Women's Branch of the Industrial Service Section.[34] In October 1918, Hog Island hired and trained women as electric welders. Women already working in social services were hired to gather specific data. Lillian Erskine, investigator of occupational diseases for the New Jersey Department of Labor, prepared a pamphlet on *The Problem of Physical Efficiency in the Shipyards* that revealed connections among transportation, housing, safety, sanitation, diet, and welfare management. Anticipating later concern with malnutrition, Erskine wrote that "one of the most serious

phases is the hasty breakfast, with its resulting undernourishment at the beginning of the day's work. . . . As a matter of fact, the undernourishment of the
American worker is an increasingly serious problem in the high-wage industries."[35]

Employment of women and the physical efficiency of workers were minor
concerns of the EFC compared with its interest in providing housing. Recognition of the problem that would be created by the expansion of war-related
industries began in May 1917, when Samuel Gompers, acting on the authority of
the Council of National Defense, appointed architect Phillip Hiss to tour the
country's factory sites and shipyards to report on housing conditions. Hiss made
his report on September 21, and the Advisory Commission of the council recommended that the War Industries Board consider the congestion of industrial
population in placing of future orders. The commission also advised the council
to appoint a committee to study the housing problem further. Otto Eidlitz, a civil
engineer and construction executive, was appointed chairman and also served as
advisor on housing to the EFC. Eidlitz immediately had a bill introduced in
Congress requesting funds, and on March 1, 1918, Public Law 102, authorizing
the USSB/EFC "to provide housing for shipyard employees through loans to
realty companies incorporated by shipbuilding companies," was signed by the
president. At the same time, a bill had been introduced to authorize the secretary
of labor to provide housing, local transportation, and other community facilities
for war needs. It is a measure of the special importance of the shipbuilding
program that President Wilson felt that the EFC should have separate funding.
After assuring Congress that all housing would eventually by administered through
the Labor Department, Wilson got two agencies and dual appropriations. Eidlitz
became head of the U.S. Housing Corporation, while J. Rogers Flannery, a
Pittsburgh lawyer and manufacturer, became director of housing for the EFC.[36]

From the beginning of the housing program, it was apparent that the architects
and planners working for the EFC hoped to accomplish more than just an immediate and temporary solution to the housing problem. Although the EFC did not
actually construct buildings, it maintained strict control over design, rental, and
management. Flannery and his staff were impressed by British experiments in
worker housing and drew on the services of advocates of the "garden city" idea,
such as Clarence Stein and Frederick L. Ackerman. According to Roy Lubove, it
was Charles Harris Whitaker, editor of the *Journal of the American Institute of
Architects*, who first sent Ackerman to England in 1917 to report on housing
developments there.[37] "One thing strikes the observer forcibly in practically all
of the larger operations constructed by the government," Ackerman wrote, describing his impressions of British housing.

These communities are complete. They are laid out along the latest ideas of housing and
town planning. They contain, beyond the cottages. . . dining halls, recreation buildings,
clubs, institutes, schools, playgrounds, churches, hospitals, stores, markets, and they are
provided with excellent roads with curbs, sidewalks, fences, hedges, and, in many cases,
trees have already been planted.[38]

Like the British, U.S. officials were motivated principally by a desire to guarantee the health and relative comfort of workers in order to increase their productivity and efficiency. Nevertheless, the discussion of public housing in the United States reveals some characteristically American concerns.

Imbued with the "garden city" ideal, Flannery and Ackerman recruited architects who shared their vision. Electus D. Litchfield's Yorkship Village in Camden, New Jersey, provided dwelling units for 1,637 families and 38 single men in 1,578 individual houses, 59 apartments, and a hotel. Built around a town square and a common, the village contained a school, football field, and gym. A streetcar line carried passengers to the shipyard and to Camden. Curved, irregular streets helped to break up the monotony of the two-story brick houses even before trees and shrubs were planted. A story in the Yorkship *News* describes the houses as

reminiscent of quaint old English village architecture, and larger structures, recalling the types of homes characteristic of Dutch or Flemish towns. Again there are colonial houses, pleasing to the most exacting advocate of the out-and-out national home design and capping the general impression of the village gained by the visitor.[39]

Advertisements for the houses emphasized "complete bath with built-in tubs, gas range, electric light, hot air heat, enameled sink in kitchen, and laundry tubs." Plans show two- and three-bedroom houses, most with dining rooms. A generation that had grown up reading and dreaming over the pages of *House Beautiful* and *Ladies' Home Journal* could at last enjoy the symbols of middle-class family life—built-in tubs and dining rooms. The architecture confirmed what Erskine had proclaimed: "Cleanliness, order, discipline, and the conviction of the men that a 'square deal' is intended are the first essential factors."[40]

In Philadelphia, architect Owen Brainard, who had worked on the New York Public Library and the Senate and House Office Buildings in Washington, D.C., was faced with a more difficult task. Locating space for almost 2,000 houses near the Hog Island yard (now the site of the Philadelphia airport) was the first problem. Maintaining the "garden city" ideal amid the long blocks of row houses in southwest Philadelphia was the second. After vacant lots were found between Sixty-first and Sixty-eighth streets and Seventy-first and Seventy-fourth streets along Elmwood Avenue, Brainard solved the second problem by arranging his houses around squares, which became playgrounds and parks. The two-story, three-bedroom row houses all had small porches, a dining room, and back yards. Corner houses were designed to be used as stores, but other services were left to the existing neighborhood. Hilton Village in Newport News, Dundalk in Baltimore, and Sun Hill and Buckman in Chester, all exhibit similar designs. Perhaps the most thoroughly documented project is Union Park Gardens in Wilmington. Wilmington had two shipyards, Harlan and Hollingsworth and Bethlehem's Pusey and Jones. As early as 1916, the local chamber of commerce had been aware of a housing shortage, and the local government hired John Nolen to study the city's housing conditions. Nolen found 4,600 men working on government contracts in the yards and predicted an increase of 1,900 in the coming months, almost all of whom would require housing. Forty-three percent of the workers were skilled, 60 percent were married, 84 percent were native-born or naturalized. The respondents desired single-family housing of stucco, poured concrete, or brick construction within fifteen minutes of the yard.[41]

Nolen went on to recommend revision of the zoning laws to provide more square feet for each house, the formation of a housing company to secure sufficient capital for the construction of worker housing, and that the proposed enterprise consider the whole problem of community development, including transportation and recreation. The Wilmington Chamber of Commerce formed a Housing Committee, which raised money to purchase land to be turned over to the government. The EFC then loaned the Housing Committee money for construction. Construction was begun in June 1918, with Christmas set as the date of completion. The area had been rolling farmland with a brook running through it. Nolen hoped to "create an area of homes, play, culture, and stores easily accessible to work and city lights."[42] The most notable feature of Nolen's plan was the arrangement of streets. Wide, straight streets carried through traffic near the streetcar tracks and on either side of the stream, while narrower, curved streets were reserved for local traffic. Small areas for rubbish pick-up were designated in front of a cluster of houses. The houses, designed by the Philadelphia firm of Ballinger and Perrot, were of four basic designs, which could be further varied by changing roof lines, porch locations, and surface materials. Most of the houses were duplexes, with three bedrooms, a kitchen, dining room, and living room. Of the total fifty-eight acres, 60 percent was designated for housing, 13.2 percent for school and playground, and 25 percent for streets. Although the density of 15.83 families per acre exceeded the recommended English figure of 12, Nolen's arrangement of lawns, parkway, and open spaces provided a distinctly suburban appearance to the community.[43]

Delays pushed the completion date back, but a few houses were ready November 30. The Armistice had caused the immediate suspension of all EFC projects that were not at least 75 percent completed. At Union Park Gardens the weekly hours of construction workers were cut from sixty to forty-five, which resulted in a strike that pushed the occupation date back still further. Although the EFC continued to loan money to the city to help pave streets, install gas and electric lines, and provide streetcar service, plans were made to sell the project to the highest bidder. EFC officials wanted to sell all the units to a single buyer, but individuals, fearing eviction, wanted to buy the houses they were occupying. An auction finally took place February 27, 1922. Several firms and a few individuals bought pieces of Union Park Gardens. The EFC received $1,573,507, or about 63 percent of its original investment. Although this was less than desired, it was more than the average return on EFC housing projects. In 1920, Ackerman concluded that the EFC projects were "attractive for general suburban development, [but] are too ambitious and expensive for practical dwellings for the general run of workmen."[44] The unskilled would have to continue to eat in the kitchen.

Occasionally, of course, EFC officials were at odds with each other on labor policy. Although the National War Labor Board, the War Labor Policies Board, and the Shipbuilding Labor Adjustment Board (SLAB) all affirmed the right of workers to organize in trade unions and to bargain collectively through representatives of their own choosing, some EFC officials resisted the spirit of the law. One troublesome issue was whether union business agents could have free access to shipyards. A circular dated February 27, 1918, to "All Shipyard Owners, District Officers, and District Supervisors," from Charles Piez, announced that the EFC

has decided that it would be hardly fair to compel the shipyard owners to allow free entry to their yards of representatives of any organization for the purpose of discussing purely personal matters with the employees. The corporation feels, however, that where there is any complaint in regard to working conditions in any shipyard doing work for it, that the representatives of the organizations should be permitted to enter the yards for the purpose of looking into the matter.[45]

As early as November 4, 1917, SLAB decided that "business agents of the different crafts shall be given access to the shop or yards at the discretion of the management." Later, SLAB allowed representatives of the different crafts to "have free access to shops or yards at all times, provided they do not interfere with or cause the men to neglect their work."[46]

Still later, in April 1918, when the shop committees were being established, SLAB permitted outside representatives chosen by the committee to come in if grievances could not be settled between the committee and management. Finally, in October, 1918, the outside representative was allowed to take part in negotiations between management and shop committee members from the beginning. In 1919, Admiral Bowles issued an order prohibiting union representatives from entering the yards, which drew a strong protest from R. W. Leatherbee, who had replaced Leon C. Marshall as director of industrial relations. In the meantime, individual shipyards continued to set their own rules. D. R. Kennedy, industrial relations manager of American International at Hog Island, informed Marshall:

Our policy here has been to give a recommended representative of each Craft employed a monthly pass with instructions that they must not take up the time of the men from their work to organize them or to collect dues from the men during working hours. We are beginning to have some real difficulty and some nasty unpleasantness because, as you so put it [sic] in your letter to the heads of the National organizations, some of the business agents are really objectionable and insist on being allowed to collect dues in the yard, and directly or indirectly use some coercion in forcing men to join their particular union.[47]

The EFC's relationship with workers and organized labor was tangled skein of ambiguous policies and conflicting philosophies. This condition was in part the result of the Wilson administration's lack of a labor policy and in part the inevitable result of hasty wartime decisions. Some light can be thrown on the situation by looking at the relationship between the Division of Industrial Relations, under Marshall, and the Shipbuilding Labor Adjustment Board, under Macy. The intricate relationships between SLAB and the Division of Industrial Relations and the conflicts between Marshall and his staff on the one hand and Piez and the shipyard owners and managers on the other was ultimately very important for the future of labor relations in the industry. Marshall emerges as the key individual in the bewildering array of government agents charged with shaping labor policy. He appeared first as economic advisor to the War Labor Policies Board, which was set up in May 1918, to

fix [wage] standards to be determined for all industries in a given section of the country after investigations disclosing the conditions of life, including the cost of living and the services rendered. . .to allocate the supply [of labor] according to the productive needs of the country. . .[and to] regulate hours of labor in the various industries and determine the needs of industry with regard to housing and transportation facilities, etc.[48]

The War Labor Policies Board, headed by Felix Frankfurter and including among its members Franklin D. Roosevelt for the Navy Department, Robert P. Bass for the USSB, and Charles Piez for the EFC, was intended to be a planning body, to formulate policies by which other branches of the government could be guided.

Marshall then became director of the Division of Industrial Relations of the EFC, and finally a member of SLAB. In 1934 he was named chairman of the National Labor Relations Board. Frankfurter's efforts on behalf of the eight-hour day are well known, but Marshall experimented with several labor reform measures and may have been labor's strongest advocate in the Wilson administration. Certainly he was one of the few who regularly sought the advice of union leaders on EFC policies. This was especially important in the case of the controversy over the admission of union business agents to the yards. On the other hand, Marshall spent a considerable amount of time exploring the possibilities of shop committees for the shipbuilding industry. These committees were not conceived as representing crafts organized by independent unions, indeed they were seen by some as an acceptable alternative to unionization. Like the idea of industrial democracy from which it sprang, the shop committee obviously meant different things to different individuals. For some, it was a way of allowing workers a voice in their own affairs, an extension of political democracy into the work place. For others it was a convenient alternative to independent labor unions, a synonym for company union. Still others saw shop committees in the context of changing definitions of work, hoping to break down the growing barriers between owners and "hired men."[49]

This concept seems closest to that held by Marshall, Seager, and the staffs of both SLAB and the Industrial Relations Division of EFC. On September 17, 1918, Marshall sent a memo on shop committees to all shipyards and auxiliary plants, summarizing a report by C. G. Renold for the British Association for the Advancement of Science. The assumptions of this report were:

1. That conditions of industrial life now fail to satisfy the immediate needs of the worker; and that work under present conditions fails to satisfy the desire of self expression.
2. That the need of self-expression depends upon power of control exercised by the worker over the materials, processes, and conditions of his work. The worker must be a cog in a machine, but unless he has some perspective and understanding of the part he plays in the general mechanism, he is bound to be subject to unrest and lack of real interest in his work.[50]

Marshall went on to point out that the "extreme subdivision of processes and trades has promoted efficiency in a material way, but at the cost of interest on the part of the worker." Mechanical efficiency could be sacrificed for "more willing work and cooperation," Marshall argued, and employers should share their power with their workers and be willing to spend time discussing even the most minor grievances.

In theory the idea was simple, but in practice it met with opposition from both employers and unions because it threatened their autonomy. Even when workers and management agreed to try shop committees, the extreme division of labor in shipyards made it difficult to coordinate their activities. The result was the adoption of the "joint shop committee," a group composed of the chairmen of the separate craft shop committees; a solution bearing a remarkable similarity to an industrial union. This was recognized by Seager, who opposed representation by departments because it would be resisted by craft unions.[51] The most serious problem for SLAB, however, was the tendency of the companies to control the shop committees through excessive paternalism or simple intimidation. Again, SLAB and the EFC turned to the employment managers to assure the proper functioning of the employees' committees. In memorandum after memorandum in the EFC files, there are suggestions for employment departments to see

that conditions are established which will arouse the confidence and enthusiasm of the workers and show them that the company's policy toward them is one of fair dealing. . . . The Employment Department brings home to the company the need and importance of encouraging and respecting such suggestions [made by employees].[52]

Like Marshall, V. Everit Macy seems to have been an advocate of industrial democracy through the shop committee. Macy is a good example of a patrician reformer who was basically aloof from both industry and labor. The heir to a fortune based first on whale oil, then on petroleum, Macy was on the boards of several banks and other corporations in New York City when Wilson picked him as chairman of the Shipbuilding Labor Adjustment Board. Although portrayed as an evangelist for capitalism and a foe of socialism, Macy himself blamed 60 percent of the Seattle strike on selfish employers and 40 percent on radical leaders who thought themselves strong enough to defy their national officers.[53]

By the end of the war, spokesmen for both management and labor praised the Macy Board, and its decisions served as the model for the "Bethlehem Agreement," which governed labor relations in the Bethlehem shipyards from January 7, 1919, to the autumn of 1921.[54]

The Shipbuilding Labor Adjustment Board, also known as the Macy Board, was conceived in the midst of shipyard strikes in the summer of 1917. Louis B. Wehle, nephew of Louis D. Brandeis and friend of Franklin D. Roosevelt, had come to Washington as a member of the law committee of the General Munitions Board. In that position he drafted a provision for contracts between the Army and private building contractors that allowed the government contractors to settle labor disputes between the builder and his employees. This led in turn to the agreement between Secretary of War Newton Baker and Samuel Gompers to create an adjustment commission composed of representatives of the Army, the public, and labor to adjust and control wages, hours, and conditions of labor in the construction of cantonments. Wehle openly espoused strong federal authority in wartime labor-management relations, and his willingness to bypass employers and, to a certain extent, organized labor in creating commissions and boards in Washington for the control of wages and working conditions is significant. He and Baker hoped to avoid the British solution to labor disputes—compulsory arbitration—by simply dictating rates and hours. "The American situation," Wehle wrote, "seemed to lend itself to postponing and perhaps completely avoiding compulsory arbitration: Skilled labor was not so highly organized as in Britain, and we had in Gompers a labor leader of great moral power, genuine patriotism, and strong influence."[55]

Wehle was anxious to avoid committing the government to the closed shop or even to using union standards to determine wages, hours, and conditions. He felt that it was enough that "for the first time in American history the United States Government, through an executive official, had negotiated on even terms with a union leader as such." In August Wehle was named general counsel of the EFC and asked by Joseph Tumulty to organize wage adjustment machinery for shipbuilding. Wehle found the situation in shipbuilding considerably more complicated than in the cantonments. Instead of one temporary employer, there were "scores of employers, owners of permanent shipyards, old and new, where ships were under construction." Some had open shops, other closed shops. There were more unions involved, and the Metal Trades Department was more independent of the AFL than was the Building Trades Department. When he failed to get Gompers to support a board that would establish standards, whether union or nonunion, which had been in force in a particular plant on July 15, 1917, Wehle turned to James O'Connell, president, and A. J. Berres, secretary of the Metal Trades Department of the AFL. They too rejected his proposal until John Donlin, president of the Building Trades Department, who had worked with Wehle on the cantonment agreement, convinced the Metal Trades officials that Wehle's intentions were good.[56]

The agreement of August 20, 1917, which established the SLAB, was vague about the structure and authority of the board but gave both union and nonunion workers considerable voice in settling disputes.

When matters concerning any plant or plants are before the board, it shall invite a person representing, and designated by the owner or owners of such plant or plants, and also a person representing, or selected by the majority of the workers in the particular craft or crafts directly interested in the disputed matters, both of said representatives to sit with voting power as associate members of said board in connection with such matters.[57]

The memorandum was signed by O'Connell, Berres, Donlin, and Gompers, as well as by representatives of the Machinists, Molders, Carpenters, Electrical Workers, Plumbers, Union of Steam and Operating Engineers, Boilermakers, Pattern Makers, Blacksmiths, Metal Polishers, and Sheetmetal Workers. Hurley and Capps signed for the USSB and EFC. Employers were not consulted in the organization of SLAB, since the government was paying for labor as well as material and because the owners were not well organized themselves. It was more difficult to find a single spokesman for the industry than it was for labor. Gompers was consulted not only on the selection of a labor representative for the three-man board but for the public member as well. Hurley was to name the EFC representative. Labor had little to lose in cooperating with the government, since most yards were not well organized and the industry had been so unstable in the past that unions had been unable to protect their members from layoffs and wage cuts. The provision for workers in a shop to elect a representative under government supervision must have seemed a golden opportunity to organize previously unorganized workers.

· The gold turned to lead after SLAB's first experience in the field. Macy, E. F. Carry, a Chicago manufacturer, and Berres constituted the original board. According to Wehle, Henry R. Seager of Columbia University was brought in as an economist, although his official title was secretary, and W. Jett Lauck, an economist with close ties to labor, was named statistician. No sooner did this group begin meeting with representatives from Pacific Coast yards than Hurley and Capps announced that they would not pay wage increases that they themselves did not approve. The ground was cut from under the board. Supported by Baker and Roosevelt, Wehle wrote Wilson that Hurley "is playing with dynamite; he is jeopardizing the honor of the government in its dealings with organized labor."[58] On September 23, Hurley, Macy, and Gompers were called to the White House, and the dispute was settled in favor of the Macy Board. Louis A. Coolidge, a United Shoe Machinery Company official, was named to replace Carry, and the board left for Seattle to try to settle the strike that had broken out. By November 4, the board had established a uniform wage scale for the entire Pacific Coast. It made substantial increases in wages and agreed to review them by February 1, 1918. It refused to sanction the union shop in Portland, where it had not existed before the war, but did encourage the establishment of shop committees that could, as a last resort, call in a representative of organized labor to negotiate directly with employers.[59]

Out of the experience on the Pacific Coast, SLAB revised the agreement of August 20, and on December 8, 1917, published a new memorandum on the adjustment of wages, hours, and conditions of labor in shipbuilding plants. The major changes were the elimination of the representatives of the company and the workers in a shop, a strengthening of the power of SLAB-appointed examiners, and a shift from the wages in force in a single plant to "the wage rate prevailing in the district" in which the shipyards were located as the basic standard. Hotchkiss and Seager argue,

These changes all worked in the direction of simplification and standardization. More definitely than the agreement of August 20, that of December 8 placed upon the international officers of labor unions the authority to represent labor even in cases having a local significance and made one board, in which the government, the general public, and labor were each represented by a single member, the instrument for all adjustments. Realization of the necessity of such a board, with power to make final decisions and to create its own machinery for enforcing them, came not because of any preconceived theory but because of the growing appreciation of the gravity of the emergency that confronted the country and of the importance of unified action.[60]

Gompers seems to have won important concessions—the district wage rate and the elimination of possible rival union representation in the bargaining process—but the faith that the board placed in the officers of the international unions was misplaced, as events in Seattle in 1919 were to prove.

The next two months were busy ones for SLAB. Strikes broke out in Wilmington, Philadelphia, and other East Coast yards. The major cause of these strikes was wages. Both wages and piece rates paid to workers in the same craft in different yards varied greatly. On February 14, 1918, the board gave its Valentine to workers in the Delaware River district. It fixed the hourly wage for skilled craftsmen at 72.5 cents an hour, or $5.80 for the eight-hour day, as compared with $5.775 on the Pacific Coast, but it allowed the creation in some crafts of second-class mechanics who received slightly less. The recognition of a second class of skilled craftsmen was, in the words of Hotchkiss and Seager, "in conformity with local custom as embodied in the uniform classification of occupations recommended by the joint committee of yard owners and employees." Arguing that a second class was only created when there was an inadequate supply of fully qualified mechanics, the decision nevertheless contributed further to the bewildering number of wage rates in shipyards. For example, the wage scale in effect October 1, 1918, on the Atlantic Coast, Gulf Coast, and Great Lakes, included 188 different job classifications and about 15 different wage rates.[61]

Nor were these the only differences between the Pacific Coast and the Delaware River awards. Uniform piece rates were established, carfare was granted when the cost to or from a yard exceeded eight cents, and the Saturday half-holiday was granted for the entire year, "in keeping with a long-established custom." A feature of the Pacific Coast award absent from the Delaware River decision was the prescription of shop committees. The board hoped that the employers and unions would establish grievance machinery on their own. When they did not, the provisions for shop committees were subsequently restored.[62]

Although the shop committees might forestall unionism, they seem to have coexisted with craft union locals in many yards, and the Metal Trades Department of the AFL approved their existence in the Bethlehem Agreement in 1919. In the context of the times, the board's support for shop committees must be seen as prolabor. So it seemed to Charles Piez when in September 1918 he wrote to Felix Frankfurter and Hurley, complaining,

I am not at all certain that in these trying times a widespread attempt to secure an immediate recourse to collective bargaining will not have unwholesome and disastrous effect on the producing capacity of our factories. . . . I feel most distinctly that this is not the time to launch a widespread attempt to democratize industry, for it must be borne in mind that, owing to conditions engendered by the war, labor has drifted from one shop to another, and that in consequence many important industries are manned heavily by 'Floaters' and irresponsibles, who have taken the place of the more fit and ambitious who have either entered the service or have sought employment in more remunerative occupations.[63]

Piez went on to express his preference for collective bargaining with labor unions rather than unaffiliated shop committees, feeling that it was unwise "to entrust the reins of government to people who have not yet reached the proper stage of development to exercise it." Piez's social Darwinism aside, the long-term significance of this attitude is clear. The shop committee, with its promise of industrial democracy and its dependence on government participation in the process of collective bargaining was less desirable from the point of view of business than the two-sided battle between company and union.

In short, it is difficult to disagree with Horace Drury's conclusion in 1921:

The practical operations of the Shipping Board have, to a very large extent, been in the hands of a small group of shipping men who represented in their former associations a group particularly hostile to trade unionism. But, on the other hand, there have been most of the time on the Shipping Board and in the Shipping Board organization individuals who have frankly sought to make the board's policy one of meeting the unions half way, and enlisting the support of these voluntary associations in the building up of the methods and agencies of adjustment which would be cooperative rather than dictatorial or one-sided in their operation.[64]

Both the Macy Board and the Industrial Relations Division took a broad view of labor relations and gave the workers and unions the benefit of every doubt. Marshall's memos are models of fairness and openness to suggestion. In trying to explain the causes of absenteeism to shipyard managers, Marshall listed four causes—overtime, high wages, alcoholism, and mental attitude—and urged employment officers to consider all possible causes in trying to reduce absenteeism in their yards. Attempting to deal with complaints received from individuals and firms, Marshall drew up a list of fifteen frequent complaints, including "that men are discharged because they belong to a union, or to a shop committee," "that men are discharged for refusing to join the union," and "that labor representatives are not admitted into the shipyards, or if admitted, make improper use of their privilege."[65]

The most conspicuous failure of SLAB and the Industrial Relations Division of EFC was in Seattle. The well-organized and locally powerful Central Labor Council of Seattle had never been happy with the Macy Board award of November 4, 1917. Skinner and Eddy, the largest of Seattle's seventeen shipyards, with over 13,000 workers, consistently scamped labor by paying wages above the board's scale. When Charles Piez tried to take personal control of the Seattle labor situation, the result was confusion and further undercutting of the authority of SLAB and the EFC. There were several factors which made Seattle a likely center of labor unrest. Workers and craft locals in that city gave unusual support to the Central Labor Council. "No matter what union a Seattle workers belonged to, he was most conscious of being a member of a *Seattle* labor organization. This intense localism was unique. . . . The Seattle labor movement caused the AFL leaders endless trouble. It stood for everything Samuel Gompers rejected— labor in politics, industrial unionism, and nationalization of key industries."[66] There was also the strong influence in the Northwest of the Industrial Workers of the World, with many Wobblies trying to capture the AFL unions by boring from within. Finally, there was simply a provincial distrust of the Eastern-dominated AFL.

The two most important issues that remained unsolved after the Macy Board award of 1917 were wages and the open shop. Because shipyard workers in Seattle were making higher wages than any other shipbuilders in the country, the board's uniform wage rate cost the government money. Secondly, shipyards in Seattle were under closed union shop agreements, whereas those in Portland and some in the San Francisco Bay area were not. "Seattle labor was particularly apprehensive that a regional standard would be used as a first step in taking away advantages its labor movement had won by its own efforts, thus helping to destroy the organization itself."[67] Even after the Macy Board allowed the Seattle yards to pay a 10 percent bonus to their workers, the unions felt cheated. Management too felt confident that Seattle yards could offset high wages with increased production if they were left free of government control. Piez's final report acknowledges that Skinner & Eddy Yard No. 1 was the second best yard in the country in performance as measured in deadweight tons per man per year.[68] Labor turnover was also low in most Seattle yards. The Armistice brought renewed demands by the shipyard unions to negotiate a new contract. In December, the Seattle Metal Trades Council announced wage demands of $8.00 per day for mechanics, $7.00 for specialists, $6.00 for helpers, and $5.50 for laborers.

Moreover, that Metal Trades Council claimed jurisdiction over workers in the wooden boat yards. The wage demand was rejected by management, and the jurisdictional claim caused some protest from unions not represented on the council, but the Metal Trades unions boldly went on strike on January 21, 1919. On February 6, they were joined by 65,000 other workers in all occupations, creating one of America's largest strikes.

The shipyard strike highlights the divisions within the EFC between those who were sympathetic toward labor and those who represented management's position. In terms of personalities, the division was between R. W. Leatherbee, who had succeeded Marshall, and Piez, who was now director general. Piez, relying on confidential reports from the EFC district manager in Seattle, was led to believe that the Federal Employment Office was dominated by organized labor and that a dozen "undesirables and unpatriotic labor men" were responsible for the unrest.[69] Leatherbee defended the leaders of the AFL, arguing that they had been "wickedly and maliciously played upon—surely on the one hand by the IWW movement—possibly on the other hand by the shipbuilders themselves—to such an extent that from all practical reasons they had little choice as to what they should do, and were forced to strike." Leatherbee reported to Piez the rumors that shipyard owners encouraged the AFL to strike in the belief that the EFC would grant the increases. From this perspective it looked as if labor and management were conspiring to test the authority of the federal government, and Leatherbee urged Piez to join with the secretary of the navy in holding firm against these pressures.[70]

A few days later, on the eve of the strike, Leatherbee prepared a long memo for one of his staff with questions about the relative influence of the AFL and IWW in the shipyard strike. The answers were penciled beside his questions. Both questions and answers suggest that the EFC had put too much faith in the national AFL leadership and its ability to enforce the Macy Board decisions at the local level. In answer to the question, Do the International Presidents of the American Federation of Labor think that the Emergency Fleet Corporation in any way violated its part of the agreement which created the Macy Board, in regard to conditions in Seattle? Leatherbee was told that some did and some didn't, but that those who did felt that the EFC should have made clear whether rates fixed by the board were maximums or minimums. Although answers to questions of IWW influence indicate that the AFL did not feel threatened by the Wobblies, they also suggest that the federation felt impotent in the Seattle situation.[71]

Throughout February and March, as Seattle's workers drifted back to work, or on to other cities, Leatherbee fought for a continuation or a substitution of the Macy Board, but on April 1, 1919, SLAB was terminated, and labor relations in the shipbuilding industry returned to their prewar status, except in the yards covered by the Bethlehem contract. The Division of Industrial Relations was discontinued a month later. Construction began to be curtailed immediately after the Armistice and contracts canceled. Men were laid off by the thousands, and the wages of those who remained were either frozen or cut. A strike involving

35,000 men in San Francisco lasted from October through December 1919, and other strikes broke out across the country, but to no avail. Although ships under construction continued to employ men through June 30, 1921, the end of the shipbuilding boom was sudden and complete. From a peak of 336,857, employment in shipyards fell below the prewar level to 75,000 in June 1920, and lower still in 1921.[72] For the next fifteen years, shipbuilding experienced a severe depression, which resulted in the permanent closing of several yards. The techniques of standardization and fabrication were abandoned. Unions lost members and contracts. Employment managers had few men to manage. The great promise of 1917 was lost.

Yet the record of the EFC remains impressive. Starting with little, the corporation launched 480 vessels before the end of the war, 117 of them steel ships built specifically for the government. At Hog Island, construction of the yard did not begin until the summer of 1917, yet the first keel was laid February 12, 1918, and the first ship launched August 5. Eventually, all 110 cargo ships ordered by the EFC were delivered by American International Shipbuilding Corporation, and 12 of the 70 troop transports. By June 23, 1921, the EFC took possession of 1,455 ships. The EFC had built two dozen new communities with over 9,000 houses, apartments, hotels, dormitories, and stores, accommodating more than 28,000 men and their families. The Employment Management Branch had trained sixty new employment managers and placed seventeen of them in shipyards; published seven bulletins on selection and placement of shipyard workers, including "Opportunities in Shipbuilding for the Physically Handicapped"; and developed standard forms to help personnel officers record and keep track of shipyard employees.[73] The government's shipbuilding program in World War I involved thousands of men with various ideas and causes to promote—standardization and fabrication of steel ships, employment management, government ownership— and conflict and criticism were inescapable. Some wanted to prove that American industry could raise production to even higher levels than had been previously attained and win the economic as well as the military war. Most agreed with Charles Schwab when he said, "Hog Island suffered from the same cause that hampered other war industries—the fact that the war ended before it had an opportunity to prove its real value.[74]

Obviously, many daily habits of shipyard workers and their employers did not change in eighteen months. Continuing conflicts over job classifications reveal the conservatism of the skilled workers. Traditionalists like Homer L. Ferguson of Newport News Shipbuilding and Dry Dock Company were anxious to pronounce fabrication a failure. Yet the intensity of daily life in 1917 and 1918 left its mark on the men in the yards and offices. Labor, having benefited from the decisions of the Macy Board, looked more eagerly to Washington for help in gaining recognition from employers and in collective bargaining. Managers and owners learned quickly too the value of organization. In 1936, when shipbuilding was again stimulated by government subsidy and the threat of war, the industry was ready to play an equal role in the tripartite agencies that were planning the future of the U.S. merchant marine. Marshall, Seager, and others returned to teaching and writing, promoting their ideas on management secure in the knowledge that their experience in the EFC proved their theories. Some, like Morris L. Cooke, were able to return to Washington in the 1930s to revive the old wartime spirit in the service of the New Deal.[75]

World War I caught the shipbuilding industry at a moment when its owners and managers were beginning to break the habits and traditions of the past. New technologies, new corporate organization, and new management techniques were slowly being introduced. The war accelerated these changes. Workers were not as eager to accept the changes wrought by prefabrication and partnerships to corporations. The crafts tried to maintain their work culture, including the hierarchies of skills and the autonomy of individual unions. The prewar culture of shipbuilding was based on paternalism, pride in craft, and a fatalistic acceptance of long periods of inactivity and limited construction. The war disrupted this condition. Business and labor saw an opportunity for growth and increased power. But where there had been two contending parties there were now three. Government managers and planners created their own occupational group with habits shaped by a belief in public interest and experience in social reform. Shipbuilding, like all business, was no longer seen as an isolated activity producing a product as the result of a contract between individuals. It was part of an organized, patterned, national culture, dominated by the values of capitalism *and* democracy. The USSB/EFC became an instrument to teach the new values of planning, cooperation, and personal fulfillment. Owners were encouraged to think in terms of mass production; managers were to bring about "industrial democracy" with government authority as a mediating force; and workers were introduced to the rewards of organized leisure and material abundance—the company team, nutritious lunches, and the separate dining room. That the promise was not fulfilled, that new habits were not completely formed, is less important than the way the experience actually worked. Culture change is uneven and subject to different interpretations by those experiencing it. Neither Hurley's toy boats nor Nolen's "garden city" could accomplish the total change from the old individualistic capitalism to the new government-corporate partnership, from an economy based on work and production to one based on leisure and consumption, but changes did take place—piecemeal, contradictory changes that continued through another cycle of boom and bust, leaving unformed still the habits of 1918.[76]

In the years since the end of the Emergency Fleet Corporation, the federal bureaucracy has expanded enormously in size and complexity, yet the pattern of development for large-scale government projects remains similar. In many ways, the National Aeronautics and Space Administration repeated the experience of the EFC. Although NASA grew out of an existing space advisory committee, it was essentially a special purpose, crash program, focused chiefly on putting a man on the moon. Its years of greatest activity, 1962-66, were hardly longer than that of the EFC. Employing 400,000 workers at its peak in 1966, NASA "managed" many more workers through its contracts with private corporations and through the coordinated activities of other federal agencies. Indeed, NASA could assume that many areas of labor management could be left to union contracts and various agencies of the departments of Labor; Health, Education, and Welfare; and Housing and Urban Development. For example, the Huntsville, Alabama, location of the Marshall Space Flight Center received one of the first model cities grants with the goal of

revision and upgrading of curriculum, teaching methods, and facilities; vocational and on-the-job employment training; employment information services; establishment of a light industry park; expanded public transportation facilities; a housing counseling service; three multipurpose health centers; and neighborhood parks and recreation facilities.[77]

All these activities were legacies of the EFC and other government projects that sought to ameliorate conditions in communities affected by federally stimulated growth.

Just as EFC had created a new shipyard at Hog Island, Pennsylvania, NASA created facilities in Hancock County, Mississippi, and New Orleans, Louisiana. Near the Kennedy Space Flight Center in Florida and the Marshall Center in Alabama as much as 30 percent of the total work force was directly employed by NASA, and many more were indirectly supported. NASA-stimulated growth forced Brevard County, Florida, to raise property taxes to support new schools, yet within three years the work force had declined over 40 percent. Although the history of labor-management relations in the aerospace industry remains to be written, it appears that NASA's record is somewhat better than the EFC's. NASA was aware of the potential social impact of its projects and sought to preserve much of what it had created. It is probably significant that James E. Webb, administrator of NASA, was a lawyer who had been a federal bureaucrat with several important agencies, whereas Edward Hurley of the USSB had been a businessman and inventor. By 1961, management demanded a greater degree of specialization and legal knowledge. Yet, like Hurley, Webb was a master of public relations as well as of administration. Webb took as his models the Panama Canal, TVA, and the Manhattan Project. "A hierarchical system of authority," Webb has written, "the hallmark of the traditionalists, is in one form or another essential."[78] But if hierarchy is the hallmark of modern management, democracy is the cornerstone of American government. Perhaps the permanent departments of government can never achieve the efficiency of the special, short-term programs, but it is through them that the best accomplishments of the special-purpose endeavors will be perpetuated and their benefits diffused throughout society.

NOTES

1. Thomas C. Cochran, *Business in American Life: A History* (New York: McGraw-Hill, 1972), p. 217.

2. David Brody, *Steelworkers in America: The Nonunion Era* (Cambridge, Harvard University Press, 1960). See also Alfred D. Chandler, Jr., *Strategy and Structure: Chapters in the History of the American Industrial Enterprise* (Cambridge, Mass.: MIT Press, 1962); Warren Van Tine, *The Making of the Labor Bureaucrat: Union Leadership in the United States, 1870-1920* (Amherst: University of Massachusetts Press, 1974); Jerry Israel, ed., *Building the Organizational Society: Essays on Associational Activities in Modern America* (New York: Free Press, 1972); and Bernard Mergen, "Blacksmiths and Welders: Identity and Phenomenal Change," *Industrial and Labor Relations Review* 25, no. 3 (April 1972): 354-62.

3. John G. B. Hutchins, "History and Development of the Shipbuilding Industry in the United States," in *The Shipbuilding Business in the United States of America*, ed. F. G. Fassett, Jr., vol. 1 (New York: Society of Naval Architects and Marine Engineers, 1948), pp. 14-60; and George W. Dickie, "Can the American Shipbuilder Under Present Conditions Compete with the British and German Shipbuilders in the Production of the Largest Class of Ocean Passenger and Freight Steamships?" *Transactions of the Society of Naval Architects and Marine Engineers* 8 (1900): 173-96.

4. Dickie, "Can the American Shipbuilder," p. 196.

5. Richard Brown, et al., "Leisure in Work: The 'Occupational Culture' of Shipbuilding," in *Leisure and Society in Britain*, ed. M. A. Smith, S. Parker, and C. A. Smith (London: Allen Lane, 1973), pp. 98, 107; Bernard Mergen, "Work and Play in an Occupational Subculture: American Shipyard Workers, 1917-1977," in *Play: Anthropological Perspectives*, ed. Michael Salter (West Point, N.Y.: Leisure Press, 1978), pp. 187-200.

6. Dickie, "Can the American Shipbuilder," p. 192.

7. John F. Metten, "The New York Shipbuilding Corporation," *Historical Transactions of the Society of Naval Architects and Marine Engineers, 1893-1943* (1944): 222-30; R.H.M. Robinson, "Fabricated Ships," *Transactions of the Society of Naval Architects and Marine Engineers* 25 (1917): 137; Craig Andrews, "Fabrication in Shipbuilding" (Unpublished paper for Curator of Marine Transportation, National Museum of History and Technology, 1973); "Henry Grant Morse," in *The National Cyclopaedia of American Biography*, vol. 29 (New York: J.T. White, 1941), pp. 242-43.

8. Richard J. Wright, *Freshwater Whales: A History of the American Ship Building Company and Its Predecessors* (Kent, Ohio: Kent State University Press, 1969), p. 81.

9. J. D. MacBride, "Manufactured Ships," *Scientific American* (March 11, 1919): 130; Andrews, "Fabrication in Shipbuilding," p. 3.

10. "Maritime Legislation of the United States in the Twentieth Century to the Enactment of the Merchant Marine Act, 1936," appendix B, "The Use and Disposition of Ships and Shipyards at the End of World War II," no. 48, June 1945, A Report Prepared for the United States Navy Department and the United States Maritime Commission by the Graduate School of Business Administration, Harvard University.

11. "William Denman," in *Who Was Who*, vol. 3 (Chicago: Marquis, 1960), p. 221.

12. Robert D. Cuff, *The War Industries Board: Business-Government Relations During World War I* (Baltimore: Johns Hopkins University Press, 1973), p. 90.

13. Melvin Urofsky, *Big Steel and the Wilson Administration: A Study of Business-Government Relations* (Columbus: Ohio State University Press, 1969), p. 203.

14. W. C. Mattox, *Building the Emergency Fleet* (Cleveland: Penton, 1920), pp. 24-25.

15. Joseph P. Cotton, "Fabricated Steel Ship Project," Memorandum, July 25, 1917,

National Archives, Record Group 32, United States Shipping Board, Construction Organization, Old General File 173-3. Hereafter cited as RG 32, followed by file numbers.

16. *Shipping Board Operations*, Testimony of Willian Denman to U.S. Congress (Washington, D.C.: Government Printing Office, 1920), pp. 3171-78; Andrews, "Fabrication in Shipbuilding," p. 14. While Goethals was organizing the structural steel trade and negotiating with the three agency contractors, Theodore E. Ferris designed a standard cargo steamer that could be built from commercial structural shapes and plates with a minimum of bending. The ship had a flat bottom and could be built in either 5,000- or 7,500-deadweight-ton capacity.

17. "Edward Nash Hurley," in *Dictionary of American Biography*, vol. 21, supp. 1 (New York: Scribner's, 1944), p. 446; Edward N. Hurley, *The Bridge to France* (Philadelphia: Lippincott, 1927).

18. "Charles Piez," in *Who Was Who*, vol. 1 (Chicago: Marquis, 1950), p. 973; *Emergency Fleet Corporation Personnel* (Washington, D.C.: Government Printing Office, 1919), p. 144; Wright, *Freshwater Whales*, pp. 182-83.

19. Mattox, *Building the Emergency Fleet*, p. 56.

20. *Emergency Fleet Corporation Personnel*, p. 139; Mattox, *Building the Emergency Fleet*, pp. 70-79; *Emergency Fleet News* (August 1, 1918): 8-9. Some of these posters are on display in the Hall of American Maritime Enterprise, National Museum of History and Technology, Smithsonia Institution, Washington, D.C.

21. *Emergency Fleet News* (June 3, 1918): 2.

22. *Emergency Fleet News* (December 5, 1918): 1, and (January 1, 1919): 9. There was an ironic end to this episode when the Ives Manufacturing Company of Bridgeport, Connecticut, went out of business in 1929. According to Louis Hertz, Hurley convinced Harry Ives that it was his patriotic duty to make and distribute a toy merchant fleet, which Ives did, even after his accountants told him that the boats were losing money. See Louis Hertz, *Messrs. Ives of Bridgeport* (Wethersfield, Conn.: Mark Harbor, 1950), pp. 134-35. The advertising copy in the 1919 Ives catalog sounds as if it had been written by Hurley himself: A boy "can get throughly interested in the great game of commerce and the big Merchant Marine of his country. He can talk it, play it, and interest his chums in it. . . . Who knows but what it may lead them into the big business of transportation by sea that is going to play such a wonderful part in the future world trade of the United States?"

23. Ernest Martin Hopkins to Morris L. Cooke, February 4, 1918, RG 32, Records of the Industrial Relations Division, 277, 43. On Bloomfield, see Claude S. George, *The History of Management Thought* (Englewood Cliff, N.J.: Prentice-Hall, 1972), pp. xii, 123, 129; Edmund M. Lynch, *Meyer Bloomfield and Employment Management* (Austin: University of Texas Press, 1970); *Dictionary of American Biography*, supp. 2, pp. 45-46; *Who Was Who*, vol. 1, p. 109.

24. Lynch, *Meyer Bloomfield*, p. ix. For recent interpretations of welfare capitalism in this period, see Daniel Nelson, *Managers and Workers: Origins of the New Factory System in the United States, 1880-1920* (Madison: University of Wisconsin Press, 1975); Stuart D. Brandes, *American Welfare Capitalism, 1880-1940* (Chicago: University of Chicago Press, 1976); and David Noble, *America by Design: Science, Technology, and the Rise of Corporate Capitalism* (New York: Oxford University Press, 1977).

25. U.S. Shipping Board and Emergency Fleet Corporation, *Report of New England Shipbuilding Conference* (Washington, D.C.: Government Printing Office, 1918), pp. 15-17.

26. USSB/EFC, *New England Shipbuilding Conference*, p. 50.

27. U.S. Shipping Board and Emergency Fleet Corporation, *Report of the Shipyard Employment Managers' Conference* (Washington, D.C.: Government Printing Office, 1918), pp. 15-16.

28. Ibid., p. 38.

29. Ibid., pp. 3-4.

30. U.S. Shipping Board, *First Annual Report of the United States Shipping Board* (Washington, D.C.: Government Printing Office, 1917), p. 7.

31. Replies to questionnaire, February-May 1918, RG 32, 233, trays 15-22, files 103, 110, 221, 301, 302, 303, 306, 504, 703, 705, 823, 904, 914, 1002, 1003, 1004, 1007, 1201, 1202.

32. Alyce Whitner to USSB, April 4, 1918; Head, Industrial Service Department, to Alyce Whitner, April 10, 1918, RG 32, 277, 47, 136-3. See tray 46, file 132-1 for letters from deserted wives.

33. List of women employed, RG 32, 277, 47, 144-1. See also, *Saturday Evening Post*, November 17, 1917.

34. *Emergency Fleet News*, October 24, 1918, p. 11; Memorandum from Clara M. Tead to Stanley King, War Department, May 16, 1918, RG 32, 279, 53.

35. Lillian Erskine, *The Problem of Physical Efficiency in the Shipyards* (Washington, D.C.: Government Printing Office, 1918), p. 5.

36. U.S. Department of Labor, *Report of the United States Housing Corporation*, vol. 1 (Washington, D.C.: Government Printing Office, 1919), p. 10; ibid., vol. 2 (1920), pp. 11-12. I am indebted to Richard Shea for the use of his unpublished paper, "The Emergency Fleet Corporation and the Housing of War Workers (With a Short History of the EFC's Housing Project in Wilmington, Delaware)."

37. Roy Lubove, "Homes and 'A Few Well Placed Fruit Trees': An Object Lesson in Federal Housing," *Social Research* 27, no. 4 (Winter 1960): 471.

38. Ibid., pp. 471-72.

39. Ibid., pp. 481-82; *Yorkship News* (April 15, 1919): 6, 11.

40. *Yorkship News* (June 1919): 19; Erskine, *Physical Efficiency*, p. 10.

41. Frederick Ackerman, *Housing the Shipbuilders* U.S. Shipping Board/Emergency Fleet Corporation, (Philadelphia: 1920); *Philadelphia Record*, September 29, 1918, magazine section; John Nolen, *War-Time Housing and Community Development*: Report to the Wilmington Chamber of Commerce, Wilmington, Delaware, 1918, pp. 11-16; Shea, "Emergency Fleet Corporation," pp. 28-30.

42. John L. Hancock, "John Nolen and the American City Planning Movement: A History of Culture Change and Community Response, 1900-1940" (Ph. D. diss., University of Pennsylvania, 1964), p. 288; Shea, "Emergency Fleet Corporation," pp. 30-32; Nolen, *War-Time Housing*, pp. 5-7.

43. Emile G. Perrot, "Recent Government Housing Development: Union Park Gardens," in *Housing Problems in America* (National Housing Conference, 1918), p. 108; Richard Childs, "The Government's Model Villages," *Survey* (February 1, 1919); Shea, "Emergency Fleet Corporation," pp. 41-42.

44. Wilmington *Evening Journal*, October 29, 1918, quoted in Shea, "Emergency Fleet Corporation," p. 45; Ackerman, *Housing*, p. 2. H. O. Trowbridge to EFC, April 26, 1918; C. W. Doten to Trowbridge, April 30, 1918, RG 32, 277, 47, 140-1.

45. Charles Piez to All Shipyard Owners, District Officers, and District Supervisors, February 27, 1918, RG 32, 273, 53806-1.

46. Henry Seager-E. C. Felton correspondence, February-June 1918, RG 32, 290, 32;

J. Caldwell Jenkins, *Codification of the Shipbuilding Labor Adjustment Board Awards* (Washington, D. C.: Government Printing Office, 1921), p. 14.

47. D. R. Kennedy to L. C. Marshall, July 5, 1919, RG 32, 273, 53806-1.

48. Willard E. Hotchkiss and Henry R. Seager, *History of the Shipbuilding Labor Adjustment Board 1917 to 1919*, U.S. Department of Labor, Bureau of Labor Statistics Bulletin, no. 283 (Washington, D.C.: Government Printing Office, 1921); Alexander M. Bing, *War-Time Strikes and Their Adjustment* (New York: Dutton, 1921), pp. 312-13; Joseph W. Powell, "Labor in Shipbuilding," in Fassett, *Shipbuilding*, pp. 271-94.

49. For Marshall's biography, see *Who Was Who*, vol. 4, p. 614. On Frankfurter, see Urofsky, *Big Steel*, pp. 272-73; Nelson, *Managers and Workers*, pp. 159-60. On shop committees, see Daniel Rodgers, *The Work Ethic in Industrial America, 1850-1920* (Chicago: University of Chicago Press, 1978), pp. 58-64; Milton Derber, "The Idea of Industrial Democracy in America, 1898-1915," *Labor History* 7, no. 3 (Fall 1966): 259-86, and "The Idea of Industrial Democracy in America, 1915-1935," *Labor History* 8, no. 1 (Winter 1967): 3-29; and Marshall to various union presidents and shipyard managers, July 2, 1918, RG 32, 273, 53806-1.

50. Marshall to All Shipyards and Auxiliary Plants, September 17, 1918, RG 32, 273, 53713-1, part 1.

51. Seager to Marshall, July 26, 1918, RG 32, 273, 53713-1.

52. Employees' Committees, n.d., RG 32, 279, tray 54.

53. "V. Everit Macy," in *Dictionary of American Biography*, vol. 12, pp. 179-80. Among Macy's many philanthropies were the National Child Labor Committee, the poor of Westchester County, and the Girl Scouts. James Weinstein, *The Corporate Ideal in the Liberal State: 1900-1918* (Boston: Beacon Press, 1968), pp. 134-35; Robert L. Friedheim, *The Seattle General Strike* (Seattle: University of Washington Press, 1964), pp. 78-79; Bing, *War-Time Strikes*, p. 26.

54. Powell, "Labor in Shipbuilding," pp. 280-83; W. Jessup to R. W. Leatherbee, February 11, 1919; and Piez to James O'Connell, February 17, 1919, RG 32, 273, 53795-3.

55. Louis B. Wehle, *Hidden Threads of History* (New York: Macmillan, 1953), p. 23.

56. Ibid., pp. 23, 40.

57. Hotchkiss and Seager, *History*, pp. 8-9, Jenkins, *Codification*, p. 8.

58. Wehle, *Hidden Threads*, pp. 45-46.

59. Ibid., p. 49; Hotchkiss and Seager, *History*, pp. 13-23.

60. Hotchkiss and Seager, *History*, pp. 13-14.

61. Ibid., pp. 24-26, 103. According to Bing, there were 101 shipyard strikes in 1917 and 138 in 1918 (Bing, *War-Time Strikes*, p. 295). Horace B. Drury gives slightly higher figures in his *History of Shipbuilding Stabilization*, pt. 1 (Washington, D.C.: Industrial College of the Armed Forces, Technical Liaison Staff, June 1947), p. 99. Drury also provides comparative figures for World War II: 29 strikes in 1942, 86 in 1943, and 156 in 1944.

62. Hotchkiss and Seager, *History*, pp. 25-26.

63. Piez to Macy, August 13, 1918, and Piez to Frankfurter, September 24, 1918, RG 32, 290, 39, and 140 (10), 127-1.

64. Horace B. Drury, "The Labor Policy of the Shipping Board," *Journal of Political Economy* 29, no. 1 (January 1921): 3.

65. Marshall to All Firms Engaged in Work for the Emergency Fleet Corporation, July 31, 1918; Marshall to Executive Heads of Divisions and Sections, August 2, 1918; and Marshall to Wolfe, October 25, 1918, RG, 32, 140 (9), 120-1; and 273, 53713-1.

66. Friedheim, *Seattle General Strike*, pp. 26-27.

67. Ibid., p. 61.

68. *Report of Director General Charles Piez to the Board of Trustees of the United States Shipping Board Emergency Fleet Corporation (Philadelphia) April 30, 1919* (Washington, D.C.: Government Printing Office, 1919), p. 118.

69. J. F. Blain to Piez, October 5, 1918, RG 32, 140 (9), 120-21.

70. Leatherbee to Piez, January 31, 1919, RG 32, 273, 53832-4, part 2.

71. Leatherbee to J. J. Casey, February 5, 1919, RG 32, 273, 53832-4, part 3.

72. Leatherbee to Piez, February 28, 1919, RG 32, 273, 53795-3, part 1; *Fourth Annual Report of the United States Shipping Board, Fiscal Year Ending June 30, 1920* (Washington, D.C.: Government Printing Office, 1921), pp. 71-72.

73. *Second Annual Report of the United States Shipping Board, December 1, 1918* (Washington, D.C.: Government Printing Office, 1918), p. 177; *Fifth Annual Report of the United States Shipping Board, Fiscal Year Ending June 30, 1921* (Washington, D.C.: Government Printing Office, 1921), pp. 130, 238, 305; "Report of the Activities of the Employment Management Branch," RG 32, 277, 2.

74. Mattox, *Building the Emergency Fleet*, p. 14.

75. William Leuchtenburg, "The New Deal and the Analogue of War," *Change and Continuity in Twentieth Century America*, ed. John Braeman, Robert Brenner, and Everett Walters (New York: Harper Colophon Books, 1966), p. 139.

76. On changes in work, see Herbert Gutman, "Work, Culture, and Society in Industrializing America, 1815-1919," *American Historical Review* 78, no. 3 (June 1973): 531-88; Daniel T. Rodgers, "Tradition, Modernity, and the American Industrial Worker: Reflections and Critique," *Journal of Interdisciplinary History* 7, no. 4 (Spring 1977): 655-81; David Montgomery, "The 'New Unionism' and the Transformation of Workers' Consciousness in America, 1902-22," *Journal of Social History* 7, no. 4 (Summer 1974): 514.

77. Mary A. Holman, *The Political Economy of the Space Program* (Palo Alto: Pacific Books, 1974), pp. 214-15).

78. James E. Webb, *Space Age Management* (New York: McGraw-Hill, 1969), p. 65.

Structure and Strategy:
The Small Manufacturing Enterprise
in the Modern Industrial Economy

JAMES H. SOLTOW

The rise of the large business corporation in the late nineteenth and early twentieth centuries appears in perspective, as Thomas C. Cochran has pointed out, to be "one of the major changes in history, comparable to the rise of medieval feudalism or of commercial institutions at the close of the middle ages."[1] Since that time, many observers have perceived the small firm as an anachronism, the logic of industrial structure holding that "large-scale production, especially when conducted in large-scale firms and plants, tends to result in maximum efficiency."[2] Thus, according to this view, small business should have disappeared as a part of the rationalization of the economy.

Yet small businesses have persisted in large numbers in America, as in other industrial nations, in the face of a major transformation of the economic, social, and political environment, "a trend that surprises many scholars not familiar with the situation," as Cochran has commented.[3] In the same setting that appeared to encourage the growth of large corporations, small firms continue to multiply in number, as indicated in Table 1. As a British economist has observed recently, "Paradoxical as it may seem, though America is thought of as the home of 'big business,' it is also in a sense the home of 'small business.'"[4]

It is true that a high rate of turnover of the business population reflected a high rate of mortality for small firms. As the *Survey of Current Business* reported in the mid-1950s, "There was an even chance that a new firm would last only two years under the same management."[5] But a hard struggle for survival among independent businessmen was not of recent origin. David Wells maintained in

This essay draws upon material contained in the author's "Origins of Small Business and the Relationship Between Large and Small Firms: Metal Fabricating and Machinery Making in New England, 1890-1957," in *Small Business in American Life*, ed. Stuart W. Bruchey (New York: Columbia University Press, 1980).

TABLE 1
Business Enterprisers and Business Firms in Relation to Population, United States, Selected Dates 1880-1960

Year	Business Enterprisers			Business Firms	
	Number (thousands)	Number per 1,000 of Population	Percentage of Labor Force	Number (thousands)	Number per 1,000 of Population
1880	1,218	24.3	8.0	n.a.	n.a.
1890	1,719	27.1	8.0	n.a.	n.a.
1900	2,198	28.9	8.2	1,660	21.9
1910	2,682	29.1	7.7	2,100	22.8
1920	2,573	24.2	6.5	2,580	24.4
1930	3,101	25.2	6.6	2,994	24.4
1940	4,378	33.2	8.0	3,291	24.9
1950	5,439	36.0	8.8	4,051	26.9
1960	n.a.	n.a.	n.a.	4,658	26.1

Sources: For business enterprisers, estimates for 1880-1930 compiled in Spurgeon Bell, *Productivity, Wages, and National Income* (Washington, D.C.: The Brookings Institution, 1940), pp. 10, 211-217; for 1940-1950, in Joseph D. Phillips, *Little Business in the American Economy* (Urbana, Ill.: University of Illinois Press, 1958), p. 4.

    For business firms, for 1900-1920, ten-year averages of number of firms in operation, centered at indicated years. Melville J. Ulmer, "Industrial Patterns of the Business Population," *Survey of Current Business* (May 1948). For 1930-1950, annual average number of firms in operation; for 1960, firms in operation on January 1. U.S., Bureau of the Census, *Historical Statistics of the United States, Colonial Times to 1970* (Washington, D.C.: Government Printing Office, 1975), p. 911. Agriculture and professional services are excluded from the tabulations of number of firms.

Note: N.a. indicates not available.

the 1880s that "90 percent of all the men who try to do business on their own account fail of success."[6] And some small firms did survive the hazardous early years to live to a ripe old age. For example, among a group of eighty small New England metal fabricating firms studied in the late 1950s, fifty-two were twenty-five years old or older.[7]

    It is clear that small enterprises must be viewed not just as survivals of the past but more importantly as economic units performing special functions and as part of the structure through which economic decisions are made in modern industrial societies. The most useful approach is to consider the individual firm as an element of the business system, which is defined by the late Arthur H. Cole as a network of diverse functional units linked together in mutually advantageous ties.[8] Recognizing that the business system as conceptualized by Cole embraces the totality of the business world or economy, we may conveniently focus on one industry to provide a setting within which to examine the operations of individual firms. One of the most striking features to be observed in an advanced economy like that of the United States is the performance of a set of industrial activities by a collection of firms in a wide range of sizes, making many different specific products, using varied technical processes, and experiencing diverse market conditions. Within the setting of an industry, one may note significant differences "between those bits of the industry where probably conservatism and caution pay best and those bits where imagination and daring produce the best results."[9] Irrespective of any trend toward larger *average* size of firm in industry as a whole, or even in any one set of industrial activities, firms of many sizes continued in operation, doing different things in different ways.

The existence of different kinds of firms implies different kinds of people who make economic decisions through these firms. Specifically, it is postulated that entrepreneurs in small business form a special group in society and possess a set of motivations and behavior patterns not randomly distributed among the population as a whole, or even among men and women in business generally. These individuals seek to play a special entrepreneurial role, one that is different from the function of executives in corporate bureaucracies. In contrast to the cooperation and teamwork expected of the "organization man" in the large corporation, the small business entrepreneur believes that he has greater scope to act according to a pattern of behavior reflecting traits of "individualism." Such an entrepreneur likes to be able "to make decisions instantly and to carry them out." He closely identifies himself with his enterprise and often derives a "sense of completeness" in seeing the total process by which his ideas were transformed into finished products. The small business entrepreneur takes satisfaction from the very multiplicity of tasks to be performed in the management of his firm.[10]

It is obvious that the type of entrepreneurial role envisaged by such individuals could be satisfactorily performed only within the framework of a small organization in which the major decisions could be made and carried out by one executive or, at most, two or three managers working together on the basis of informal, personal association, as opposed to a formal, bureaucratic relationship. If the size of the firm became too large for the owner-manager to make and carry out decisions by himself, the entrepreneur was faced with a dilemma: He would be operating inefficiently with a pattern of direct management, or he would have to devise a bureaucratic structure of management.

In short, if an entrepreneur wished to play a role within the framework of a small organization congenial to his personal attitudes and goals in life, he would have to adopt a set of objectives that a small firm could achieve. Thus, we would expect to find in the behavior of the small firm and its entrepreneur a different relationship between strategy and structure from that characteristic of the large corporation. As Alfred Chandler has noted in his analysis of the experience of the giant enterprise, the strategy of growth, based on awareness by entrepreneurs of opportunities through expansion, required a new structure of administration to carry out operations in an efficient manner. In Chandler's words, "Structure follows strategy."[11] But this formulation may be turned around in developing a hypothesis appropriate to the analysis of the small firm: Among most members of

the small business population, structure, or the organizational form, is an important determinant of strategy, or the kind of activities carried out by the firm.

However, it was not easy for the aspiring small entrepreneur to develop an
appropriate strategy that would bring true satisfaction. Traditionally, large numbers of small businessmen have entered what turned out to be for them "blind
alleys"—relatively routine kinds of operations in which low entry requirements
in terms of capital, skills, and imagination resulted in extremely limited opportunity even for those who survived the high degree of competition.[12] Some small
firms have attempted to operate on the fringes of an industry dominated by an
oligopolistic "leading core."[13] Other enterprises have functioned as "satellites,"
serving as a distributor of the products of one large corporation or as a supplier to
a single large customer in a modern version of the putting-out system.[14] At best,
owner-managers found little sense of independent entrepreneurship in these situations because of low incomes, the instability of operations, and/or the necessity
of sharing with a large firm some of the decision-making functions with respect
to pricing and even investment.

There was a type of strategy that entrepreneurs could employ in order to attain
some measure of success for a small firm—success being defined roughly as the
ability to stay in business, to earn over a period of time a return on capital beyond
a wage for management, and to exercise a degree of independence in decision
making. The successful small firm acquired a strong market position as a small
firm by adapting to a niche in the market that afforded some degree of isolation
from complete and direct competition with other firms, both large and small.[15]
On the one hand, it exercised a strategy of size, turning small size into a positive
advantage by operating in a segment of industry where the competitive tides ran
in favor of smallness of the firm.[16] (We shall see later some of the specific tactics
for carrying out this strategy.) On the other hand, to provide protection against
the direct competition of many other small firms, this type of enterprise developed a basis of product differentiation by providing unique services for customers and acquiring a reputation for dependability and reliability. To avoid
establishing a dependent relationship, the small company normally sought to
spread its sales among as many different customers as possible, preferably to
those in different industries. The small firm, however strongly entrenched in its
niche, had to be flexible enough to adjust to changes in technology, markets, and
industrial structure.[17]

In any economy, only a relatively small number of firms successfully carried
out this kind of strategy. At any given time there existed an objective structure of
opportunity deriving from such forces as the state of technology and science,
income levels, population distribution, and the current structure of the industry.
Specifically, the opportunity for the small enterprise lay in occupying the inter-
stices or niches that developed in the process of industrial growth. But the overall
economic situation could be regarded as creating only incentives for entrepreneurial activity. As Glade has suggested, we can distinguish "a structure of
differential advantage in the capacity of the system's participants to perceive and

act upon such opportunities."[18] What is important then, from the point of view of the individual entrepreneur, is the ability to perceive the nature of the potential opportunity through interpretation of the environment and to take appropriate action to capitalize on it. As Edith Penrose has observed, "The 'subjective' opportunity is a question of what [the firm] thinks it can accomplish" in terms of developing a strategy or set of objectives.[19] But the opportunity is also limited by the resources at the entrepreneur's command—not only financial resources but even more importantly technical and managerial abilities. As Arthur Cole has stressed, entrepreneurship requires a solid operational base to be effective. In addition to determining the objectives of the enterprise, it is necessary to make decisions and to carry them out along several channels: develop an organization, secure adequate financial resources, acquire efficient equipment, and develop markets.[20]

Although analysis of statistical data may indicate some of the general characteristics of a business population, only a study of the histories of individual enterprises will reveal the patterns of strategy and the bases of decisions made by entrepreneurs. How did individuals holding certain generalized goals perceive opportunities, discern problems, and take what they believed to be appropriate action, using the resources at their command? In the next section, we shall direct our attention to the historical experience of small firms producing various types of metal fabrication and machinery.

***

The generalizations that follow are based upon a study of the histories of eighty small companies, fabricators of metals or makers of machinery, located in eastern Massachusetts and founded at various times during the period from the 1890s to the 1950s. Since few records were available by which to gain an understanding of the nature of entrepreneurship within the small firm, it was necessary to seek data from each company about its origins, policies, and activities. The historical accounts of the individual companies were intended to furnish more than case studies of "small business problems." Rather, they were compiled to provide empirical data needed to understand the history of small business as an economic and social institution, stressing the role of individual decision making.

Metalworking includes all types of industries that use metals as raw materials. Some establishments have specialized in the intermediate stages of processing metals, such as foundry work or stamping, the product of which other firms would use to make a variety of items. Other establishments have concentrated on the manufacture of specific products, either consumer goods or producer goods. Within these broad categories there existed many sorts of market and product differences, as well as a variety of techniques and processes, which thereby provided an abundance of opportunities for different kinds and sizes of enterprises. (See Table 2.) Many metalworking firms in New England in the middle of

TABLE 2
Distribution of Establishments, by Number of Employees,
Metalworking Industries, Massachusetts, 1909 and 1954

Number of Employees[a]	Number of Establishments		Percentage of Total Number	
	1909[b]	*1954[c]*	*1909*	*1954*
1–5	279	—	33.9	—
1–4	—[d]	938	—	31.4
6–20	233	—	28.3	—
5–19	—	972	—	32.5
21–50	155	—	18.8	—
20–49	—	476	—	15.9
51–100	84	—	10.2	—
50–99	—	243	—	8.1
101–250	49	—	5.9	—
100–249	—	170	—	5.7
251–500	10	—	1.2	—
250–499	—	88	—	2.9
501–1,000	7	—	0.8	—
500–999	—	52	—	1.7
1,001 and over	7	—	0.8	—
1,000 and over	—	50	—	1.7
Total	824	2,989	—	—

Source: U.S. Census of Manufactures (Washington, D.C.: Government Printing Office), 1909 and 1954.

[a]Wage earners only in 1909; all employees in 1954.

[b]Foundry and machine-shop industries. This broad classification embraced most types of metal fabricating and machinery making. The Census Bureau in later years classified as separate industries, or reclassified into other categories, many products included here in 1909, such as engines and tractors, power pumps, steel barrels, textile machinery, welded iron and steel products, machine tools, machine tool accessories, and ice-making apparatus.

[c]Total of major industrial groups 33 (primary metal products), 34 (fabricated metal products), 35 (machinery, except electrical), 36 (electrical machinery, equipment, and supplies), 37 (transportation equipment), and 38 (professional, scientific, and controlling instruments; photographic and optical goods, watches and clocks).

[d]Dash indicates not applicable.

the twentieth century employed the new technology based upon advanced scientific concepts, while others continued to emphasize the older tradition of mechanical skills. But there was considerable interaction between these two kinds of technology because the growth of science-based industries created a need for the application of mechanical skills to produce new types of equipment and components.[21]

SUPPLY OF ENTREPRENEURS

Most of the founders of the companies studied entered independent business in the same or a closely related field to that in which they had previous experience as employees. Their backgrounds showed a strong technical orientation, particularly among those who were skilled bench workers or college-trained engineers. Even office employees usually had closely observed the production side of the business in which they worked. Similarly, many of the engineers and skilled workers who became entrepreneurs had gained some knowledge of the office side as the result of managerial or supervisory experience.

In the highly specialized lines of metalworking, the technical and business knowledge required could normally be gained only from the inside of the industry. On the basis of their experience prior to entering independent business, potential entrepreneurs learned not only what could be produced from the technical point of view but also what could be marketed. On the basis of his knowledge of the industry, the entrepreneur could recognize the niches in the business world that the small firm could profitably occupy. For example, the general observer might have recognized a trend toward increased use of metal stampings in the 1920s, but the individual with experience in the industry, determined to start his own enterprise, knew what specific kinds of stampings a small firm could produce at a profit and for what types of customers.

With the increasing complexity of technology and business, formal academic training and managerial experience have become increasingly important. Although skilled workers continued to enter business for themselves in the mid-twentieth century, as they had in the period prior to World War I, limited education and bench skills were usually no longer adequate. But the high level of education and more extensive experience that appeared to have become prerequisites for successful operation of a small business did not impose as great a limitation upon freedom of entry as might be expected at first glance. Rising educational levels of the population as a whole and multiplication of management positions in large corporations provided a growing proportion of working people with skills and experience.[22] Indeed, it would not be an exaggeration to regard big business as an increasingly important training school for potential small entrepreneurs.

Some entrepreneurs looked to the operation of their own enterprises primarily as a path to economic advancement. For men with limited educational backgrounds, like shop workers, there usually existed little chance to advance as an employee beyond the level of foreman in the shop.[23] The only apparent method for the highly skilled individual to maximize his income was to set up his own shop based on his technical abilities. College-trained engineers, on the other hand, entering independent business from the 1920s on usually made this choice as an alternative to seeking advancement through a career in a large corporation, where they were more likely than shopworkers to be promoted to the top. These enterprisers found the role of business bureaucrat, at whatever level they might have worked in the bureaucracy, unsatisfactory, even when they held reasonably remunerative positions. They often expressed a dislike for what they regarded as the tactics necessary to advance within a business bureaucracy ("office politics"), a sense of violation of one's own moral and technical code contained in certain corporate policies, and the lack of interest on the part of superiors in "doing new things in new ways." Many had careers marked by a considerable amount of job mobility as they searched for opportunities that they believed to be suitable to their training and temperament. In short, they were men and women who would not accept the limitations employment imposed upon their individualism.

Although ambition to become an independent businessman provided strong motivation, the new entrepreneur had to carry out his enterprise within the context of the overall economic situation existing at a given time. Hopes and desires alone would not create a firm. Most entrepreneurs launched their firms with some objectives, typically attempting to fill a need in the business world before that need had become widely recognized. On the basis of their experience in industry, some founders had developed definite ideas about new products or substantial improvements in existing ones, ranging from a machine to sharpen saw blades (invented in 1904) to novel types of microwave equipment (conceived in 1955). One entrepreneur introduced a unique metal-finishing process into New England in the 1920s, when he obtained exclusive regional rights from the patent holder. Other founders envisaged novel types of service to offer, such as a system of specialized equipment for industrial users; or they sought opportunities in industries where problems involving application of new techniques remained to be solved.

FINANCING NEW ENTERPRISE

Perhaps no question has been as thoroughly debated with less conclusive and generally accepted answers than the "adequacy" of capital for small business.[24] Yet one point is clear: Small firms have not obtained investment funds in the same way as large, well-known corporations have. Special considerations, both economic and noneconomic, shaped the financial policies of small businessmen. In the first place, the cost of making a public offering of a small issue of stock through organized security markets was prohibitive. Furthermore, owners of small enterprises have usually been reluctant to share ownership and possibly control with outside investors. It might be true, as some writers have suggested, that the entrepreneur in small business should seek equity financing more actively and that he "should take courage in the knowledge that risk capital is being bet on him."[25] However, the originator of a small business typically put into his enterprise not only all of his financial resources but much personal effort as well as his determination to become an independent businessman. He regarded as unfair the ability of outsiders to reap some of the fruits of his labor when they offered to back him financially only after his ideas had begun to show promise, for few investors would make commitments of capital on untried ideas of new-born enterprises.[26] At best, it would be difficult to reconcile the divergent goals of managers seeking independence in a business of their own and outside financiers aiming for a high return on investment.

Personal savings of the original entrepreneur, sometimes supplemented with funds from relatives and friends, constituted the most important source of initial capital for these new enterprises. On the basis of the data about the New England metalworking firms, it would be difficult to draw meaningful conclusions about trends in minimum amounts of capital required to enter independent business. Throughout the period since 1890, the amount of investment at the start appeared to depend less upon conceptions of minimum capital requirements than upon the amount of funds possessed by the founder at the time of entry.

In view of the emphasis placed upon "independence," it is not surprising that the keystone to financial policy was reinvestment of company earnings. Even firms begun with relatively small amounts of original capital could, if they proved unusually successful, rely to a considerable extent upon corporate savings to finance growth. Reputation in the business community gained through previous experience as a salaried manager was a key factor in obtaining bank financing and in establishing credit with suppliers. Dollars secured through bank loans and materials acquired on credit released funds already held by entrepreneurs to be invested in fixed assets. In furnishing working capital, it could be said that "outsiders" made significant investments in small manufacturing firms. Resourcefulness of entrepreneurs could be considered as a capital asset. Need for funds could be minimized, particularly in the crucial early stages, by adapting machinery, converting to their purposes low-cost plant facilities, using unpaid or underpaid family labor, and keeping cash withdrawals for personal expenses at a minimum.

Penrose has drawn attention to the relationship between the financial resources that a firm can attract and the "very particular and possibly very rare sort of entrepreneurial ability [that] is required to launch successfully a new firm on a shoestring." She maintains that "difficulties attributed to lack of capital may often be just as well attributed to a lack of appropriate entrepreneurial services."[27] There is much in the financial histories of the Massachusetts metalworking firms to support these observations. Thus, the question of the "adequacy of small business financing" may well turn on the adequacy of individual small businessmen in tapping sources of funds and then making the best use of those available to them.

OWNERSHIP AND MANAGEMENT

The corporation was the characteristic form of legal organization among our group of New England metalworking companies. Most firms incorporated at the time of origin or in the early years of operation. But these corporations did not resemble the "modern corporation" analyzed by Berle and Means. Rather, small manufacturing enterprises preserved a close identity of ownership and management. In actual operation, they were similar to proprietorships or partnerships in spite of their use of the corporate form. Indeed, lenders often required the principal owners of small corporations to pledge personal property as collateral for short-term loans, regardless of the condition of the corporate balance sheet.

Direct management was typical in these companies, in contrast to the hierarchy of managers found in the large corporation. Yet owners of small enterprises met the problems of administration in a number of specific ways. In firms started by men who assumed all managerial responsibilities, at least in the initial stages, versatility was a basic requirement. Some companies followed the traditional pattern of the family as the unit in business, with brothers, brothers-in-law, cousins, or even husband and wife dividing the responsibilities of administration. Managerial groupings dependent upon family relationships usually relied on chance to assemble individuals with complementary talents. Thus, some entrepreneurs whose ability lay on one side of the business consciously selected a partner or partners whose experience and skills would complement their own. Such an arrangement might intentionally include men with different temperaments as well as different talents, so that neither excessive optimism nor overcaution would unduly influence the firm's decision making. But experience sometimes illustrated the adage that "there is no way for two people to be equal partners in any business" when basic disagreements on policy developed between partners.

Personal considerations played a major role in decisions by entrepreneurs about the location of their new enterprises. Because all of the founders were residents of New England and desired to remain, there was little chance that any would have begun operations outside the region. The original entrepreneur appeared sometimes to make his decision about where to plant his firm on the basis of "preference for 'consumer location,' that is, where he would like to live." But he did not ignore "the question of 'producer location,' that is, the best place to earn a living."[28] On the basis of previous experience in the industry in which he entered independent business, the potential entrepreneur had a fairly clear idea of what kind of business might succeed in the New England economic environment. In contrast to most theory, which assumes that the entrepreneur decides first what to produce and then the most economical location, the sequence of decision making in practice could be stated in this way: locate in New England, or more specifically a community in eastern Massachusetts ("consumer location preference"); and then determine what products could be manufactured in the area with the capital (human and money) at his command.

In recruiting and dealing with production workers, small manufacturers employed a paternalistic approach, stressing the importance of personal relationships and fostering what they sometimes called a "family atmosphere" in their plants. To diminish the potential advantage that workers might derive from unions, employers provided wages and other economic benefits comparable to those received by labor in unionized plants. For these reasons, as well as the expense to unions of organizing small plants, few of the metal-fabricating companies had to engage in collective bargaining with representatives of organized labor. In seeking to discourage unionization of their work forces, owners were primarily concerned about potential union interference with their managerial prerogatives in directing their work forces, which they believed would limit their flexibility of operations. In labor relations as in financial policy and other areas of decision making, entrepreneurs emphasized "independence."

In organizing productive facilities, entrepreneurs normally leased or purchased an available existing building, which might require renovation, rather than construct a new, special-purpose structure. Similarly, they usually started business with used machinery or equipment that they improvised. Technical knowledge enabled them to adapt low-cost plant space and equipment to their specialized needs so as to minimize capital outlays. Cost data were lacking, but owners of companies housed in older buildings and using machinery purchased on the second-hand market might have argued that any increase in operating and maintenance costs resulting from such practices would have been offset by lower fixed costs.[29]

THE SMALL FIRM AND THE MARKET

Regardless of the ingenuity that small manufacturers might apply to their financial and production problems, their efforts would come to little unless they considered carefully their product and marketing policies. Defining product lines, securing customers, establishing channels of distribution, and determining prices were all crucial matters for the new enterprise. For a small manufacturing enterprise to succeed, the entrepreneur had to make the key decisions about the kinds of goods and services to be offered and the clientele to be served within the framework outlined earlier—the adoption of a strategy of size to avoid direct competition with large corporations and the establishment of product differentiation to minimize potential competition from other small firms.

One tactic to carry out the strategy of size in the metalworking industries was to specialize in the manufacture of products with a limited total demand. The large corporation oriented to mass production and mass distribution was not likely to enter such fields, but a small enterprise could produce and market such items profitably. The following illustrate specialty items produced by metalworking firms, each of which was among only a few sellers in its specific national market: (1) metal core plugs for uses in the tarpaper, floor covering, and newsprint industries, produced in a stamping plant employing forty workers; (2) a special type of screen plate for paper mills, made by a company with thirty employees; (3) miners' cap lamps, turned out in a plant with about forty workers; (4) a specialized air valve produced by a firm with fifteen employees. A complete list would be a long one, ranging from electronic clips to ships' clocks.[30]

Other companies, in employing a strategy of size, specialized in a specific process. These included such varied operations as machine shops, sheet-metal fabrication, screw-machine products, metal stamping, structural-steel fabrication, electroplating, heat treating, and metal finishing. These establishments normally served local or regional markets, primarily because of the need for maintenance of close relations between producer and customer during the fabricating process. Much of the custom work, done to the order of individual customers, involved nonstandarized design for special applications and special attributes of quality. Again, this was not a fruitful field of operations for the large corporation with its mass-production and mass-distribution facilities.

By utilizing a strategy of size, small manufacturers in metalworking were able to protect one flank by entering fields where they did not engage in head-to-head competition with big business. Successful adaptation to a niche that afforded a strong market position required, in addition, that the firm "do something different" from what could be done by any hopeful entrant into business with a small amount of capital. If owners of small companies wanted to advance beyond merely routine operations that might be pushed to the wall at any time in the competitive jungle characterizing many industries composed of small firms, they had to adopt a policy to encourage product differentiation. For the small metalworking firm selling to well-informed and price-conscious industrial buyers, differentiation had to be based on special services to customers, reputation for dependability and reliability, and personal sales representation.

In providing service, the small manufacturer applied his detailed knowledge of sources of materials and parts and of production, designing, and scheduling to meet the unique needs of particular customers, often taking on the kind of work regarded by the run-of-the-mill producer as "too difficult." Sometimes, just being a person that people liked to do business with was a significant, if intangible, competitive factor. The seller's way of doing business, his reputation for fair dealing, courtesy, efficiency, and all the personal links attaching his customers to himself were taken into account by buyers.[31]

New entrepreneurs usually determined the segment of metalworking in which they could gain a foothold, given the resources at their command at the time of entry, on the basis of their previous experience. With their background in industry, owners of new enterprises had a fairly clear idea of potential markets, customers, and often even the individuals in charge of purchasing the products they had to sell. A reputation in the industry derived from experience as a salaried manager also helped the new entrepreneur to obtain initial orders from customers who were as concerned about quality and ability to deliver as about a quoted price. Most companies, even when they had passed beyond the initial stage, continued to rely upon the efforts of owners to handle sales. In an enterprise that emphasized service and attention to the special needs of customers, the decision about the profitability of a particular order was a crucial one that could not be delegated to a salesman. The chief executive in a small firm, as the only man with knowledge of all aspects of company operations, had to determine the ability of his plant to produce what was required by a potential customer.

Although many manufacturers necessarily relied upon one or two customers when they started operations, they moved to spread their sales among more clients as they enlarged production because of the risks of such dependence. Most obvious was the danger of a change in the customer's policy, such as to "pull in" to its own plant work previously contracted out, but there was also the problem of economic pressure applied by a large firm that dominated a small company's sales.

No enterprise could afford to rest entirely upon its past achievements to maintain its market position. Even the firm strongly entrenched in its niche, based upon specialization in products or services, could find its position threatened by external circumstances such as changes in technology, markets, or industrial structure. The entrepreneur alert to the trend of developments began to develop a new set of objectives while his firm still possessed the ability to make a transition. He usually built upon the base of specialization in which his enterprise had acquired a special competence through experience. For most metalworking companies, the technological base or the possession of a special competence involving machines, processes, skills, and raw materials was the significant factor determining the direction in which the firm would grow.

***

Many observers have stressed the importance of economic integration and large-scale production in modern industry; others, like Allyn Young, have demonstrated that "industrial differentiation has been and remains the type of change characteristically associated with the growth of production." Young stressed the importance of "the increase in the diversification of intermediate products and of industries manufacturing special products or groups of products."[32] Within the intricate nexus of economic activities reflecting a complex division of labor among firms of varying size, entrepreneurs sought to adapt to niches in which small enterprises could carry on efficient and profitable operations.

Yet the structure of division of labor by firm cannot be taken as given, since it may vary considerably even among advanced economies, the structure influenced in different ways by varying economic and sociocultural factors. In the 1890s, observers pointed out that the division of labor by firm was considerably more extended in American than in European industry.[33] This "lag" in specialization in Europe as compared with the United States has persisted beyond the middle of the twentieth century. A study of the history of a group of small metal-fabricating companies in Belgium carried out in the mid-1960s points to some of the differences in industrial structure between this Western European nation and the United States. [34] These forty-odd enterprises, like their American counterparts, emphasized direct management by owner or owners (regardless of the legal form of ownership), financial "independence" (which meant reliance largely on reinvestment of profits to finance expansion), paternalism toward employees, successful adaptation to a niche through development of a special-ized set of products or services, and flexibility in adjusting to changes in the economic environment. However, the small Belgian firms not only produced generally a wider range of products (in styles and sizes) than did companies of like size in the United States, but they also were more vertically integrated. Small enterprises in Belgium specializing in particular final products normally produced most of the components they required, in contrast to American product specialists of this size, who concentrated on final assembly and contracted the manufacture of parts to process specialists, many of which were themselves small firms.

If the extent of the market is considered to be the principal economic force determining the division of labor,[35] the large size of the American economy is the most obvious explanation for the more extensive specialization found in the United States. But social and cultural factors also contributed to differences. Since the nineteenth century, American industrialists have assigned a higher value to efficiency than did their European counterparts, who continued to em-phasize to a great extent noneconomic considerations like "the cult of prowess" in defining the scope of their operations.

As sociologist Jesse Pitts explains in his study of French society, "Specializa-tion implies the necessity of focusing on a limited area of problem solving," which is seen to be contrary to the "belief in a man's capacity for top perfor-mance in any area he may choose." The emphasis on prowess suggests display of unusual skill in producing goods whose value was determined in large part on the basis of aesthetic qualities as seen by the producer; this attitude tended to dis-courage standardization in industry, which in turn impeded specialization. From the technical point of view, use of standardized components would interfere with the ideal of making as nearly perfect a product as possible.[36] As David Granick has pointed out in his perceptive analysis of Soviet metal fabricating, "Standard-ized parts and subassemblies are seldom the best—if no consideration were given to the production economies resulting from larger-scale output—that could be utilized in each final product taken individually."[37]

The high value assigned to prowess reinforced the goal of avoiding a situation of "dependency which goes with specialization." Dependence upon outside sup-pliers seemed to involve risks for the manufacturer, who saw himself as only one of a number of customers having to "compete" for the specific attention of the producer of essential components. In addition, rather than be placed in a situation where disagreement might take place concerning the quality of work done by outside suppliers, industrialists often preferred to perform the job in their own plant or shop.[38]

Regardless of the weight one may attach to any specific set of factors encour-aging a relatively high degree of vertical integration in Belgian small industry, the situation itself tended to create a vicious circle. Emphasis on prowess and catering to the special demands of individual customers limited the ability of the small firm specializing in the assembly of finished industrial products to engage in series production and indirectly encouraged it to maintain its own facilities to make components. This in turn discouraged the possible organization of process specialists who might have achieved some success, as in the United States, by applying their functional skills to the solution of problems common to the manufacture of a wide range of finished products. Then, the absence of division of labor by firm in the form of a fine network of subcontractors and suppliers served as a further justification for assemblers of final products to engage in the manufacture of components. Contributing to the difficulty was a turnover tax in Belgium, then levied on each transaction between firms. The cumulative effect of this tax created a further obstacle to the formation of a pattern of division of labor among firms.[39]

***

Despite the prominent position of the giant corporation in twentieth-century America, opportunities continued for the small enterprise to adapt to a niche in the market affording a strong market position. Some lines of technological development actually favored small scale of operations.[40] Significantly, the bias toward efficiency in American society, as well as the large size of the domestic market, contributed toward an elaborate division of labor by firm in the United States. The existence of a network of process specialists made it possible for product specialists to concentrate their resources on developing facilities for final assembly and on marketing, at the same time having access to the services of experts in the machining, stamping, cutting, and shaping of metals. Similarly, the presence of such a body of product specialists constituted an encouragement for process specialists in many narrowly defined lines in an industry like metalworking.

As we indicated earlier, the objective structure of opportunity that existed at any given time created incentives for entrepreneurial action. Ability to perceive and to act upon opportunities in the economic environment was not evenly distributed in the population. Entry into independent business involved the investment not only of money capital but even more importantly of human capital—technical skills and business capability to determine objectives and to perform the many other tasks of entrepreneurship. Ingenuity was also a necessary characteristic, as the new entrepreneur had to be resourceful to devise expedients to meet problems that had no textbook solution. An essential ingredient in establishing a new firm was persistence in what some have called "getting through the knothole," the first few years of long hours, low monetary returns, and often discouraging circumstances. These were the "qualified" individuals who took advantage of the opportunities for small enterprise in the framework of twentieth-century American industry.

A final point to emphasize is that the existence and performance of the small business sector in an advanced economy not only provided positions in society for individuals with special kinds of motivation and talent but also held important implications for the operation of the economy as a whole—a point underscored in the recent suggestion of a British economist that a more vigorous and numerous small business sector in Britain now would not represent industrial backwardness but rather would contribute to greater productivity in that nation's economy.[41]

NOTES

1. Thomas C. Cochran, *American Business in the Twentieth Century* (Cambridge: Harvard University Press, 1972), p. 40.

2. P. Sargant Florence, *The Logic of British and American Industry: A Realistic Analysis of Economic Structure and Government* (London: Routledge and K. Paul, 1953), p. 48.

3. Thomas C. Cochran, *Social Change in America: The Twentieth Century* (New York: Harper & Row, 1972), p. 98.

4. S. J. Prais, *The Evolution of Giant Firms in Britain: A Study of the Growth of Concentration in Manufacturing Industry in Britain, 1909-1970* (Cambridge: Cambridge University Press, 1976), pp. 143-44. Prais notes that enterprises with under one hundred employees accounted for a larger proportion of total manufacturing employment in the United States than in the United Kingdom.

5. B. C. Churchill, "Age and Life Expectancy of Business Firms," *Survey of Current Business* (December 1955).

6. David A. Wells, *Recent Economic Changes* (New York: D. Appleton and Company, 1889), p. 351.

7. James H. Soltow, *Origins of Small Business: Metal Fabricators and Machinery Makers in New England, 1890-1957* (Philadelphia: American Philosophical Society 1965), p. 7.

8. Arthur H. Cole, "Meso-Economics: A Contribution from Entrepreneurial History," *Explorations in Entrepreneurial History* 2nd ser., vol. 6 (Fall 1968): 3-33; "Aggregative Business History," *Business History Review* 29 (Fall 1965): 287-300.

9. John Jewkes, "Are the Economies of Scale Unlimited?" in *Economic Consequences of the Size of Nations*, ed. E.A.G. Robinson (New York: St. Martin's Press, 1960), p. 102.

10. Soltow, *Origins of Small Business*; Orvis F. Collins and David G. Moore, *The Enterprising Man* (East Lansing, Mich.: Bureau of Economic and Business Research, Graduate School of Business, Michigan State University, 1964).

11. Alfred D. Chandler, Jr., *Strategy and Structure: Chapters in the History of the Industrial Enterprise* (Cambridge, Mass.: The M. I. T. Press, 1962), p. 14.

12. See Kurt B. Mayer and Sidney Goldstein, *The First Two Years: Problems of Small Firm Growth and Survival* (Washington, D. C.: Small Business Administration, 1961); Mabel Newcomer, "The Little Businessman: A Study of Business Proprietors in Poughkeepsie, New York," *Business History Review* 35 (Winter 1961): 477-531; and Joseph D. Phillips, *Little Business in the American Economy* (Urbana: University of Illinois Press, 1958).

13. Harold G. Vatter (*Small Enterprise and Oligopoly: A Study of the Butter, Flour,*

Automobile, and Glass Container Industries [Corvallis, Ore.: Oregon State College Press, 1955]) observes that in these kinds of industries "small enterprise is often dependent enterprise, i.e., it surrenders part of its power to make independent decisions to large concerns, some of which may be its competitors" (pp. 110-11). For example, leading manufacturers of glass containers controlled entry by means of patents on equipment and containers but allowed a number of small concerns to exist as long as the latter followed price and output policies determined by the leaders. As one executive stated in the 1920s, "There is...the question as to what is to be done with the outsiders when dominated. How many shall be allowed to survive and at what price?" (p. 88).

14. A spokesman for Sears, Roebuck and Company summarized policy toward small suppliers in 1947: "Our concern is not with 'How much does a manufacturer make on his production for us?' but 'What does he do with those profits?' We feel that adequate sums should be plowed back into the business.... As a matter of fact, in all our important lines we require such a research program, with an agreed sum of money appropriated, the character of the research problems agreed upon, and the program paid out of a definite apportionment of the unit price." Boris Emmet and J. E. Jeuck, *Catalogues and Counters: A History of Sears, Roebuck and Company* (Chicago: University of Chicago Press, 1950), p. 402.

15. See Richard B. Heflebower, "Toward a Theory of Industrial Markets and Prices, "*American Economic Review: Papers and Proceedings* 44 (1954), for a valuable theoretical analysis of niches in markets.

16. W. Arnold Hosmer, "Small Manufacturing Enterprises," *Harvard Business Review* (November-December 1957): 111-22, elaborates a concept of strategy of size.

17. Howard F. Bennett, *Precision Power: The First Half Century of Bodine Electric Company* (New York: Appleton-Century-Crofts, 1959), shows the ways by which a small company retained a strong market position over a long period of time by consistently adapting to changing technology and industrial structure. By contrast, Theodore F. Marburg, *Small Business in Brass Fabricating: The Smith & Griggs Manufacturing Company of Waterbury* (New York: New York University Press, 1956) illustrates how failure to adapt resulted in deterioration of market position and ultimate demise of the firm.

18. William P. Glade, "Approaches to a Theory of Entrepreneurial Formation," *Explorations in Entrepreneurial History*, 2nd ser., vol. 4 (Spring-Summer 1967): 245-59, suggests the use of a type of bilevel situational analysis to formulate hypotheses about entrepreneurship.

19. Edith T. Penrose, *The Theory of the Growth of the Firm* (New York: John Wiley & Sons, 1959), pp. 41-42.

20. Arthur H. Cole, "An Approach to the Study of Entrepreneurship: A Tribute to Edwin F. Gay," *Journal of Economic History*, supp. 6 (1946): 1-15.

21. Various aspects of the history of New England industry, especially metalworking and machinery making, are discussed in the following: National Planning Association, Committee of New England, *The Economic State of New England* (New Haven: Yale University Press, 1954); Arthur D. Little, Inc., *Report on a Survey of Industrial Opportunities in New England* (Cambridge, Mass.: Arthur D. Little, 1952); Seymour Harris, *The Economics of New England: Case Study of an Older Area* (Cambridge, Mass.: Harvard University Press, 1952); Charles E. Artman, *Industrial Structure of New England*, part 1 of the Commercial Survey of New England, Domestic Commerce Series, no. 28 (Washington, D.C.: Government Printing Office, 1930); Martha V. Taber, *A History of the Cutlery Industry in the Connecticut Valley*, Smith College Studies in History, vol. 41

(Northampton, Mass.: Smith College, Department of History, 1955); George S. Gibb, *The Saco-Lowell Shops: Textile Machinery Building in New England, 1813-1949* (Cambridge, Mass.: Harvard University Press, 1950); Thomas R. Navin, *The Whitin Machine Works Since 1831: A Textile Machinery Company in an Industrial Village* (Cambridge, Mass.: Harvard University Press, 1950); Charles W. Moore, *Timing a Century: A History of the Waltham Watch Company* (Cambridge, Mass.: Harvard University Press, 1945).

22. In 1890, only 1.3 percent of the population in the appropriate age group graduated from college, compared with 18.7 percent in 1950. These percentages were developed by dividing the number of college graduates into one-fifth of the total population, age 20-24. Based on data in U.S., Bureau of the Census, *Historical Statistics of the United States, Colonial Times to 1957* (Washington D.C.: Government Printing Office, 1975), p. 10, and *Statistical Abstract of the United States: 1955* (Washington, D.C.: Government Printing Office, 1955), p. 123.

23. See John S. Ellsworth, Jr., *Factory Folkways: A Study of Institutional Structure and Change* (New Haven: Yale University Press, 1952). In his study of a New England factory, Ellsworth points out: "On paper the organization charts look like a simple promotional ladder, with workers at the bottom, foremen on the next step, assistants to managers on the next, and so on up. In practice this works only in exceptional cases.... The worker who could start at the bottom and work up would be a remarkable exception. He might go as far as foreman but probably no farther, and there are intimations that even this modest rise is coming to require more than mere plant training and experience" (pp. 151-52).

24. Two studies made by specialists in the late 1950s reached these respective conclusions: (1) "A review of financing facilities available to small business leads to the conclusion that they are inadequate." (2) "Financing appears to have been adequate for the sector as a whole [i.e., small business] in the postwar period." Federal Reserve System, *Financing Small Business: Report to the Committees on Banking and Currency and the Select Committees on Small Business*, 85th Cong., 2d sess. (Washington, D.C.: Government Printing Office, 1958).

25. Paul Donham and Clifford L. Fitzgerald, Jr., "More Reason in Small Business Financing," *Harvard Business Review* (July-August 1959): 96.

26. A Boston investment banker with an interest in small business pointed out to this writer that he and other investors like himself followed a policy of supplying only "second money" to small enterprises, in effect forcing the original entrepreneur to use his own resources to finance the discovery of any mistakes.

27. Penrose, *Theory of the Growth of the Firm*, pp. 38-39.

28. Edgar M. Hoover, *The Location of Economic Activity* (New York: McGraw-Hill Book Co., 1948), p. 4.

29. The owner of a metal-fabricating firm argued that a company could "tax itself out of business by erecting fancy buildings" because of increased real estate tax assessments.

30. Patrick G. Porter and Harold C. Livesay, "Oligopoly in Small Manufacturing Industries," *Explorations in Economic History* 7 (Spring 1970): 371-79, argue that concentration in small industries (those with total product value of less than $100 million annually) typically occurs in "survivors from the nineteenth century," activities "closely related to the older, agrarian-based economy of the nineteenth century." Their observation that "very few of the small oligopolies in this century are in new industries" may be correct in terms of their use of the Census Bureau definition of *industry*. However, the product lines for segmented markets, to which we have referred here, do not coincide with the concept of industry as applied by the Census Bureau and used by Porter and Livesay. Heflebower comments that "markets for most products (broadly conceived) tend to settle

into segments among which there are varying degrees of elasticity of substitution and of intersegment mobility" ("Toward a Theory of Industrial Markets and Prices," p. 123). Whether particular articles are the products of "old" or "new" industries may not be entirely relevant, as we stressed earlier the importance of interaction between the older set of activities based on mechanical skills and the newer science-based sector in New England metal fabricating and machinery making.

31. Hosmer, "Small Manufacturing Enterprises," p. 121. A survey of purchasing practices of large corporations made in 1959 concluded with this rule for sellers in industrial markets: "Make the buyer feel important. Assure him that you appreciate his business. Don't take him for granted. He expects *personal attention*" ("How to Use Emotional Factors That Trigger Industrial Sales," *Steel: The Metalworking Weekly*, April 6, 1959). But such practices are as old as American manufacturing industry. Theodore F. Marburg points to the importance of personal sales representation in establishing product differentiation in the brass industry in the 1830s in "Historical Aspects of Imperfect Competition: In Brass Manufacturing During the 1830s," *Tasks of Economic History*, supplemental issue of the *Journal of Economic History* 3 (December 1943): 36.

32. Allyn A. Young, " Increasing Returns and Economic Progress," *Economic Journal*, 38 (1928). Edward Ames and Nathan Rosenberg, "The Progressive Division and Specialization of Industries," *Purdue Faculty Papers in Economic History, 1956-1966* (Homewood, Ill.: R. D. Irwin, 1967).

33. See, for example, W. D. Forbes, "European vs. American Shop Methods," *American Machinist* 14, March 19, 1891. H.F.L. Orcutt, "Machine Shop Management in Europe and America," pts. 1-8, *Engineering Magazine* 16-17 (January-August 1899).

34. James H. Soltow, "Entrepreneurial Strategy in Small Industry: Belgian Metal Fabricators," *Proceedings of the American Philosophical Society* 115 (1971).

35. George J. Stigler, "The Division of Labor Is Limited by the Extent of the Market," *Journal of Political Economy* 59 (1951).

36. See Jesse R. Pitts, "Continuity and Change in Bourgeois France," in *In Search of France*, ed. Stanley Hoffman (Cambridge, Mass.: Harvard University Press, 1963). Pitts argues that "specialization implies the necessity of focusing on a limited area of problem solving," which is perceived to be contrary to the "belief in a man's capacity for top performance in any area he may choose" (p. 43).

37. David Granick, *Soviet Metal-Fabricating and Economic Development: Practice Versus Policy* (Madison: University of Wisconsin Press, 1967), p. 45

38. David Landes has observed in mid-twentieth-century French industry "an overintegration extremely harmful to efficient production—the manufacturer does not like to rely on outside help or cooperation. The system of subcontractors and suppliers that creates in American industry a sort of division of labor on the factory level is still relatively neglected in France." "French Business and the Businessman: A Social and Cultural Analysis," in *Modern France: Problems of the Third and Fourth Republics*, ed. Edward M. Earl (Princeton, N.J.: Princeton University Press, 1951), p. 338.

39. Institut d'Etude Economique et Social des Classes Moyennes, *Le Problème fiscal de la sous-traitance* (Brussels: Institut d'Etude Economique et Sociale des Classes Moyennes, 1966). By contrast to the turnover tax, a "value-added" tax does not have a cumulative effect; thus, it does not discourage performance of different economic functions in different firms.

40. See, for example, John M. Blair, "Technology and Size," *American Economic Review, Papers and Proceedings* 38 (1948): 121-52.

41. Prais, *Evolution of Giant Firms in Britain*, p. 160.

New York's Electricity: Establishing a Technological Paradigm

HAROLD ISSADORE SHARLIN

One of the paradoxes of the present American industrial scene is that automobiles, steel, textiles and electric utilities, industries that were once responsible for U.S. world industrial leadership are now said to be technologically backward. These enterprises were once the very source of technological innovation but have become conservative in marketing and technologically stagnant—an object of serious concern to the national economy.

Is this decline an inevitable course for aging industries?[1] Must a mature industry lose the resilience necessary to meet competition? Does federal policy cause the loss of dynamism? Can government policy cure the problem of industrial aging, or is the problem indigenous to all technology-based industries? Regulation cannot be the root cause because the electrical utilities were most vital during an era of the severest type of regulatory restraint. The telephone industry, also a regulated monopoly, rather than being inhibited by regulation, has maintained technological world leadership for over one hundred years.

When the so-called sick industries are compared, in order to discover why they are laggard, two elements appear in common. It is these that constitute the technological paradigm. First, all of these industries began with a technological breakthrough. And, second, each developed a market (usually a mass market) peculiar to the given technology.

The technological paradigm has been a guide to decision making and an obstacle to change. For electrical utilities the paradigm has bound the technology of generation, transmission, and distribution to a concentrated market in which the largest users pay the lowest price per kilowatt-hour; it has made the industry resistant to such changes as conservation, decentralization, and the use of renewable resources. But the example of the telephone industry indicates that a technological paradigm can undergo change. The links that bind a particular technology to a specific market will be discovered through historical analysis of the way a paradigm is established. Such an analysis will indicate opportunities for substituting links rather than resorting to drastic, forced, and disruptive change.

Electric utilities are the most constrained of any industry. Production is controlled by a government policy that allocates natural resources, and distribution is regulated by public utility commissions. The threatening cloud of public ownership seems always to hover on the horizon of a utility's business environment. Yet, with all of these constraints, electric utilities have been among the country's most dynamic industries and have grown in capacity and diversity, at least until recently.[2] A rapidly evolving technology was the most important strategic device in utilizing an expanding market potential as well as coping with a shifting government policy. The decline in technological innovation[3] has meant a loss of dynamism in the utility industry because a company's strategic response to market opportunities and government regulation no longer has the flexibility that turns outside pressures into business opportunities.

In the 1980s, electric utilities face a new set of problems and opportunities: basic changes in the market, in which growth is slowing down; new regulatory restraints that now include such things as life line pricing; new energy resource constraints due to environmental restrictions; and a decline in technological innovation.

Is the slowdown of technological innovation a permanent condition signifying that the technological paradigm has become a static liability instead of a means to dynamic change? Does popular opposition to economic growth require new corporate strategies for a business environment with no new markets and therefore a technological paradigm frozen in place?

Utilities have variables in common, such as the natural resources used for energy, the relations with their public utility commissions, and the public-private power picture; the Niagara Mohawk Power Corporation of New York had to take all of them into account in a corporate strategy that developed over the years. In addition, the corporation and its predecessors are important to the history of electric power because they made the critical decision between alternating current (a.c.) and direct current (d.c.) power and were a part of one of the country's most disputed public-private power controversies.

The reason for unraveling this intricate story of the evolution of an electric utility is that Niagara Mohawk, like other utilities, will plan its future strategy from its present position within the energy market, vis-à-vis the government and in the stream of technological change. Past decisions have placed the company in the locus of a business environment that is determined by the intersection of three planes: the market, government policy, and technology.

ENTREPRENEURSHIP AND TECHNOLOGICAL BREAKTHROUGHS

The first large-scale electric power project as contrasted with electric lighting project in the United States was at Niagara Falls, New York. Edison's Pearl

Street Station project supplied electric lights, not power. The magnitude of the first Niagara Falls power project was a result of the strategy followed by entrepreneurs who, in 1890, saw beyond the nineteenth century. The strategy that was chosen dealt with state regulation and tapped a market potential equal to the magnitude of the energy source. The entrepreneurs chose a technology that dealt with both the market and regulation at the same time.

The first step in developing the corporate strategy, the decision to build a centralized power station rather than produce the power in a series of isolated plants within factories, was in response to action taken by the state of New York to preserve the scenic value of the natural phenomenon. The state acquired land along the Niagara River above and below the falls. There was no need to pass regulations prohibiting factories along the Niagara River because the state's use of eminent domain scotched plans by the entrepreneurs to build water-powered factories on its banks. The state's action resulted in a plan for a single water inlet to develop hydraulic power, and this plan evolved into the concept of a central electric power station.[4] There were three steps in the evolution of the concept of a central a.c. electric generating station: (1) centralize the power by building a power station with a few water turbines instead of building over 200 factories with their individual water-wheel power; (2) choose a method for transmitting the power from the central station to the point of use (electricity was chosen over wire rope or air pressure as a transmitting medium); (3) use a.c. instead of d.c. The first two steps led to the third decision, which was the truly pioneering action. Another step in the evolving corporate strategy was the decision to market the electricity as industrial and commercial power, that is, for the electric motor to power street railways and factories. This was a decision against the slow-growth alternative of the domestic lighting market, the primary market for electricity up to that time. That decision, ironically, ruled out the city of Niagara Falls as a possible industrial market, so a means was needed to transmit power twenty miles away to Buffalo, the nearest industrial town. The strategy that emerged combined all these elements: a central station; marketing the electricity as a power source rather than as a medium for electric lights; and competing in a large and immediate market twenty miles away instead of tapping the local market.

For the entrepreneurs, the strategic choice was inescapable: a centralized, alternating-current generating station that transmitted the electric power at high tension to Buffalo. That landmark strategy, formulated in 1893, has shaped the world's electric power industry.[5] The current strategy of the Niagara Mohawk Power Company (successor to the original Niagara Power Company) has evolved from the first strategy and contains the same elements: centralized production; concentration on an industrial market; and use of the most advanced technology.

In the original decision several transmission technologies were considered. To settle the question of the best means for power transmission, the corporation established an International Niagara Commission, which conducted a worldwide competition for the best central station technology and the most efficient transmission system. As another part of the third prong of the corporate strategy, using the most advanced technology, the corporation hired a physicist, a hydraulic engineer, and an electrical engineer as technical consultants, all of them among the most prominent men in their fields. The idea of employing the best technical thinking was a forerunner of the corporate research and development (R&D) department now used by high-technology industries. In the final analysis, the corporation's board of directors, a group of financiers with little technical background, made all the crucial decisions. Then, as now, the corporate decisions were made by integrating the several aspects of the corporate strategy.

Earlier attempts to underwrite a power project at Niagara Falls had failed because the businessmen were not "capitalists."[6] The project was a high-risk venture associated with the entrepreneurial spirit. Even the more cautious mill over wheelpit plan contained large market and technical uncertainties. The task of selling small shares of so speculative a venture was too much for the small group of local boosters at Buffalo. A large sum of venture capital was quickly raised after a group of New York financiers designed a scheme that would pay a high return but required a very large investment of capital. The money subscribers included a number of speculators who had financed Edison's original electric lighting venture, which had paid good returns on their money.[7]

The amount of money raised for the new Niagara Falls power scheme was very large for the times, over $2.5 million, from sources that expected a high rate of return. The expectation in turn gave a more daring character to corporate decision making. Even though the entrepreneurs had no technical background, they ruled against the cautious engineering advice of experienced people such as Edison and Kelvin who recommended the d.c. system.[8]

The shapers of technological paradigms are the entrepreneurs, who, although they may understand the technology incompletely, sense a market, imagine how that market might be tapped, and create the manufacturing plus sales structure. It is the entrepreneurs who combine technology with market techniques. For example, Frederick Pabst won a national and international market for his beer by combining the technology of refrigeration and bottling with a well-managed sales network.[9] Isaac Merritt Singer's acumen was applied to setting up district sales offices for the newly invented sewing machine. The DuPont company, beginning with smokeless powder, diversified and became one of the largest corporations in the world by using the company's developed munitions technology to expand into synthetic materials markets.[10] In each case, the entrepreneur was not the primary inventor but contributed to the diffusion of the technology by developing a market.

Luck is a major ingredient in entrepreneurial risk taking. The unanticipated uses of the new technology plus the unexpected extent of the market combine to give surprisingly high returns on investment. Niagara was a case in which the return was higher than the speculators anticipated. The first power at the Niagara project was produced in 1895, and the planned 100,000-horsepower capacity was quickly installed. The demand rapidly caught up with the enormous increase in electric power capability. An unanticipated and sizable market for Niagara's electric power materialized when Pittsburg Reduction Company (later Alcoa) and Carborundum built plants less than a mile from the generating plant site.[11] These electrochemical plants were large consumers of direct current power. The irony, therefore, was doubled by the unanticipated appearance of large consumers of direct current power in the immediate vicinity of the falls. Direct current was associated with an electric lighting load and alternating current with electric motor power. But the new electrochemical industry used large amounts of d.c. electricity. None of the engineers had planned for demand in large blocks of d.c. electricity. Would the entrepreneurs have chosen a.c. over d.c., and would they have made the decision to transmit the power twenty miles to Buffalo if electrochemicals had figured into their plans for Niagara?

If the undertaking had been a public one, the new generating station would have closed the chapter in the development of the falls because the demand for Niagara power had so rapidly reached its capacity. The great success of the entrepreneurs stimulated them to further expansion. In 1900, five years after beginning operation, the Niagara Power Company increased its capital and doubled the generating capacity at the falls,[12] demonstrating again that success in a venture capital enterprise breeds more venture capital.

TOO LARGE TO BE PRIVATE?

The Niagara Falls Power Company attributed its rapid growth to the strategy of emphasizing the sale of power to industry. The corporation began the policy of offering lower rates to industrial users of power than to domestic household customers and gave industry special concessions for purchasing power in bulk. The company boasted that it had converted the small town of Niagara Falls, New York, to one of the chief electrochemical and electrometallurgical centers in the world.[13] The population of the town increased by almost 300 percent from 1900 to 1930, compared with the 70 percent growth rate for the rest of New York State and the 60 percent population increase for all the United States.[14]

The utility holding company fever touched the Niagara Falls Power Company in 1929. A holding company, Niagara Hudson Power was formed through the integration of fifty-nine separate companies, including Niagara Falls Power. Before consolidation, these companies had been vertically integrated in that they performed the three functions necessary for producing and marketing electric power: generation at a central station; transmission to load centers at a high voltage; and distribution directly to consumers of electric power. The consolidation made the Niagara Hudson Power Company the largest electric utility in the world.[15] The formation of the Niagara Hudson Power Company capped a decade of holding company expansion, from 1919 to 1929, throughout the country. By 1929, 60 percent of electric power production in the United States was controlled directly or indirectly by seven holding companies.[16]

The growth in the production and use of electric power was dramatic in the early years of development. From 1882, the date of Edison's first central station at Pearl Street in New York City, until 1929, electric power production doubled every five and a half years.[17] The growth nationally, dramatic as it might seem, was a logical extension of the Niagara Falls Power Company strategy. The Niagara Hudson Power Company acquired systems, for example, that were centralized, served primarily industrial loads, and used alternating current technology, which by then had become standard.

Improvement in technology was gradual and along the lines originally established. The increase of the maximum transmission voltage, for example, proceeded in gradual steps. The highest voltage attained in 1892 for transmission of electric power was 10,000 volts. The relatively high voltage capability for that period was the reason alternating current was chosen. Transmission technology followed the course of ever higher voltages, and step by step the maximum voltage reached 220,000 volts in 1920.[18] The expansion of electric utilities, therefore, followed the strategy laid down in 1895—centralized generating stations, industrial market, and the most advanced technology. But technological innovation was not nearly as rapid as it had been.

Why did the electric utilities fail to maintain the rapid pace of technological development that characterized the beginning of the industry? In this technological conservatism, electric utilities resemble other established high-technology industries. The automobile industry, for example, fixed on a technological paradigm of the mass-produced internal-combustion engine car for a mass market and changed hardly at all over the next fifty years. The electric utilities increased efficiency by gradually raising transmission voltage and improving generation, but no basic changes have been made in the technological paradigm of the industry since Niagara.

The telephone industry, if it is not judged an exception to the idea of inevitable industrial decline, suggests that there is an alternative to the technological life cycle theory that contends that, as it ages, each new technologically based industry loses its innovative capacity and declines. A striking feature of the telephone industry's history is that each time the industry was on the point of saturating a market, a new technology opened a new market opportunity.

When the manually operated switchboard reached its capacity for handling calls, the invention of the dial system vastly increased call handling capacity, and soon every American home had a telephone.[19] Direct long-distance dialing opened another untapped market. At the moment satellite communication is extending the reach of every American telephone to the whole world market and long-distance transfer of computer-stored information offers another new and extremely large market opportunity.

There is no reason to believe that the American telephone system, the best in the world, has developed its last technological paradigm. On the other hand, an industry that is unable to adapt constantly the technological paradigm may become moribund. The electric power industry is frozen into a particular technological paradigm and cannot adapt, in the present condition, to change.

A technological breakthrough has on occasion occurred as, for example, in the form of system interconnection. Horizontal integration, the tying together of vertically integrated electric power systems by means of holding companies, was a method of overcoming one of the disadvantages of electricity as an energy source. Since electricity cannot be stored, achieving maximum system efficiency is difficult where demand varies. By joining power systems with different demand patterns, it is possible to minimize the dips and peaks in demand through the judicious balancing of supply and demand by passing power back and forth between integrated systems.[20] The economic difficulties of interconnection were ironed out through the holding company device.

Edison and businessmen who followed his lead had done well in promoting direct current central stations for supplying electric lighting loads, but as the limits of lighting loads were reached, alternating current used primarily for power was seen as the coming opportunity for business investment. Between 1913 and 1926, the proportion of electricity used for power had increased from 32 percent of the total amount of the electricity generated to almost 50 percent of the total.[21] In 1899, the water wheel and the water turbine were the major sources of industrial power, and electricity supplied only 1.8 percent of the total used. The transition to electric power took less than three decades. By 1927, 49 percent of the total industrial power was electricity.[22]

Textile mills were the first to convert from water wheels to electric motor drive for machinery. But steel mills were the largest consumer of electric power. A steel mill that made rails had machinery that was turned by 6,000-horsepower motors.[23] Another major user of electric power was street railways. By 1902, 94 percent of all street railways were electrified.[24] Eventually, the growth in demand for electric power used for motors and electrochemical processes far exceeded the growth in demand for electric lighting. That the growth in industrial demand would eventually exceed the domestic electric lighting demand was anticipated by the entrepreneurs at Niagara Falls in 1890.[25]

The prediction became determinant. In the United States, domestic and rural use of electricity was far behind Europe, where household consumption was given precedence. The difference between the direction of growth of electricity in Europe and the United States was that growth was determined in the United States by private strategy and in Europe by public policy. The private strategy aimed at rapid growth and the result by 1927 was that the United States, with one-half of the total world electric power capacity, far exceeded the European rate of growth in the use of electricity.[26]

In addition to faster growth as a justification for an industrial market strategy, the Niagara Hudson Power Company argued that its hydroelectric source of energy dictated that 85 percent of its market be for industrial use. With a constant flow of water as the energy source, the cost of producing hydroelectricity is virtually the same over a wide range of output, that is, hydroelectric dams operate with a virtually costless fuel. So the more electricity that is produced hydroelectrically, which is the ultimate in economics of scale, the less the per-unit cost will be. The Niagara Hudson Power Company gave large discounts to industries that contracted for power on an annual basis and argued that "if this power were sold only for residential and farm use, its cost would be so great that people would return to candles and kerosene lamps."[27]

Technological paradigms are established through an accretion of response to both market and technological changes. Decisions for centralization and in favor of long-range transmission of electricity were in response to New York State's defense of the environment at Niagara and Niagara Hudson Power Company's search for a ready large-scale market. The national growth in demand for industrial power was aided by the utilities' technological paradigm, and the market growth helped, in turn, to fix the paradigm's form. Hydroelectricity, a major source of electrical energy in the early period of growth, gave further impetus to the industrial market orientation because an industrial demand more closely matched the continuous nature of the hydroelectric supply.

Centralization, long-range transmission, the use of alternating current, and interconnection of systems was the resulting complex paradigm of these and other individual decisions. Remarkably, this unplanned accretion had a resilience that enabled the electric utility industry to adapt to revolutionary changes in the American economy for ninety years after its start in 1882. Not the least of these changes was the mechanization of the home that contributed to the compounding growth in electricity demand.

A measure of the adaptability of the paradigm was that, although utilities concentrated on the industrial market, they launched campaigns for the all-electric kitchen and then the all-electric home. The proportion of residential use of electricity increased from 5.5 percent of total sales in 1920 to 25 percent of the total in 1970.[28] The shape of the paradigm remained the same but was bent considerably to adapt to social change.

Liberals in the 1930s opposed the social consequences of the electric utility strategy that favored industrial customers. The liberal view, which became a New Deal plank, was that the new benefits of scientific research should benefit the people directly rather than by roundabout means, as the utilities argued was best. The distributional issue was linked to conservation of natural resources. Franklin Delano Roosevelt made public power a primary issue in his political platforms. In 1929, in his inaugural address as governor of New York, he said that hydroelectricity "is our power" and that corporations "act as the people's agent in bringing this power to their homes and workshops."[29]

Public power in liberal political terms meant rates set at a low level for domestic and rural users without regard for economic efficiency. In the election of 1930, public power was an issue in several states, including New York, Wisconsin, Montana, Colorado, and Alabama. The policy of public control of electric power was based, said the Natural Resources Commission in 1934, on the American democratic principle that

the gains of our civilization are essentially mass gains and should be administered for the benefit of the many rather than the few; our priceless resources of soil, water, and minerals are for the service of the American people, for the promotion of the welfare and well-being of all citizens.[30]

The movement for public power in New York State was begun by Alfred E. Smith and was continued under Roosevelt's governorship. The basis for the argument in favor of public power in New York was that the electrical energy produced from the Niagara and Saint Lawrence rivers, since they were natural resources, rightfully belonged to all the people. The Niagara Hudson Power Company's counter to the liberal position was that their strategy of favoring industrial customers produced economic growth that benefited all the people in the state by providing more jobs as well as cheaper electricity for the home.

Advocates of public power took a social approach to the question of the direction of electric power development; they advocated a cut in domestic electricity rates that would expand domestic demand so much as to make this plan economically viable. To counter that argument, the private power advocates cited the Tennessee Valley Authority (TVA) experiment as proof of the sound economic argument that economies of scale dictated lower electricity rates for industry and that the social benefit in the form of lower domestic rates would follow. Proof of this contention could be found in the time curves that showed a nationwide decrease in domestic electric rates. With the public power argument derived from a social basis and private power rebuttal founded on an economic basis, the only possible solution to the public-private controversy was a political one.

Which of the methods of controlling the direction of growth in the use of electricity, corporate strategy or public policy, was more responsive to change? Immediately after the formation of the Niagara Hudson holding company, the corporate strategy responded quickly to changes in the business environment. When the 1929 depression caused industrial sales to slump, the corporation's market strategy shifted emphasis to domestic and rural sales.[31]

Niagara Hudson's domestic market was cultivated at the same time by a chain of electric appliance stores that sold water heaters, refrigerators, electric irons, and vacuum cleaners to their customers. By 1931, the corporation was operating ninety-four of these appliance stores.[32] When electric power sales fell in 1930, the decline was kept to 5.9 percent because the decrease in industrial sales was offset by a 9.7 percent increase in sales to domestic customers and 35 percent increase in rural sales.[33] The corporate strategy of emphasizing industrial sales had responded successfully to the question of what would happen during a period of industrial decline.

LOSING TO PUBLIC POWER

The twenty-year agitation for public control of power in New York achieved a symbolic victory under Governor Franklin D. Roosevelt. In 1931, the New York legislature established the Power Authority of the State of New York (PASNY) with the mandate to develop hydroelectric power in the Saint Lawrence River.

Niagara Falls, the other major waterpower resource in the state, was left under private control.

The declared principle of New York State under the Power Authority's charter was that waterpower resources were the people's inalienable property. Electricity had made waterpower an energy source that could be widely distributed. Riparian rights had a long tradition, but how were those rights to be interpreted if the power was transmitted to users many miles away? Modern technology made inalienable rights difficult to interpret. Roosevelt chose a policy of having the state produce hydroelectricity and transmit the power to distribution centers, but he favored having private utilities sell the electricity on the retail market.

Development of Saint Lawrence waterpower was delayed by political and diplomatic difficulties, so the Power Authority turned its attention to capturing Niagara Hudson's rights to generate power at Niagara. The Power Authority's opportunity came in 1936, when the Niagara Hudson Power Company applied to the Federal Power Commission (FPC) for an amendment to its license to develop power at Niagara. The Power Authority, acting as an intervenor in the amendment hearing before the FPC, opposed continuation of the private corporation's license on the grounds that

the power company's use of the water has not been in the public interest. It develops less than two-thirds of the power which might be realized from the existing diversions [of water from the Niagara scenic display to that of power use]. It discriminates against the public in favor of a few industrial customers.[34]

It was not in the public interest, the Power Authority charged, for a private enterprise to use public resources and to sell the energy derived from that resource primarily to industrial customers. It was charged that the corporation's strategy of selling eighty percent of the electricity to industrial customers was a misuse of the license privilege.[35] The corporation responded by citing the TVA and other public power company practices of promoting the sale of power to industry in order to keep electric rates low for everyone. "Electricity cannot be stored," so the response went, and, it was necessary and desirable to sell to customers with high load factors, that is, to factories where electricity was used at a more constant rate than households with their intermittent use of electricity, still mainly for lighting.[36]

The Power Authority supplied evidence at the FPC hearing to show that domestic rates could be lower without a strategy that favored industrial users. Ontario Hydro, a publicly owned Canadian company, used hydroelectric power obtained from Niagara Falls to supply a primarily rural and domestic market. Ontario's Hydro rates for household customers were anywhere from 33 percent to as much as 66 percent lower than Niagara Hudson's domestic electric rates.[37]

Niagara Hudson's reply to the charge of rate discrimination was that the differences in rates resulted from "two fundamentally different policies of operations and rate making."[38] In other words, there could be no resolution of the public versus private rate controversy because one argument was based on a policy that had social goals and the other used economic reasoning. Perhaps householders supplied by Ontario Hydro enjoyed more of the conveniences of electricity than residential consumers on the American side, but, on the other hand, economic growth on the American side was at a faster rate. The manifestation of the two separate pricing systems was that, on the American side, the Niagara Hudson system had outstripped demand and was buying power from Ontario Hydro, where the market had not kept up with the supply.

In the United States, rate setting for social purposes has the weight of historical tradition behind it in the form of the preference clause that is inserted in all licenses that the Federal Power Commission has granted. New York State made use of the same principle in the Power Authority's enabling legislation. Generally, the preference clause requires that the power company give priority to domestic and rural demand in marketing electricity. The preference clause is applied where there are competing users for electric power. The clause as inserted in all licenses states that municipally and cooperatively owned electric power companies will have first claim to the power available.

The Power Authority Act declared that hydroelectric power obtained from the Saint Lawrence should be primarily for domestic and rural customers, on the grounds that the power derived from that waterpower resource belonged to the people. The act was explicit: Sale to and use by industry "shall be a secondary purpose," that is, the sale of power to industry was only to be allowed when that was the way of keeping domestic and rural rates low.[39]

The public policy of preference to household use of electricity and the private corporate strategy of price concessions to industrial users can be made compatible since no specific quantitative division of power between the two types of users is contained in either the policy or the strategy. Even when the Congress required that 50 percent of the power developed at the new Niagara Falls station be reserved for domestic and rural use, the requirement was not enforced because there was not at first enough rural and domestic demand to consume 50 percent of the power available.[40]

The idea that public power should be used primarily for domestic and rural service is a goal and not a policy that can be followed literally. The Power Authority under the chairmanship of Robert Moses interpreted the enabling act in a policy that was similar to the strategy of the private company. The Power Authority has sought industrial buyers for electric power as good business practice. Contrary to the enabling Act, industrial users were not "secondary" customers, and, Moses argued, as the private power companies once had, bulk sales to industry would keep domestic and rural rates low. The public power ideology was impossible to implement as a practical matter. Moses followed a policy similar to the private strategy in spite of what he called "vociferously urged conflicting points of view" and the "clamor" of special interest groups.[41]

The changing relationship between public policy and private strategy in the generation and distribution of New York's electricity has revolved around a historically established technological paradigm. The choices, public as well as private, in the past were made between alternatives. Some of these alternatives either no longer pertain or carry less weight. Rational policy analysis requires that the changed conditions be taken into account so as not to base present policy on outworn premises. The changes in the electric utility business environment, such as slower demand growth, availability of energy sources, and pollution control policies, are forcing changes in strategy that may or may not be accomplished within the established technological paradigm.

Producing change in industries that were originally based on a technological breakthrough seems difficult to accomplish, paradoxically. The steel industry finds modernization difficult; the automobile was laggard in adjusting to the new realities of the world oil supply simultaneously with more stringent requirements for pollution control; and utilities are resisting pressures to change distribution strategy. On the generation side of electric power systems, there is public insistence that new sources of energy such as geothermal and solar be used, and, at present, these new sources cannot be accommodated easily to the centralization of generation that the established paradigm requires.

Reluctance to make technological change may be less a matter of stubborn conservatism than a dependence on a paradigm that has been a long-time guide to decision making. The paradigm is a device for relating product to use in much the same way that a production process, mass or specialized, is matched to a market.

The technological paradigm is a model, that is, it is a representation of the essential characteristics of a business's relation to the market.[42] The model may be implicitly employed by business and, even though no reference to a paradigm is made, decisions will be consistently made as though the decision maker had a model in mind. Sometimes the model can be quite explicit.

Alfred Sloan described General Motor's venture into diesel locomotives as having been an "enterprise within our scope" in that diesels were durable products that had motors. GM followed its own model and mass-produced fifty locomotive engines rather than follow the steam locomotive model of custom building. GM treated diesel locomotives like its automobiles and began with a stock of standardized repair parts and a service system before the first diesel was sold.[43] The paradigm, being a model, can be transferred to another industry if the concept is transferred by analogy rather than by trying to establish an identity. For example, GM first tried their diesel locomotive in passenger service in a too-close analogy with their passenger auto business but then changed to switching engines, and the idea was successful.[44]

The basic requirement of the technological paradigm is a dynamic relation with the market, meaning that a technological innovation imposes the need for new markets. The paradigm developed by AT&T for the telephone is a good example of the need to shift an idea.

The paradigm of the telephone, established during its first years, is person-to-person communication, with each subscriber able to choose from an expanding subscriber pool. The paradigm shifts but has not changed fundamentally. Each technological innovation has enlarged the pool of potential conversation partners. Bell stumbled on the technical principle of the telephone, talking over a wire, but it was his business partners who thought to enlarge the market potential by having a telephone exchange so as to increase greatly the potential number of point-to-point connections.

Instead of being restrained by the paradigm, the telephone company has grown with it. The dial replaced the switchboard operator, automatic long-distance dialing further expanded the potential list of contacts, and satellites have greatly increased the number of calls made each year.[45] The original paradigm, conversation over a distance with a pool of potential partners, remains the same. But each new technological breakthrough has been adopted to the benefit, not the detriment, of the telephone company. The technological history of the telephone company appears in sharp contrast to the technological history of steel, textiles, and electric power, industries in which technological change has meant decline in American competitiveness with the rest of the world and in serious domestic economic straits.

A number of authors have analyzed the conservatism of electric utilities in an effort to explain why they are so resistant to change and why utilities have been unable to adapt to a changing business environment.[46] The question of electric power companies' conservatism is important to the issue of new sources of energy, whether nuclear or solar, and to the ability to adjust to a variable growth curve. The explanations for the electric utilities' entrepreneurial conservatism is usually given as the effect of regulation, an aging management, technological fixation, or merely as the characteristic of a mature industry. One or the other of these explanations seems to apply to the steel, textile, and automobile predicaments but leaves telephones as an aberration.

Change for a technology-based industry has always been a matter of a shift of the paradigm, either within the same market or into a new market. Given those choices, a public utility can shift its paradigm by either using a technology to expand within the same market, as the telephone industry has done, or using a technology to seek a new market, as GM did with the diesel locomotive.

The particular situation that utilities find themselves in translates the choices into (1) using energy source technologies, such as nuclear power, synthetic fuels, or fluidized bed coal burning, to expand their industrial market or (2) using solar power, low head hydroelectric, or other decentralized energy sources to create a new type of domestic market. The new market might be one of decentralized distribution that supplies domestic demand directly rather than treating the domestic as secondary. This type of paradigm shift would be a revival of the New Deal program of electricity as an agent of social change. The new wave of environmentalists see this as a paradigm shift in which "the monopoly of the big power companies would be broken, and we would have at least the technological basis for that decentralized, pastoral existence so many of us claim to want."[47]

Utilities must choose, if they plan to make a paradigm shift, between these two alternatives since they are not complementary. Possibly, the original paradigm may be shattered by the dictates of regional differences, and neighboring utilities may differ by opting for different choices. Any number of alternatives are possible. One possible innovation would be to allow generation to become a competitive industry, leaving transmission and distribution a regulated monopoly.

A respite in the pressure to change has been provided by successful utility-sponsored programs in electric energy conservation.[48] But eventually the electric power industry will have to make a choice and either make a paradigm shift and remain as viable as the telephone industry or tenaciously keep the original technological paradigm and languish in the same way as steel and textiles.[49]

NOTES

1. Simon Kuznets, "Technological Innovations and Economic Growth," in *Technological Innovation: A Critical Review of Current Knowledge*, ed. Patrick Kelly and Melvin Kranzberg (San Francisco: San Francisco Press, 1978), pp. 335-56, esp. p. 338.

2. Federal Power Commission, *The 1970 National Power Survey*, pt. 1 (Washington, D.C.: Government Printing Office, 1971), pp. 1, 10, 12.

3. This commonly repeated statement is given empirical support in Bruce A. Smith, "Technological Innovation in Electric Power Generation, 1950-1970" (Ph.D. diss., Indiana University, 1974), pp. 45-60.

4. Edward D. Adams, *Niagara Power: History of the Niagara Falls Power Company* 1886-1918, 2 vols. (Niagara Falls, N.Y.: privately printed, 1927), I: 142-44.

5. Harold I. Sharlin, "The First Niagara Falls Power Project," *Business History Review* 35 (Spring 1961): 58-74.

6. Ibid., p. 62.

7. Matthew Josephson, *Edison: A Biography* (New York: McGraw-Hill, 1959), p. 363.

8. Sharlin, "First Niagara Falls," pp. 66-72.

9. Thomas C. Cochran, *The Pabst Brewing Company: The History of an American Business* (1948; reprint ed., Westport, Conn.: Greenwood Press, 1975), pp. 102-79.

10. Alfred D. Chandler, Jr., *Strategy and Structure: Chapters in the History of the American Industrial Enterprise* (Cambridge, Mass.: MIT Press, 1962), pp. 78-85; Chandler, *The Visible Hand: The Managerial Revolution in American Business* (Cambridge: Harvard University Press, 1962), pp. 303-5.

11. Victor C. Clark, *History of Manufacturers in the United States*, 3 vols. (New York: McGraw-Hill, 1929), III: 2.

12. Ibid.

13. "Reply Brief on Behalf of Applicant, The Niagara Falls Power Company," June 1, 1940. "Before the Federal Power Commission. In the Matter of the Application by The Niagara Falls Power Company for Amendment of License Issued March 2, 1921, as Amended, for Project No. 16 so as to Include Therein Authority to Divert an Additional 275 Cubic Feet of Water Per Second Through Said Project" (Washington, D.C.: Federal Energy Regulatory Commission, formerly the Federal Power Commission), p. 145 (hereafter cited as FPC file).

14. "Water Power and Control Commission v. Niagara Falls Power in Supreme Court of New York," June-December 1938, FPC file, p. 26.

15. Payson Jones, "A Survey of Niagara Hudson Power," *Financial Survey*, 2, no. 5 (June 1930).

16. Federal Power Commission, *National Power Survey, 1964*, 2 vols. (Washington D.C.: Government Printing Office, 1964), I:18-19.

17. National Resources Committee, *Technological Trends and National Policy* (Washington D.C.: Government Printing Office, 1937), p. 250.

18. FPC, *National Power Survey, 1964*, pp. 13-14.

19. Harold I. Sharlin, *The Making of the Electrical Age: From the Telegraph to Automation* (London: Abelard-Schuman, 1963), ch. 2.

20. Interconnection on a major scale was first proposed in 1920. The scheme was called Superpower and was to form a power grid from Boston to New York. Pennsylvania also had a power grid plan called Giant Power, which was an ambitious project proposed in 1925. Neither plan was funded.

21. William E. Mosher, ed., *Electric Utilities: The Crisis in Public Control* (New York: Harper & Brothers, 1929) p. xv.

22. Committee on Recent Economic Changes, *Recent Economic Changes in the United States*, 2 vols. (New York: McGraw-Hill, 1929), I: 125-26.

23. Clark, *History of Manufacturers*, III: 168.

24. Ibid., p. 165.

25. George Forbes, "Electrical Transmission of Power from Niagara Falls," *Journal of the Institution of Electrical Engineers* 22 (1893): 502-3.

26. CREC, *Recent Economic Changes*, I: 79.

27. Niagara Hudson Corporation, *Annual Report* (Niagara Falls, N.Y.: Niagara Hudson, 1929), p. 27. The same argument was used ten years later in the company's "Reply Brief, Niagara Power Before FPC," June 1, 1940, pp. 375-76.

28. U.S. Bureau of Census, *Historical Statistics of the United States, Colonial Period to 1970* (Washington, D.C.: Government Printing Office, 1975), p. 831.

29. Bernard Bellush, *Franklin D. Roosevelt as Governor of New York* (New York: Columbia University Press, 1955), p. 209.

30. Quoted by Leland Olds in "Toward a Federal Power Policy," in U.S., Congress, House, National Resources Committee, *Energy Resources and National Policy, Part I*, 76th Cong., 2d sess., Document 160 (Washington, D.C.: Government Printing Office, 1939), p. 426.

31. Niagara Hudson, *Annual Report (1929)*, p. 25; and interview with Minot H. Pratt by Jack L. Mowers, January 16, 1973. Recorded in Mowers, "Niagara Mohawk History" (unpub. ms.).

32. Niagara Hudson, *Annual Report (1929)*, p. 22; and *Annual Report* (Niagara Falls, N.Y.: Niagara Hudson, 1931), p. 6.

33. Niagara Hudson Corporation, *Annual Report* (Niagara Falls, N.Y.: Niagara Hudson, 1930), pp. 6-7.

34. The hearings were prolonged into 1940. The brief, from which all the information about the Power Authority's charges were obtained, can be found as an appendix to the Power Authority's ninth annual report. See "Brief of the Power Authority of the State of New York Before the Federal Power Commission, March 1, 1940," also published as "In the Matter of the Application of the Niagara Falls Power Company to Include in Project No. 16 Authority to Divert an Additional 275 Cubic Feet of Water per Second," in *New York Legislative Documents, One Hundred and Sixty-Third Session*, 19, nos. 76-90, document no. 87 (Albany: State of New York, 1941), p. 26. Hereafter cited as PASNY, "Application of the Niagara Falls Power Company."

35. Ibid., pp. 34-35.

36. Niagara Hudson Corporation, "Reply Brief, Niagara Power Before FPC," June 1, 1940, p. 372.

37. PASNY, "Application of the Niagara Falls Power Company," p. 35.

38. Niagara Hudson Corporation, "Reply Brief, Niagara Power Before FPC," June 1, 1940, p. 385.

39. Power Authority of the State of New York, *First Annual Report* (Albany: PASNY, 1932), pp. 97-98.

40. Power Authority of the State of New York, *Power Marketing* (New York: PASNY, [1957]), p. 4.

41. Power Authority of the State of New York, *Power Marketing* (New York: PASNY, [1961]), p. 3.

42. Edith Stokey and Richard Zeckhauser, *A Primer for Policy Analysis* (New York: Norton, 1978), ch. 2.

43. Richard S. Rosenbloom, "Technological Innovation in Firms and Industries: An Assessment of the State of the Art," in Kelly and Kranzberg, *Technological Innovation*, pp. 225-56.

44. Ibid., p. 226.

45. Sharlin, *Electrical Age*, ch. 2.

46. Smith, "Technological Innovation in Electric Power." See note 3 above. Arturo Gandara, *Electric Utility Decisionmaking and the Nuclear Option* (Santa Monica, Calif.: Rand, 1977).

47. Sheldon Novick, *The Electric War: The Fight over Nuclear Power* (San Francisco: Sierra Club Books, 1976), p. 144. See also chs. 28-31, for a historical account of the centralization versus decentralization paradigms.

48. Washington *Post*, June 2, 1981.

49. The theory of technological paradigm was first developed in an unpublished background paper that I wrote in 1978 for the Office of Technology Assessment, U.S. Congress. A published version of the theory, still not fully explicated, can be found in Harold Issadore Sharlin, "What's Historical About Science and Technology Policy?" *Public Historian* 2, no. 3 (Spring 1980): 26-38.

Modernization and Habitual Change: A Model Explored Through American Autobiography

STANLEY BAILIS

Professor Thomas C. Cochran has given us a wide-ranging and remarkably coherent account of modernization in America. This he has done through studies of the changes wrought by industrialization and entrepreneurship since 1830 and by the inner revolution of values that has been going on since 1870 at least.[1] His approach to these matters has been a pragmatic blend of history and the social sciences—a search of the recorded past for regularities that are posited in formal theories to account for change.[2] His findings indicate a disruptive process, with traditional American lifeways in flux by 1870, and a subsequent upsurge of continuous change that left the major intact social roles and institutions of 1900 either greatly altered or dysfunctional by 1970.[3]

Cochran's account advances a provocative explanatory claim: that our large-scale social and cultural transformations have been mediated primarily by individual departures from roles, from the conventionalized patterns of interpersonal conduct that ordinarily give enduring form and effect to institutions.[4] In the following essay I wish to consider how departing from roles became the common practice that it must have been after 1900 if this claim is true.

Historians seldom deal with this sort of question, according to Cochran, because data pertaining directly to roles seem rare. Instead, they examine large institutional changes, which can be recognized more readily in available records.[5] Still, if these aggregate events were rooted in individual acts, then the latter remain to be explained once the course of change has been charted and its institutional forms described.

How are we to investigate the behavioral bases of large-scale change historically? Perhaps this is a conceptual problem—a matter of how we regard the documents we have, not of an actual lack of documentation. Suppose we can explain the provenance and practice of departing from roles conceptually. Suppose we can also specify an available class of documents that should contain indicators of our conception if it is correct. Then we should be able to use these documents to evaluate our conception and explore its implications.

Such are the possibilities I wish to pursue. I have three main aims: (1) to detail a model in which departing from roles is made out to be a generalized habit that becomes stronger in persons and more common in populations if and as modernization proceeds; (2) to sketch a way of evaluating this model through published autobiographies by Americans born early in the inner revolution; (3) to consider the explanatory import of our model and evidence for the study of change in America generally and for the particular theme of business and its environment.

***

J. Robert Oppenheimer once observed:

This world of ours is [new because of] the prevalence of newness, the changing scale and scope of change itself. . . . This world alters as we walk in it. . .the years of man's life measure not some small growth. . .or moderation of what he learned in childhood, but a great upheaval. . . . Yet this is the world that we have to live in. [Its] very difficulties. . .derive from growth in understanding, in skill, in power. To assail the changes that have un-moored us from the past is futile, and in a deep sense, I think, it is wicked. We need to recognize the change and learn what resources we have.[6]

The outlook expressed in these remarks is a rationale for the habitual response to which our model is addressed: Recurrent change, however disturbing, is a pervasive condition that must be accepted and dealt with as an inevitable consequence of human advancement. Surely, we may suppose, a people possessed of this outlook would behave so as to sustain and even advance the condition of recurrent change, would depart so often from so many roles as to sunder institutions again and again.

But surely this is to suppose something very unusual. For departures from roles are usually resisted by people who usually associate their well-being with adherence to familiar routines. It is this basic conservative impulse that keeps human interactions repetitive and human aggregates stable. Indeed, it is because roles perdure that we can identify cultures and social structures, institutions and organizations, traditions, customs, and values.[7]

Then how does a protean disposition develop in persons, spread through populations, and effect institutional as well as individual change? These are the questions our model must answer, both in principle and in historically applicable ways.

Modernizing societies are the principal contexts for which these questions have been explored by scholars interested in the comparative study of large-scale change.[8] Hence, a review of what has been found out about modernization, and of what has remained puzzling about it, will serve to indicate the sorts of things our model must cover.

Modernization is now usually understood as the set of transformations by which a people comes to gather its lifeways around the requirements of using inanimate sources of power and tools that are both highly sophisticated and extremely specialized.[9]

Industrialization is primary in importance if not in time. Defined as growth in the number of people who work at power-driven machines for pay, it depends on the emergence of several conditions, including money-based markets, capital formation, guaranteed credit, routine applications of science and entrepreneurship to economic functions, coordination of specialized production factors, commercialization and mechanization of agriculture, improved transportation and communication, mobility of persons and property, impersonal performance criteria, participatory national politics, and widespread education for minimal verbal and arithmetic literacy.[10]

Sociocultural characteristics that impede these developments must be transformed if industrialization is to go on. The demographic transition is significant here. It produces a young and growing population that abandons agriculture for urban employment in manufacturing and services, that fills newly distinguished jobs by meeting steadily rising skill requirements and demands for trained professionals.[11] The stratification system opens to this new mobility of persons and positions from which newly important tasks are performed.[12] Concomitant increases in specialization make social units less self-sufficient and more interdependent, thereby fostering the growth of bureaucracies that specialize in the coordination of specialized units. This growth, together with improved transportation and communication, facilitates centralization.[13]

What follows is mass culture, in which persons who are widely separated in social and physical space nevertheless interact in temporally immediate if anonymous ways. Within this framework, interpersonal relationships become more definite, more delimited, and more often defended by appeal to objective or scientifically rationalized standards than to custom.[14]

Several psychological changes are associated with these transformations. Lerner has pointed to the emergence of "high empathicness"—a capacity for repeatedly rearranging one's self-system by incorporating new sorts of persons and their situations, new environmental features, and new behavioral obligations.[15] Others have claimed that the scientizing of social relations requires beliefs and values conducive to an unhampered search for new knowledge, a positive approval of innovation, and a high tolerance for ontological uncertainty.[16] Still others have linked strong achievement motives in adults to child-rearing practices that mirror the emphasis an industrial order puts on innovation, entrepreneurship, and technical skills.[17] And Inkeles and Smith have documented a modernized personality type in which most of the aforementioned traits are organized around a strong sense of personal efficacy, openness to new experiences, faith in planning, and readiness for social change.[18]

Such are the main components of modernization. When its consequences begin to coexist—when a people is industrialized, urbanized, bureaucratized, mobilized, politicized, scientized, and ready for more—then we have an instance of modernity.

The hallmark of modernity is change—rapid, continuous, pervasive change. Recently emerged forms of the sociocultural system display a heightened proclivity for systemic change, a marked constitutional bent for generating and incorporating novelty.[19]

This is a familiar point, but it has not been completely explained. In order to explain something, we must be able to show that a regular relation of dependence exists between it and a set of conditions from which it should follow theoretically as a matter of course.[20] Nothing quite so clear connects modernization to a heightened proclivity for change.

First, it isn't clear that modernization constitutes anything as uniform as a set of conditions. Our summary of the process is a constructed type—a composite image of characteristics that social scientists have found to be more or less usual and associated in industrialized societies and either separated or nonexistent in traditional milieus. But the actual qualities and amounts of these attributes vary enormously for given degrees of industrialization in different cases. And the modernization sequences of different populations have been quite varied with respect to their order, timing, and exact content.[21] So we must wonder in what sense different instances of modernization might constitute sets of conditions that are similar, or that at least operate similarly toward a heightened proclivity for change.

Second, modernization and its consequences appear to be anomalous for theories of culture change from which they ought to follow. Such theories generally assert that novelties are accepted into a way of life on the basis of their compatibility with it.[22] But modernization has occurred in different cultures that have not become identical as a result of it.[23] How can we account for the acceptance of similar changes by different cultures, let alone a similar proclivity for change in cultures that remain distinct?

Third, what are we to make of individual characteristics amounting to increased readiness for change? Thought to operate at the level of basic personality, these traits have been found in persons who were traditionally reared and only as adults exposed to modernized structures like factories, schools, and the media.[24] What psychological processes can have offset the ostensibly fixed effects of early personality development? How do traits that favor change develop in time to support emerging modernization where already modernized structures are few or absent? And how, in any case, does individual readiness for change produce aggregate sociocultural effects?

These three lines of explanatory questioning derive from what is known about modernization and indicate what must be covered in the model I wish now to present.

***

Modernization is a way of life as well as a process of change. Any way of life has shaping effects upon those who live it, effects that are brought about through learning processes and constitute the habits that ordinarily stabilize social interaction. Our model rests on the idea that the same learning processes can, and under modernization do, produce strong habits that make other habits subject to change in socially influential ways.

More specifically, the model advances four claims:

1. Individuals can acquire a learned response that favors behavioral modification—a habit of thinking, feeling, valuing, and acting that facilitates change in other habits.

2. Any of the varied patterns in which modernization occurs is a set of conditions under which this habit of habit change will be acquired through learning processes that are cross-culturally effective and available to persons of almost any age. Moreover, this habit will be learned as a role performance directive, as a behavioral prescription or rule that people follow in the process of trying to express and justify their occupancy of social positions or statuses.

3. The habit of habit change will become stronger in individuals and more widely distributed in populations if and as modernization proceeds.

4. Spreading a strong habit of habit change among individuals increases the likelihood that their interactions will be nonrepetitive at all levels of organization and hence conducive to a heightened proclivity for large-scale sociocultural change.

Let us consider some grounds for taking these claims to be plausible. The first suggests that people can learn to treat situations as if something about them requires abandoning established responses rapidly in order to seek and adopt new ones. This may sound very like the standard behaviorist notion that behavioral change is mechanically determined by the hedonic value of environmentally contingent rewards and punishments. But such a formulation won't do.[25] Our claim pertains to the meanings that people assign to reinforcements in given situations. Hence, we must have a way of regarding behavioral change as an intentional act that people learn to use with some degree of ease and alacrity.

Students of concept learning have contributed to such a view through experiments involving ambiguous problems with several parts.[26] For example, a subject is given several cards containing strings of letters and is told to sort them into two groups according to a predetermined but undisclosed principle. The subject tries to solve the problem completely on every trial by sorting cards according to a principle that he thinks up, say, that all cards with the same first letter go in the same group. Following each attempted solution, the experimenter gives positive or negative reinforcement by indicating whether a single card is correctly placed or not. The subjects must then stand pat or construct another solution.

The relevant observation for us is that subjects were prone to change their solutions following positive reinforcement as well as negative. This happened, evidently, because they couldn't tell what was correct about a solution that had been called correct. The correctness of a single card seems actually to have confirmed a number of alternative principles that the subjects had in mind and that they had to try. Although the subjects did become less inclined to try alternatives as they approached completely correct solutions, they never reached a zero point. Positive reinforcement never quite eliminated the tendency to consider alternatives, and negative reinforcement never became the only basis for change.

These points indicate that the activities involved in learning are purposive and inventive, not mechanically determined. Subjects appear to have been guided more by imaginative thinking about information conveyed on every trial than by the simple hedonic value of reinforcements. And their responses seem never to have become completely automatic or devoid of alternatives. In short, there is a Promethean quality in human learning that provides an active and ever-present capacity for behavioral change in response to the meaning of reinforcement.

Still, these subjects did make diminished use of alternatives once satisfying behaviors were found. Hence, we must still ask how an inclination toward behavioral change might become a strong habit. What conditions increase the ease and alacrity with which people abandon established habits to seek and adopt others? Answers can be found, I think, in more conventional learning experiments, provided our Promethean view of the process is kept in mind.

Consider a relatively ordinary discrimination learning experiment in which the subject must learn to pull the lever of a pinball machine some predetermined distance.[27] The subject knows only that a red light will flash whenever his response is correct. He does not know what a correct response is, nor does he know that the experimenter will change the definition of correctness every time the subject has made twenty correct pulls.

In the first phase of this experiment it takes the subject about 31 tries to get 20 correct pulls. Almost all of the correct pulls come in a row at the end of the sequence, so that the subject experiences a run of positive reinforcements. The definition of correctness is then secretly changed, and this time it requires about 179 pulls before 20 correct responses are made. Again, almost all of the correct responses come at the end of the sequence. Significantly, most of the sixfold increase in the number of trials needed to get 20 correct responses consists of unrewarded repetitions of the previously correct response coming at the start of the sequence. The same essential pattern—runs of reinforcement followed by nonreinforcement—continues through subsequent sequences. But as the experiment proceeds, the subject becomes increasingly adept at learning the new response, in the sense that he ceases to make large numbers of repetitions of previously rewarded but now incorrect pulls. What has happened?

In essence, the subject has learned to treat nonreinforcement following a run of reinforcements as a sign that he should try something different, that he should stop using the hitherto rewarded response and begin seeking an alternative to it.[28] Following this interpretation regularly leads to a speedy return of reward, whereas not following it regularly lengthens the interval before reinforcement is regained.

Hence, the subject's increasing efficiency at acquiring new responses manifests his *interpretation* of reinforcement patterns. In addition to learning a collection of lever-pulling responses, the subject has developed a principle about the way his world works. This principle—that established responses should be abandoned and new ones sought when nonreinforcement follows a run of reinforcements—is the essence of what I mean by a habit of habit change. A world of constantly changing reward criteria is the necessary condition for this habit's development. And if, as was earlier suggested, learning is a deliberate, exploratory, alternativistic process, then this necessary condition is also sufficient.

Still, our example is rather narrow because it deals with a single situation and type of response. If we are to make use of the habit of habit change in social analysis, we shall have to show that it can be both generalized and transferred, that is, that people can come to see many substantively different situations as alike because they contain the pattern of nonreinforcement following a run of reinforcements, and that these people can also learn to act in situations they interpret this way by abandoning established habits and seeking new ones. Without this we should have to suppose that the habit of habit change is relearned separately in every context, with the result that change of behavior would always show the delayed form observed at the outset of our pinball machine example.

A basis for this sort of point has been well developed by the Professors Harlow in their fascinating experiments on set learning.[29] In essence, the Harlows showed three things: (1) that experience with many different examples of a given type of problem leads to the development of a general type of solution—a learning set—so that new instances of the problem can be solved in a couple of tries instead of the hundred or more tries that were needed at the outset; (2) that learning sets will support efficient reversals of response when the criteria of reward are reversed; (3) that learning sets developed for different types of problems can be linked, so that when one solution-type fails another will be used. Again, the result is very rapid learning of new responses.

Through all of this, it seemed to the Harlows that their subjects—sometimes monkeys, sometimes children—were forming hypotheses about the nature of their problems and developing alternative solution strategies that could be used, reversed, and substituted on the basis of information conveyed by reinforcement patterns. Their subjects were learning to learn—developing learning sets.

What then of people whose social learning occurs in a world where the cessation of reward *does* happen often in varied contexts, where cessation *does* mean that reinforcement criteria have changed, and where hesitancy to change *does* prolong nonreward? In such a world, people should acquire the habit of habit change in a generalized, transferable form—as a learning set that leads them swiftly to abandon habits that have ceased to be rewarded and to go soon in search of new responses.

But in what sense does modernization constitute such a world, given the diversity of sequential patterns and cultural contexts in which it occurs? And how do habits—even learning sets—become relevant to roles? These questions point to our model's second claim. They may be addressed, I think, through the idea that all sociocultural milieus are learning recipes[30] for those who participate in them and that all social participation takes place through role performances that employ learning sets.

Taken together, these ideas subsume the following imagery:[31] Any society is a collection of persons who are interdependent in that they control each other's opportunities for satisfying wants and needs. Such collections of people are divided symbolically and functionally into groupings or organizational units—families, classes, schools, occupations, regions, neighborhoods, religions, and so forth. Within these groupings people occupy positions or statuses that are defined in terms of what incumbents are supposed to give and get apropos of the unit's meanings and purposes. At any moment, a person occupies several statuses in various of these units—a status set. Through time, people leave some statuses and enter others—as a consequence of aging, for example—so that they also have status sequences.

When statuses are considered behaviorally, they constitute roles, that is, the sorts of things one must do toward others in order to express or justify occupancy of a given position. The acting out of such behavioral prescriptions constitutes role performance, and the patterns of interactions that link these performances constitute role relationships. The collection of persons with whom one has role relationships is a role set. It is fundamentally toward the members of one's role sets that one acts for the purpose of satisfying wants and needs. The responses of these people, in turn, determine whether satisfactions are gained or not. In this sense, the expectations about one's behavior that are held by one's role set are a reinforcement schedule, a network of criteria that determine which of one's behaviors will be deemed correct and which will not and, hence, which will be rewarded and which will not. Because this point holds for all of the statuses one occupies at any time, and over time, one's milieu is a learning recipe.

Throughout life, the members of one's role sets present a collection of learning problems to be solved. One must figure out how to deal with them separately and together so as to achieve the satisfaction of wants and needs. The rules or directives one develops for coping with these problems are learning sets, generalized and transferable prescriptions for deciding what kinds of problems are afoot and what types of solutions may resolve them.

The relevance of this imagery to our concerns with modernization and the habit of habit change may be suggested by raising three questions:[32] Do the patterns of interaction one has developed for some part of a role set provide a reliable basis for interacting with the rest of it? Do the patterns of role performance one learned for some status that one has now left provide a reliable basis for interacting with persons who now occupy that same status? Do the patterns of role performance one has learned in anticipation of occupying some status provide a reliable basis for interaction when one comes actually to occupy that status? It is the essence of our second claim that all three questions must be answered negatively for modernizing milieus.

This is so because of the way that the transformations that characterize a modernizing society operate at the level of role relationships. Increasing mobility, specialization, and the development of mass culture make it likely that persons will have numerous role sets composed of people who have different and often incompatible expectations about how one should behave. Industrialization directed by the blending of entrepreneurship and scientific technology creates a new world of products, experiences, and opportunities for every generation, so that the parental past relates poorly to the filial present. The emerging emphasis on acquired skills and personal achievements tends to diminish the significance of ascribed positions and to make the status sequence a series of surprises that confound what in the past was expected.

In all these respects, and numerous others that could be mentioned, a modernizing milieu confronts its members repeatedly with situations in which patterns of interaction that have been learned at the hands of others turn out to be of limited and temporary use because others are now using different criteria of reward. Stripped of details, this is the configuration of "nonreinforcement after a run of reinforcements" that strengthens the habit of habit change because retrieval of reward, that is, of responses from others that lead to the satisfaction of one's wants, depends upon discovering behaviors that will meet the new criteria. It is the recurrence of this configuration across many different role performance contexts that makes the habit of habit change into a learning set—a generalized tendency to abandon established responses and to seek new ones in all situations that, however they may differ in detail, nevertheless contain the essential cue of nonreinforcement following a run of reinforcements. It is because this learning set directs the playing of roles that it hastens change in role relationships, which are, after all, the fundamental units of social structure and culture. And it is because similar learning sets are known to develop under similar conditions across many types of primates including man that we may suppose the process of set learning to be cross-culturally effective as well.

This line of reasoning leads to our third claim: It is because the process of set learning depends upon the *forms* of situations rather than on their substantive details that we may expect *any* modernization sequence to engender the habit of habit change—to strengthen it in individuals and to widen its distribution in populations *if and as* modernization proceeds. But our reasoning may at this point seem to be entering a circle, insofar as modernization is held to produce the habit of habit change, upon which it also depends.[33] A brief discussion of this issue is in order.

Our reasoning would indeed be circular if it assumed that a well-established habit of habit change is as necessary to the onset of modernization as it is to the furtherance of that process. But no such point is intended. The onset of modernization must be traced to quite other factors—to the Reformation and the confluence of nationalism, capitalism, and science in the early Western European and British instances, and, in later instances, to the impact of industry accomplished through cultural contacts that have been more often matters of conquest and exploitation than of anything more benign. Rather, our point is that *if* modernization begins and proceeds at all—and it quite often does not[34]—it will begin to

constitute a set of conditions making for the habit of habit change. And, reciprocally, if the habit of habit change is engendered, it will enhance the progress of
modernization so that as modernization goes on, the habit of habit change will
become stronger and more widespread.[35] Nor is the dispersion of this trait any
kind of mystery if it is accepted that persons who acquire it are also agents who
spread it through their role sets by acting upon its dictates. It is in this sense that,
as the component processes of modernization converge to yield modernity, a
behavioral basis for continuous rapid change emerges at the level of role performance.

Our final claim raises the question of how an essentially individual trait can
produce a systemic proclivity for change. An answer lies, I think, in an interpretation of role relationships as the basic units of sociocultural dynamics.

Culture consists of the rules of right behavior that a people share. Social
structure, by contrast, consists of the material patterns of interaction that obtain
among specific categories of persons and groups. It is through role relationships
that people acquire culture and participate in social structure, that they learn how
to behave for the purpose of completing collectively important tasks in collectively acceptable ways as well as for the purpose of satisfying their own present
and future wants. In effect, it is through role interactions that people serve as
determinants of each other's behaviors and thereby create the patterns of thought,
feeling, and action from which social structure and culture are inferred.

In populations that lack a strong and widespread habit of habit change, there is
a marked tendency for novel ways of playing roles to be quashed—deliberately,
perhaps, through acts of disapproval, but generally because role mates do not
take unfamiliar acts that disconfirm *their* expectations as grounds for abandoning
their own established responses and seeking new ones. This persistence in familiar ways tends to inhibit novelty in the behavior of would-be innovators. But, as
we have been arguing, the tendency to abandon and search is conventional where
the habit of habit change is common and strong. This tendency amounts to
approval of novelty and necessarily imparts an element of instability to role
relationships that appears at more aggregate levels of observation as diminished
sharing of the same rules of right behavior and reduced repetitiveness of material
interaction patterns. The notion of a heightened systemic proclivity for change
refers precisely to these sorts of observations.

This completes the description of our model. We have tried to present a
connected set of reasons for believing that a habit of habit change exists, that it
develops in circumstances that are characteristic of the modernization process in
general, and that it will support a heightened proclivity for change in any milieu
where it is both common and strong.

Let us turn now to the task of evaluating the model and exploring its implications in terms of the American case.

***

Virtually all of the component processes of modernization were underway or
about to begin in the United States by 1870, and the nation was approaching

industrial maturity when the twentieth century began. Ahead lay a panoply of changes amounting to outright reversals of cultural precept and social practice in such critical areas as religion, child training, education, race relations, ethnicity, class and gender identifications, sexuality, science, business organization, and the role of government at home and abroad.[36]

These developments constitute the large-scale, disruptive changes that Cochran contends were mediated by departures from roles. They also evidence that bent for systemic change which our model is intended to explain. Granted that our model's explanatory object—the link between emergent modernity and increasing change—has existed in the American milieu since the late nineteenth century at least. What of our model's main explanatory construct? Did the habit of habit change exist in the same milieu? Was it strong and widespread? Did it function as a role performance directive?

Certainly it should have. Americans born between 1870 and 1890 began their lives under conditions of emergent modernity, which, according to our model, should have spread the habit of habit change among them. Few participants in a modernizing milieu can escape recurrent encounters with situations in which novel behaviors alone are reinforced. Since it is the form of such encounters, not their specific content, that engenders the habit, it should have developed in persons no matter what their social and cultural locations might have been.

And if the habit existed as it should have, then the model that explains it also explains the practice of departing from roles—the behavioral link between emergent modernity and the ready incorporation of culturally dissonant change.

But did it exist? To answer this question, hence to evaluate our model, we shall have to make the habit of habit change discernible in historical documents that pertain to individual and interpersonal levels of activity and that should contain evidence of the trait if it existed at all.

Let us consider the matter of discernibility first. What sorts of information about a person would indicate that he or she had a strong habit of habit change and used it as a role performance directive? To begin with, such a person should be given to regarding his milieu as changing and himself, therefore, as repeatedly obliged to cope with situations in which it is not clear how he should act. Such a person should also be given to discriminating between those unfamiliar contexts in which accustomed responses will do and those in which a search for fresh behavior patterns is appropriate. Where such a person decides to seek a fresh response, he should pay close and explicit attention to his steps, so that he may recall which of his actions worked. For this sort of attention to procedures to be effective, it must be anticipatory, based on an expectation that new or alternative behaviors may become relevant. Insofar as the habit of habit change is a role performance directive, we should expect persons who have it to judge themselves and others in its terms by asking whether the acts of abandoning familiar responses and seeking and adopting new ones have been properly done. Finally, we should expect that a person who has a strong habit of habit change will place few role relationships beyond its scope.

Now our model implies that the habit of habit change is a coherent pattern in which behaviors of the sort just described entail each other so that, as the habit grows in strength, each of its behavioral components becomes more reliable until the performance of any one is tantamount to performance of all the others. It is, then, the presence of the completed pattern and not just the presence of its elements in isolation that indicates presence of the trait.

But even this sort of information must have two additional characteristics if it is to serve as a basis for evaluating our model. First, the pattern itself must be found associated repeatedly with a person's efforts to express or justify occupancy of particular statuses—with the role performances that link individual behavior to its social conditions and consequences. Second, this association must be found in persons with manifestly different status sets and sequences. Otherwise, we should have no basis for arguing that the habit of habit change is elicited by forms rather than contents of social experiences and that the trait, its conditions, and its consequences might all have been widely distributed in the American milieu.

It remains to say where we might find such information about a historical population. A source is suggested by the idea that consciousness lies on the personal side of role. By *consciousness* I mean the awareness we have of ourselves as agents and objects of our experiences. This awareness supports our ability to associate decisions about how to act with feelings about the apparent consequences of having acted in that way. It is the continuity of self-awareness— the capacity to remember pasts and to project futures—that makes human learning a deliberate, imaginative process rather than something that is mechanically dependent on external controls.

The content of consciousness is socioculturally derived. Our concepts and beliefs, our values and preferences, our behavioral repertoires, all are learned at the hands of others through social intercourse and all are used in our subsequent interactions. It is in this sense proper to think of "consciousness" in terms of social learning—socialization and enculturation—and to refer its operations to role performance.

This socially relevant form of self-awareness should be revealed, I believe, in autobiographies. Such documents provide an explication of one's own life story, an account of how one understands one's past or, at least, of how one wishes to have that past understood by others. It is hard to see how one could prepare an autobiography without giving information about the salient types of problems he and his contemporaries faced, about how and in what contexts these problems were met and handled, and about the expectations and standards that he and others had about coping with such problems.

Moreover, and more importantly, it seems reasonable to assume that persons who have a learning set as pervasive as the habit of habit change is supposed to be would surely reconstruct their personal histories in its terms. We can derive this assumption analogically from our model: Role performance directives based on learning sets consist of generalized rules for recognizing and coping with the various types of situations that commonly arise in the course of social interaction. However these rules are learned, they endure through recurrent application to present or anticipated situations, which are taken to resemble past ones. Thus, role performance directives are intrinsically associated with the acts of reconstructing past circumstances, and the production of an autobiography is just such an act. The making of such a document should be guided by the same sorts of factors as affect the reconstructive aspects of role performance itself. Autobiographers consequently should tell quite different stories depending upon whether they have or lack the habit of habit change.

In addition to being potentially relevant and at least analogically valid sources of the information we seek, autobiographies are abundant for the generation of Americans native-born between 1870 and 1890.[37] Hence, it is possible to assemble several by persons who were differently located in the social and physical space of their milieu. It should, then, be possible to use autobiographies to determine whether the habit of habit change could have been widely distributed in this population.

That it could have been is suggested by a small study of ten autobiographies of Americans born between 1870 and 1890.[38] Six of the ten cases examined were positive in the sense of containing all the elements of the pattern of the habit of habit change in large amounts.[39] One case was ambiguous in that it contained the whole pattern but devoted very little space to its presentation.[40] Of the three negative cases, one did not present its information according to the pattern sought,[41] and two presented scant amounts of information in uncompleted patterns.[42] None of the cases lacked at least some elements of the pattern. In general, the main difference between positive and negative cases was that authors who were judged to have the habit of habit change wrote as if they needed to express all elements of the pattern in order to make sense out of their stories, whereas those who lacked it seemed content to offer ad hoc remarks on the subject of change.

None of the six positive cases had more than eighteen out of forty-one locational characteristics in common, and most differed on twenty-five or more, including those which are generally regarded as influential determinants of social behavior.[43] Hence, it does seem that bearers of the habit of habit change could have turned up in a great variety of places in the milieu under study. Insofar as locational characteristics control the content of formative experience, it follows that factors accounting for the development and composition of the habit of habit change could have occurred in substantively very different contexts and yet have affected individuals in rather similar ways.

Certainly these results are not enough to support the claim that a strong habit of habit change was widely dispersed in the population of Americans native-born between 1870 and 1890. But they do lend support to the more modest claims that we set out to consider:

—that autobiographies do contain the sorts of information that our model requires;

—that this information will permit us to characterize autobiographers as having or lacking the habit of habit change;

—that positive cases could emerge under widely different socialization conditions in an incipiently modernized milieu;

—that, in view of our negative cases, we need not suspect the habit of habit change of being an artifact of autobiography itself.

In these respects, our findings do lend credibility to our model's formulation of the behavioral bases of social change and to our suggestion that such a formulation can be usefully applied to and evaluated on historical data.

But the point of such an exercise is not simply its doing. Surely it is necessary to identify the interpretive implications of what the exercise discloses. Let us turn to this matter, first regarding the theme of business and its environment illustratively, and then speculatively by way of conclusion.

***

The emergence of modernity in America owes much to business activity, which has here served commonly to link economic development with sociocultural change. This is obviously so of industrialization per se, but it is true of much else besides, if only because so little in America has escaped the transforming impact of industry.

The image of business as a factor in change has been made familiar by students of entrepreneurship.[44] In essence, entrepreneurs are those who can see fresh business opportunities in a society's needs, wants, circumstances, and resources and who are willing and able to bear the risks of innovation. Such persons serve as agents of change by purveying novelties that alter the lifeways of the people they touch.

Entrepreneurs work toward their rewards—conceived as returns to investments of psychic and risk capital—under at least two processes that may be considered limiting sociocultural conditions: acceptance and routinization. The first pertains to the initial adoption of a proffered novelty and determines what profits, power, and prestige will flow to those who at first control an innovation. The second pertains to the copying of an innovation that follows its initial acceptance and that reduces the flow of rewards to entrepreneurs as their imitators increase and as the novelty of their offering becomes commonplace.

These two processes can entrain a third, usually called ramification: As an innovation becomes more fully incorporated into a way of life, it begins to influence areas of behavior at some remove from those it originally affected, thereby inviting additional innovations. Taken together, acceptance, routinization, and ramification tie the innovative behavior of entrepreneurs to the form and content of change and to its rate and frequency as well.

The dynamics suggested in this imagery are a special case of those used in our model to account for the habit of habit change. Each of the processes involved requires the acquisition of new behaviors, and the manner in which this happens at later stages of the sequence determines a pattern of reinforcements for persons who were active at earlier stages. Thus, if acceptance is swift and large, entrepreneurs should experience the equivalent of a run of reinforcements for their innovative acts; and if the copying that mediates routinization is also extensive, such runs should come to an end, thereby completing the pattern of nonreinforcement following a run of reinforcements that conduces to the habit of habit change. Similarly, if routinization succeeds, those who indulge in imitation may experience runs of reinforcement, whereas those who participated in the initial acceptance of the innovation may find the run of benefits for their alacrity reduced through obsolescence, lowered costs of copied forms, and the like.

Ultimately, if the ramified effects of an innovation are great, then ample opportunities are created for further innovation. When seized, these opportunities reinstagate the whole cycle and provide for that repetition of the sequence, which, because it continues to include the necessary reinforcement pattern, furthers the process of set learning that makes for the habit of habit change. Reciprocally, the further development of this habit facilitates movement through the whole sequence of processes. Hence we have here a self-accelerating sequence that is rooted in entrepreneurial activity and that should lead to the phenomena of rapid, frequent, pervasive change that mark the overall course of modernization.

Given this reasoning, we should expect successful entrepreneurs under modernization to have been much subjected to reinforcement conditions that make for the habit of habit change and, therefore, to have learned its crucial lesson: that successful courses of action, even novel ones, will eventually run out of value, so that time spent persisting in such behaviors is likely to be time lost from the task of developing fresh ones that can sustain a flow of rewards. Persons so disposed are likely to make innovation into a standard business strategy and, hence, to increase the transforming influence of business activity upon the environment at large. In addition, such persons are particularly likely to bring the effects of large-scale change to bear upon the way they play their own roles and, as members of the role sets of others, upon the manner in which business itself is done—even to the point of promoting departures from established notions of how to succeed in business.

In a society in which business counts for a very great deal, this latter sort of change is of major significance. One familiar example of it is the decline of laissez faire as a pattern of business enterprise during the twentieth century. This trend is considered extensively in the autobiographies of Bernard Baruch and Marriner Eccles.[45] Their books can be used to illustrate the sense in which behaviors that appear to have been based on the habit of habit change contributed to the transformation of a major culture pattern.

The life stories told by Baruch and Eccles contain three similarities that invite our attention. First, both men indicate that they achieved pecuniary success early on through entrepreneurial careers that they pursued deliberately in terms of laissez-faire doctrine.[46] Second, both men tell how their encounters with major changes in the circumstances of American society served to convince them that laissez faire was fast becoming an inappropriate, ineffective, and even dangerous approach to business activity.[47] Third, both men describe themselves as entering into public affairs for the purpose of helping to move a reluctant community of private enterprisers away from the laissez-faire persuasion toward acceptance of a publicly planned and regulated approach to doing business.[48]

The autobiographical accounts of these three matters suggest that Baruch and Eccles operated under conditions conducive to the habit of habit change in both the private and public aspects of their careers and that they also acted in both contexts as if they possessed that characteristic. As businessmen they repeatedly departed from established patterns in order to espouse fresh forms of business activity that subsequently made for great changes in their environments. As public figures they abandoned the great American success formula and helped to promote an alternative that is still in the process of altering the way American business is done. In both respects, they operated much as entrepreneurs under modernization should.

Baruch began his Wall Street career in 1891, when, at the age of twenty-one, he became an office boy in the brokerage firm of A. A. Houseman & Co. By 1896, he was a partner in that firm, and by 1902 he was worth about $3.2 million—a fortune that he claims to have amassed in five years' time. Speculation was Baruch's chief game, and he sketches his strategy for it simply: Sell on a rising market, buy on a falling market, and keep enough cash to allow waiting for growth to make dear what was cheaply bought. Underlying this strategy was Baruch's unusual capacity for mastering vast amounts of detailed information about the internal organization and surrounding economic conditions of particular companies. For it was on this basis that he decided which among a group of companies with falling stocks could be salvaged and made to grow through competent management. Significantly, Baruch makes it clear that his strategy depended upon two features of the laissez-faire world: an unregulated market that permitted buying stocks on small margins; and repeated sharp swings of the business cycle in which the down side was regularly followed by rapid expansion of business activity. Also significant is the fact that Baruch ranks failure to notice changes in the situations of companies about which he had gathered information as a chief cause of such speculative errors as he made.[49]

For all his success, Baruch was in two ways troubled. Socialized to strong social welfare and humanitarian concerns by his parents, he could not see these values realized in his speculative games. Driven by powerful speculative urges, he felt restrained by the fact that, as a broker, he was playing with other people's money and spending time on other people's undertakings rather than his own.[50]

Baruch attacked his second problem first by retiring from the Houseman firm in 1903 in order to operate as an independent speculator with no accounts. But the industrial expansion that followed the panic of 1903 changed his plans. New sources of supply for raw materials were needed, and Baruch departed from the realm of securities speculation to undertake investment and developmental activities in new companies that sought to make the needed supplies available. In this he managed to preserve his speculative independence by repeatedly getting out of companies when they began to pay dividends and then using his profits to launch another. At the same time, he saw in this new realm an answer to his misgivings about the social value of his operations. He was now contributing to the creation of real wealth; not just money, but useful things that could alter the lot of mankind by improving it.[51]

In the vagaries of the stock market and the business cycle lie the conditions surrounding Baruch that may be taken as conducive to the habit of habit change. In the structure of Baruch's speculative strategy, in his rapid shift from speculative undertakings to resource development, and in his repeated departure from newly successful firms for the sake of fresh ventures lie indications that Baruch possessed that habit. In the social transformations wrought by industrial growth, to which he contributed much, lie evidence of the entrepreneurial link between business activity and accelerating change. What of his departure from laissez faire?

Baruch's experiences with the development of raw materials after 1903 indicated to him that the normal processes of business activity could not be relied upon to satisfy the nation's demands in time of war. Thoughts on this point began to press in on him during 1915 as the war in Europe spread and as Baruch became convinced that America would have to enter the conflict. Accordingly, he began to formulate a plan for mobilizing the economy toward preparedness by means of a national committee on which all of the major industries that supply the armed forces would be represented. Through the good offices of Secretary of the Treasury William G. McAdoo, the plan received presidential attention and was implemented in 1916 as the Advisory Commission of the Council of National Defense. It was Baruch's effectiveness in this context, particularly his ability to develop committees for each of the major supplying industries, that later led to his appointment as chairman of the War Industries Board.[52]

At the core of Baruch's thinking from the first was the importance of government control over business at levels that were unthought of and unthinkable under the prevailing doctrines of laissez faire. For Baruch, the essential novelty of the situation was clear: Modern war is total and must depend as much on the productive performance of nations as it does on the armies that actually fight. Since the required rates and coherencies of production would be impossible under laissez-faire procedures, the procedures became unthinkable to Baruch. So he operated in the Advisory Committee and in the War Industries Board to offset the effects of laissez-faire thinking—at first among industrial leaders and eventually among persons from most segments of the economy whose gatherings Baruch saw as microcosms of the economy in which the forces of supply and demand were interacting through virtual representatives. Indeed, in the committee structure that actually implemented the necessary levels of centralized control, Baruch saw the onset of contacts between government and business that he later believed had replaced the market mechanism with public planning and regulation as the basic instrument of economic decision making in America.[53]

Similar points can be made about Eccles's career, although the details are rather different.[54] In 1912, at the age of twenty-two, Eccles inherited substantial wealth and interests in several going concerns from his father, David. But David was Mormon and polygynous, and the major share of his holdings went to the sons of his first wife, Marriner's older half-brothers. Dissatisfied with his kinsmen's business procedures, Eccles eventually determined either to have their policies changed or to separate his interests from theirs—in either case, to depart from the pattern of business activity that had raised his family from rags to riches in one generation.

Being young, inexperienced, and relatively unknown, Eccles failed of his first alternative and attempted the second. But his half-brothers were intransigent. They would neither buy, nor sell, nor trade, nor facilitate his efforts to do the same. Frustrated, Eccles sought fresh ventures of his own. Beginning in 1919 with the purchase, management, and subsequently very profitable sale of the Sego Milk Company to Pet Milk, he followed an entrepreneurial career that by 1928 had made him a major figure in more than twenty firms in the intermountain West and richer by far than he had begun.

Early in this process, Eccles had his way with his brothers. But he was led by that triumph into an untoward career. By 1920, his half-brothers' principal firm, the Oregon Lumber Company, was on the verge of failure. Eccles assembled a voting trust that controlled 51 percent of the company's stock. This the half-brothers, who owned 44 percent, decided to buy. Unable to raise the required cash, they offered bank stocks as partial payment. Thus, at the age of thirty, Eccles became president of two banks in Ogden, Utah, which merged into the largest in that city and among the largest in the state. Profits from the sale of Sego Milk later made cash available for expansion, which was used to buy or to start several additional banks. Unable to manage these banks efficiently, Eccles and his associates decided to expand still further, that way to justify an adequate overhead staff. By 1928, they succeeded and established the First Security Corporation, a bank holding company that was among the first of its kind.

Eccles claims never to have intended himself for a banking career. Yet it was in banking that his propensity for change became most evident.[55] The First Security Corporation, itself an innovation, placed Eccles as its president at the center of the banking industry in the intermountain West. After 1929, the threat of bank panics was always large and often realized. Eccles managed to survive them all without losses to his depositors, mainly by departing quickly and often from established banking practice. For instance, by lending currency to competing banks, he managed to help them stay open, thereby preserving confidence in banks in general and reducing the size of runs on his own. Similarly, by inviting commercial transactions while other banks were discouraging them, he generated currency flows in to cover flows out, which again preserved confidence in his own banks. And by calmly servicing the withdrawal demands of savings depositors during a run, indeed by staying open for longer hours while other banks were closing, he yet again built confidence that reduced the size and duration of the runs themselves.

Besides indicating how Eccles may be said to have exhibited the habit of habit change, these examples pertain to three further points. First, it was in the unrelenting nature of the difficulties that beset the banking industry after 1929—in the fact that the usual expansionary boom did not follow the bust—that Eccles saw reasons for abandoning the faith in laissez faire that he claims to have held unquestioningly until 1928. Second, in the success of his efforts to offset banking disasters, Eccles claims to have found the prototypical forms of policies for public planning and regulation of business activity that he began to espouse after 1930, policies that stressed economic interdependency as against raw competition and the importance of money flows to confidence and consumption, which he took to be the main supports of a modern industrial economy. Third, this same innovative success served as the basis for his nomination to the governorship of the Federal Reserve System in 1934, from which position he pursued his policies against the norm of laissez faire.

Thus, for Baruch around 1915 and for Eccles around 1930, events that were changes in themselves—total war, unrelenting depression—brought home the imperative of further change, even change away from the established formula for business success. In this, however, we may note a significant flaw in Baruch's account. For him, it was the way in which mobilization for World War I was conducted that brought most American businessmen to acknowledge and to accept a new role for government in business affairs and, consequently, to act in ways that constituted the decline of laissez faire.[56] But Eccles, already a significant business figure during the war, claims that nothing of the kind had occurred to him or those around him until after 1929.[57] And in his own account of activities in and through the Federal Reserve System, this process of acknowledgment and acceptance is presented as by no means complete within the business community by 1950.[58]

Plainly, then, we ought not to attribute a major process of sociocultural change like the decline of laissez faire to any particular set of events at any particular time or place. For such processes ultimately consist of many persons acquiring those fresh behaviors which constitute the change in question, persons whose own new behaviors beget change in the behavior of those around them. In a large and heterogeneous society, this sort of process is rather more likely to happen to different persons at different times and places on the basis of different particular experiences. In this sense, it is the alacrity with which Baruch and Eccles departed from laissez faire and the influence that their earlier entrepreneurial successes enabled them to have over others[59] that constitutes their special contribution to the process. As this alacrity and influence were consequences of the habit of habit change, so was their contribution to the decline of laissez faire.

***

For all their similarities, Baruch and Eccles had markedly different backgrounds and beliefs. Born twenty years apart, they were very differently raised, Baruch by Jewish parents of modest means in Camden, South Carolina, to the age of ten and thereafter in New York City, Eccles by wealthy Mormon parents in various parts of Utah and Oregon. Baruch's parents were monogamous and held strong humanitarian concerns; Eccles's father was polygynous and regarded self-help alone as proper. Baruch finished college and considered medicine before entering business; Eccles finished high school only and was trained for business from the age of eight by a father for whom thrift, work, and productivity were moral motifs. Baruch, an Easterner, acquired wealth through speculation and constructive enterprise; Eccles, a Westerner, inherited wealth and increased it mainly as a banker, something that Baruch denies ever having been. Philosophically, Baruch was a rationalist convinced that immutable laws govern both stability and change in human affairs. Eccles, by contrast, was a historicist for whom epochal changes were changes entire, capable of obviating all and any rules of human conduct. Hence, although they sometimes agreed on points of policy,[60] they could also differ fundamentally—as in 1933 when Baruch insisted that the abiding laws of supply and demand necessitated a balanced budget, while Eccles espoused deficit financing as the only workable course in a world where consumption had replaced thrift as the basis of economic survival.[61]

Given that Baruch and Eccles both possessed the habit of habit change, their differences return us to the idea that this characteristic can develop in persons with different social locations and, hence, that it could have been widely present among Americans born after 1870. Supported also by the set of autobiographies mentioned earlier, whose authors did not even have careers in common, this idea invites interpretive speculation. What follows from the way the habit of habit change appears in autobiographies by Americans of the period who experienced their milieu from different points of vantage?

Two features of the autobiographies I have examined seem to have rather large implications. First, although the vast changes and the great events that occurred during the lives of our authors are mentioned, they are no sooner named than their scope and coherence are translated into the narrow, disparate, and particular stuff of mundane experience. In essence, it was immediate personal encounter that mattered most to our authors, who concentrated most on what they coped with. Insofar as change is concerned, they coped with nothing as much as unfamiliar others—persons and groups who were, so to speak, bearers of what else was going on.

This point is related to a second, namely, that our authors tended not to discriminate between unfamiliar circumstances that might require novel behavior and those that might not. While they did mention such a distinction, they seemed nevertheless to act as if its positive side alone had weight, particularly in instances involving unfamiliar others. In short, our authors displayed a strong tendency to alter their behaviors in line with the vicissitudes of social participation presented to them by a shifting array of role sets that were both diverse and inconstant.

This sounds very like the peculiar amalgam of changefulness and conformity that observers of the American scene have noted from early on. In this century the syndrome has most often been seen as evidencing a lack of inner convictions and a high need for external approval. But this imagery suggests more lassitude and less burgeoning heterogeneity than I found in American autobiographies. The concept of a habit of habit change presses for a different view:

—Behavior suggesting lack of convictions could as easily be produced by people who believe that change is necessary and proper and that temporary accommodation is its instrument.

—Behavior suggesting need for external approval could be produced as well by people whose need is to solve the problems of social intercourse that unfamiliar others present.

This view suggests the existence of a strong principle of action that eschews resistance to change. The mentality that might sustain such a principle is familiar enough: Our world is new in that it daily alters, often undoing what just yesterday seemed sound. Unsettling, yes; and sometimes so harsh. But this constantly transforming reality grows from and enlivens our best capabilities—imagination, understanding, knowledge, skill, and power. Even if we lament our repeatedly lost pasts, then, we must not reject our repeatedly new presents. Rather we must grasp their basis in change and cope with its forms, again and again.

Even if this sort of mentality implied by the habit of habit change exists, though, we are left with an evaluative quandary. Many commentators on the present American scene have judged us to be living through a harried search for new values and to be meanwhile stuck in a drifting tentativeness that has no clear direction.[62] Yet others have taken us to be verging upon a bright new morality that counters an earlier cultural imperative toward competition, conflict, and the imposition of values with an urge to accommodate—indeed to incorporate—the ways of others and at least empathically to resemble them.[63]

In a sense, this quandary faces us with a crucial question about modernization. Is it a tutelary process instructing us on how to live in the world of shrinking distances and consequently proximous diversities that it creates? Or is modernization a deceptive experience that takes us through an exhilarating moment of wealth and surprise toward indifference, fatalism, and decay?

I am inclined to be somewhat cynical about such choices. But it has been aptly observed that cynics are merely scared optimists defending themselves against disappointment. In such a vein let me suggest that people possessed of the habit of habit change may just be able to best the process—not through any superior force or virtue, but by becoming confused enough to wonder and, by wondering, to seek and maybe even to find the better way. Whether this shall have been so, only Clio knows. And her daughter will tell.

NOTES

1. Thomas C. Cochran and William Miller, *The Age of Enterprise: A Social History of Industrial America* (New York: Harper & Row, 1961); Thomas C. Cochran, *Railroad Leaders: The Business Mind in Action, 1845-1890* (Cambridge: Harvard University Press, 1953); Cochran, *The Inner Revolution: Essays on the Social Sciences and History* (New York: Harper & Row, 1964); Cochran, *The American Business System: A Historical Perspective, 1900-1955*; (1957; reprint ed., New York: Harper & Row, 1962); Cochran, *Social Change in Industrial Society: Twentieth Century America* (London: Allen & Unwin 1972).

2. Cochran, *Social Change*, chs. 1, 2; Cochran, *Inner Revolution*, chs. 1, 2.

3. Cochran and Miller, *Age of Enterprise*; Cochran, *Inner Revolution*, ch. 1; Cochran, *Social Change*, pp. 29-54; 140-55.

4. Cochran, *Social Change*, pp. 14-28.

5. Ibid., p. 28.

6. J. Robert Oppenheimer, "Prospects in the Arts and Sciences," *Perspectives USA* 2 (Spring 1955): 10-11.

7. Peter Berger, *Invitation to Sociology: A Humanistic Perspective* (Garden City, N.Y.: Doubleday, 1963), chs. 4, 5, 6; George Peter Murdock, *Culture and Society* (Pittsburgh: University of Pittsburgh Press, 1965), ch. 8; Peter Marris, *Loss and Change* (Garden City, N.Y.: Doubleday, Anchor Press, 1975), pp. 1-25, 111-31.

8. Wilbert E. Moore, *The Impact of Industry* (Englewood Cliffs, N.J.: Prentice-Hall, 1965), pp. v-viii; Michael Zuckerman, "Dreams that Men Dare to Dream: The Role of Ideas in Western Modernization," *Social Science History* 2 (Spring 1978): 332-45; Daniel Scott Smith,"'Modernization' and American Social History," *Social Science History* 2 (Spring 1978): 361-67.

9. Marion J. Levy, Jr., *Modernization and the Structure of Societies*, 2 vols. (Princeton: Princeton University Press, 1966), provides a comprehensive survey of this view.

10. These points are covered in Levy, ibid., and Moore, *Impact of Industry*, and can be pursued more specifically in the following: Ralph Braibanti and Joseph J. Spengler, eds., *Tradition, Values and Socioeconomic Development* (Durham, N.C.: Duke University Press, 1961); Manning Nash, "Some Notes on Village Industrialization in South and East Asia," *Economic Development and Cultural Change* 3 (1955): 271-77; Manning Nash, "Social Prerequisites to Economic Growth in Latin America and Southeast Asia," *Economic Development and Cultural Change* 12 (1964): 225-42; Dudley Seers, *The Limitations of the Special Case*, Yale University Economic Growth Center, Paper no. 28 (New Haven: Yale University Press, 1963); Eli Ginsberg, ed., *Technology and Social Change* (New York: Columbia University Press, 1964); Cyril S. Belshaw, *Traditional Exchange and Modern Markets* (Englewood Cliffs, N.J.: Prentice-Hall, 1965); Fred W. Riggs, *Administration in Developing Countries* (Boston: Houghton Mifflin, 1964); Everett E. Hagen, *On the Theory of Social Change* (Homewood, Ill.: Dorsey Press, 1962).

11. Wilbert E. Moore, *Social Change* (Englewood Cliffs, N.J.: Prentice-Hall, 1963), pp. 40-41, 98-101; Kingsley Davis, "The Demographic Transition," in *Social Change: Sources, Patterns and Consequences*, ed. Amitai Etzioni and Eva Etzioni (New York: Basic Books, 1964) pp. 187-94. Other views on this matter are identified and ably summarized by Zuckerman, "Dreams," pp. 337-38, and fns. 16 and 17, pp. 343-44.

12. Bernard Barber, "Change and Stratification Systems," in Etzioni and Etzioni, *Social Change*, pp. 203-13.

13. Levy, *Modernization*, pp. 19-26, 38-46, 79-82; Riggs, *Administration*, chs. 1, 2; Amitai Etzioni, *Modern Organizations* (Englewood Cliffs, N.J.: Prentice-Hall, 1964); Neil J. Smelzer, "Toward a Theory of Modernization," in Etzioni and Etzioni, *Social Change*, pp. 258-74.

14. Levy, *Modernization*, pp. 60-66, 133-74; Riggs, *Administration*, pp. 63-67. Compare Julian H. Steward, *Theory of Culture Change* (Urbana: University of Illinois Press, 1954), ch. 4, and Steward, "Evolutionary Principles and Social Types," in *Evolution After Darwin*, ed. Sol Tax, 3 vols. (Chicago: University of Chicago Press, 1960), II: 169-86.

15. Daniel Lerner, *The Passing of Traditional Society* (New York: Free Press of Glencoe, 1964), pp. 49-54 and *passim*. Similar effects have been described by Alexander H. Leighton and Robert J. Smith, "A Comparative Study of Social and Cultural Change," *Proceedings of the American Philosophical Society* 99 (1955): 79-88.

16. Nash, "Social Prerequisites," p. 266; Margaret Mead, "The Implications of Culture Change for Personality Development," in *Readings in Anthropology*, ed. Morton H. Fried, 2 vols. (New York: Crowell, 1959), 2: 515-27; and Fried, "Culture Change and Character Structure," in *Identity and Anxiety*, ed. Maurice R. Stein et al. (New York: Free Press, 1960), pp. 88-97.

17. Burkhard Strumpel, "Preparedness for Change in a Peasant Society," *Economic Development and Cultural Change* 13 (1965): 203-16; John H. Kunkel, "Values and Behavior in Economic Development," *Economic Development and Cultural Change* 13 (1965): 257-77; James N. Morgan, "The Achievement Motive in Economic Behavior," *Economic Development and Cultural Change* 12 (1964): 243-67; Hagen, *Theory of Social Change*; Wilbert E. Moore, "The Social Framework of Economic Development," in Braibanti and Spengler, *Tradition*, pp. 57-82; David C. McClelland, *The Achieving Society* (Princeton: Van Nostrand, 1961); and Paul Meadows, *Industrial Man: Profiles of Developmental Society*, Syracuse University Maxwell Graduate School Center for Overseas Research, Publication no. 14 (Syracuse: Syracuse University Press, 1965), ch. 7.

18. Alex Inkeles and David H. Smith, *Becoming Modern: Individual Change in Six Developing Countries* (Cambridge: Harvard University Press, 1974).

19. Virtually all of the sources cited in our discussion of modernization develop this point.

20. Ernest Nagel, *The Structure of Science: Problems in the Logic of Scientific Explanation* (New York: Harcourt, Brace & World, 1961), p. 4.

21. Moore, *Social Change*, pp. 90-93, and generally in *Impact of Industry*; Smelzer, "Modernization," p. 260. Levy, *Modernization*, also deals with this point throughout his two volumes.

22. Gilbert Kushner et al., *What Accounts for Sociocultural Change? A Propositional Inventory* (Chapel Hill: University of North Carolina Press, 1962). Compare Anthony F. C. Wallace, *Culture and Personality* (New York: Random House, 1961), ch. 4.

23. Moore, *Social Change*, chs. 5, 6.

24. These points are developed at length in Lerner, *Traditional Society*, and Inkeles and Smith, *Becoming Modern*.

25. For example, the behaviorist vision insists that the speed with which habits are gained and lost depends upon the reinforcement conditions under which they are learned. Thus, intermittent reinforcement is said to produce habits that are slowly acquired and slow to change, whereas regular reinforcement is supposed to engender rapid learning of

habits that can be rapidly extinguished. But social learning is generally conceded to occur under conditions of intermittency because no one is ever treated as always right. How, then, can the behaviorist vision be used to explain social situations in which established habits are rapidly abandoned and replacement habits rapidly learned? Similar questions are raised by "transfer of learning" experiments, which show habits acquired under regular reinforcement to resist change by interfering with subsequent learning (see Henry Ellis, *The Transfer of Learning* [New York: Macmillan, 1965], pt. 1); and by "concept learning" experiments, which show that response change can follow both reinforcement and nonreinforcement of behavior (see Patrick Suppes and Madeleine Schlag-Rey, "Observable Changes of Hypotheses under Positive Reinforcement," *Science* 148 (1965): 661-63). Such questions certainly suggest that some variable—something like "meaning" or "interpretation"—must intervene between reinforcement conditions and the characteristics of habitual response.

26. The following experiment is reported in Suppes and Schlag-Rey, "Observable Changes of Hypotheses."

27. This experiment is described by Fred S. Keller, *Learning: Reinforcement Theory* (New York: Random House, 1954), pp. 18-22.

28. This sign or cue appears precisely because reinforcement begins to occur on every trial as a discriminated response is learned and because it is in the midst of such runs of reinforcement that the definition of correctness is surreptitiously changed.

At the start of the experiment, while the subject is acquiring his first specific pulling response, he simply follows the experimenter's advice that the red light will flash to a correct response and not to an error. His difficulties begin when this advice can no longer be applied unambiguously to the light's absence. During the acquisition of a first specific response, nonreinforcement can only mean that an act is incorrect. But after some response has been mastered, nonreinforcement may mean either that correctness has been redefined or that the subject has inadvertently begun making a small error. Additional responding is the only means of testing such alternatives. Since the subject has no reason to expect redefinition of correctness, and since the established response *has* been reinforced, he tends at first to respond repeatedly in the hitherto rewarded manner. It is this very reasonable hesitancy to leave the vicinity of reward that produces a large increase in the number of pulls needed to acquire the second correct response. As the experiment continues, however, the subject becomes increasingly convinced that nonreinforcement after a run of reinforcements means not that he has begun to err but that a new response is now in order.

29. This work is carefully discussed in Ellis, *Transfer of Learning*, p. 3-85. Ellis also reprints H. F. Harlow's classic paper of 1949, "The Formulation of Learning Sets" (pp. 119-39). See also Gregory Bateson, *Naven* (Stanford, Calif.: Stanford University Press, 1958), epilogue, esp. pp. 285-286.

30. Neal E. Miller and John Dollard, *Social Learning and Imitation* (New Haven: Yale University Press, 1941), pp. 5 ff.

31. The ideas in this paragraph and the two after it are drawn from the following sources: Alfred Kuhn, *The Study of Society: A Unified Approach* (Homewood, Ill.: Richard D. Irwin, Dorsey Press, 1963), pp. 317-412; George C. Homans, *Social Behavior: Its Elementary Forms* (New York: Harcourt, Brace & World, 1961); Murdock, *Culture and Society*; B. F. Skinner, "The Design of Cultures," *Daedalus* (Summer 1961): 534-46; O. K. Moore and D. J. Lewis, "Learning Theory and Culture," *Psychological Review* 59 (1952): 380-88; Orville G. Brim, "Socialization Through the Life Cycle," in

Socialization after Childhood: Two Essays, ed. Orville G. Brim and Stanton Wheeler (New York: Wiley, 1966),pp. 3-49; Robert K. Merton, *Social Theory and Social Structure* (Glencoe, Ill.: Free Press, 1957), pp. 368-86; John H. Kunkel, *Society and Economic Growth: A Behavioral Perspective of Social Change* (New York: Oxford University Press, 1970).

32. Mead, "Implications of Culture Change for Personality Development," and "Culture Change and Character Structure."

33. Zuckerman, "Dreams," advances this point, pp. 332-34.

34. S. N. Eisenstadt, *Modernization: Protest and Change* (Englewood Cliffs, N.J.: Prentice-Hall, 1966), esp. chs. 6, 7.

35. Zuckerman ("Dreams," pp. 334-39) points to a number of studies that identify developments in Europe and Britain between the sixteenth and late eighteenth centuries that appear to mark the onset of modernization. These developments include delayed marriage, family planning and declining fertility, nucleation of the family, the notion of childhood as a distinct social category, empathic relations between parents and children, residence styles emphasizing privacy, decline of magic and rise of "rational" religious faiths, and appearance of science and of the work ethic itself. Because these developments antedate extensive technological advances in agriculture and industrialization, Zuckerman takes them to indicate that the modern mentality emerged before and brought about the material conditions to which this mentality is usually attributed.

Granting all this, we must suppose that modernization did begin without benefit of the habit of habit change precisely because the developments in question took something like three centuries to occur. It is after these developments converge with industrialization that changes of similar consequence begin to happen over and again in diminishing periods of time and hence to constitute the reciprocal relationship between advancing modernization and the habit of habit change. Cochran makes a point compatible with ours by indicating that industrialization preceded the inner revolution in America (*Social Change*, chs. 2, 3). A similar point may be drawn from the work of Lerner, *Traditional Society*, and Inkeles and Smith, *Becoming Modern*, who are, after all, noting the absence of even a modern mentality in traditional societies of the present day and the emergence of something like the habit of habit change and its effects following participation in modernized structure.

36. For a summary survey of these changes see Cochran, *Social Change* generally and, in particular, pages 31-39, 41-47, 49, 52-67, 79, 83, 90, 94-115, 120, 133-47, 150, 157.

37. A bibliography of about 1,000 cases, arranged chronologically by date of publication and giving the authors' occupations and ages at time of writing, is available in Stanley Bailis, "Role, Change and Modernity" (Ph.D. diss., University of Pennsylvania, 1970), pp. 212-344. The bibliography is virtually exhaustive for autobiographies by Americans native-born 1870-1890 and published in monograph form to 1969. Two recent and interesting bibliographical essays on American autobiography are Albert E. Stone, Jr., "Autobiography and American Culture," *American Studies: An International Newsletter* 11 (1972): 22-36; and Robert F. Sayre, "The Proper Study: Autobiographies in American Studies," *American Quarterly* 29 (1977): 241-62.

38. The ten cases were: Rheta Childe Door, *A Woman of Fifty* (New York: Funk & Wagnalls, 1924); Sherwood Eddy, *Eighty Adventurous Years* (New York: Harper & Row, 1955); J. Oscar Langford, *Big Bend: A Homesteader's Story* (Austin: University of Texas Press, 1952); Alfred C. Gilbert, *The Man Who Lives in Paradise* (New York: Holt, Rinehart and Winston, 1954); Arthur E. Hertzler, *The Horse and Buggy Doctor* (New York: Harper & Row, 1938); Mary Kingsbury Simkhovitch, *Neighborhood: My Story of*

Greenwich House (New York: Norton, 1938); Louise Randall Pierson, *Roughly Speaking* (New York: Simon & Schuster, 1943); Sophie Tucker, *Some of These Days* (Garden City, N.Y.: Doubleday, 1945); Hughie Call, *Golden Fleece* (Boston: Houghton Mifflin, 1942); Gustavus T. Kirby, *I Wonder Why?* (New York: Coward-McCann, 1954). See Bailis, "Role, Change and Modernity," pp. 151-209, for a complete discussion of the content analytic methods used in this study, the specific hypotheses tested, the results, and special problems involved in this way of using autobiography.

39. Ranked from most to least positive, these were Dorr, a Midwestern journalist; Eddy, a Midwestern lay evangelist and YMCA functionary abroad; Langford, a Southern and Southwestern homesteader; Gilbert, a Northwestern businessman with an M.D.; Hertzler, a Midwestern doctor; and Simkhovitch, a Northeastern social worker.

40. This was Sophie Tucker, a Northeastern entertainer who traveled extensively.

41. This was Pierson, a Northeastern journalist and housewife.

42. These were Call, a Western sheep rancher's wife, and Kirby, a Northeastern lawyer.

43. For example, with regard to career and its course and setting—clearly the most critical factors affecting autobiographical content—we had six different occupations beginning in four different places, proceeding in five different physical settings under conditions ranging from extended poverty and insignificance to continuous wealth and fame, and finishing in three different decades.

44. Opening statements of the view on which the following sketch is based are in Arthur H. Cole, ed., *Change and the Entrepreneur: Postulates and Patterns for Entrepreneurial History* (Cambridge: Harvard University Press, 1949). Some more elaborated studies are: Bernard Bailyn, *The New England Merchants in the Seventeenth Century* (Cambridge: Harvard University Press, 1955); Alfred D. Chandler, Jr., *Henry Varnum Poor, Business Editor, Analyst and Reformer* (Cambridge: Harvard University Press, 1956); Cochran, *Railroad Leaders 1845-1890*; Sigmund Diamond, *The Reputation of the American Businessman* (Cambridge: Harvard University Press, 1955); William Miller, ed., *Men in Business: Essays in the History of Entrepreneurship* (Cambridge: Harvard University Press, 1952); Milton J. Nadworny, *Scientific Management and the Unions, 1900-1932, a Historical Analysis* (Cambridge: Harvard University Press, 1955); Harold C. Passer, *The Electrical Manufacturers, 1875-1900: A Study in Competition, Entrepreneurship, Technical Change, and Economic Growth* (Cambridge: Harvard University Press, 1953).

45. Bernard Baruch, *My Own Story* (New York: Holt, Rinehart and Winston, 1957); Baruch, *The Public Years* (New York: Pocket Books, 1962); Marriner Eccles, *Beckoning Frontiers: Public and Personal Recollections*, ed. Sidney Hyman (New York: Knopf, 1951).

46. Baruch, *My Own Story*, pp. 85-265; Eccles, pp. 35-53.

47. Baruch, *My Own Story*, pp. 305-327; *idem, The Public Years*, pp. 17-23; Eccles, *Beckoning Frontiers*, pp. 54-127.

48. Baruch, *The Public Years*, pp. 23-84; Eccles, *Beckoning Frontiers*, pp. 128-81, and as a theme throughout the rest of the book.

49. Baruch, *My Own Story*, pp. 85, 89-92, 186, 192, 247-65.

50. Ibid., pp. 177-78, 185-86.

51. Ibid., pp. 188-92.

52. Ibid., pp. 192, 308-16; *idem, The Public Years*, pp. 17-70.

53. Ibid.

54. The following details are from Eccles, *Beckoning Frontiers*, pp. 35-53.

55. The following details on banking and public policy are from Eccles, *Beckoning Frontiers*, pp. 54-127.

56. Baruch, *My Own Story*, p. 308.

57. Eccles, *Beckoning Frontiers*, p. 54.

58. Ibid., pp. 394-499.

59. Baruch, *My Own Story*, p. 311; Eccles, *Beckoning Frontiers*, p. 84.

60. Baruch, *The Public Years*, p. 269.

61. Eccles, *Beckoning Frontiers*, pp. 98-103.

62. Cochran, of course, invokes this imagery in *Inner Revolution*, ch. 1, and *Social Change*, chs. 2. 3, 11. Similar points are developed, for example, in Margaret Mead, "Implications of Culture Change for Personality Development," "Culture Change and Character Structure," and *Culture and Commitment: A Study of the Generation Gap* (Garden City, N.Y.: Doubleday, Natural History Press, 1970); and David Riesman et al., *The Lonely Crowd* (New Haven: Yale University Press, 1950).

63. For example, Charles A. Reich, *The Greening of America* (New York: Bantam, 1971); and Theodore Roszak, *The Making of A Counter Culture: Reflections on the Technocratic Society and Its Youthful Opposition* (Garden City, N.Y.: Doubleday, 1969). Cochran also describes this view in *Social Change*, chs. 2, 3, 11.

A City Too Busy to Hate: Atlanta's Business Community and Civil Rights

RONALD H. BAYOR

Business leaders have often had a significant impact on their urban environments, helping to shape policies from political reform to housing improvements. Rarely, however, has the business community aided social change in an effort to forge a new policy. During the civil rights struggles of the early 1960s, businessmen in many Southern cities were faced with crucial decisions when serious racial clashes disrupted their communities. In Atlanta, business leaders slowly and reluctantly helped move their city to an acceptance of the changes in racial customs. An analysis of their role in this crisis and the basis for their decisions will be the focus of this essay in an effort to note the impact that urban business leaders can have on a city's most serious social problems.

Atlanta became a center of business activity in the South after World War II. It served as a distribution and communications center for the Southeast as well as the main Southern city for banking, finance, and retailing. Substantial economic growth was indicated by the increase in the number of manufacturing plants from 1940 to 1960 (89.7 percent) and in retail sales (525 percent). In 1959 alone, 64 new factories were set up in Atlanta and 114 new offices and warehouses. Georgia ranked seventh in the country in 1960 in the number of new firms brought into the state in the previous ten years, and fourth for the previous seven years.[1]

As Atlanta's economy boomed, the business community became a more important segment of the city's power structure. Since Atlanta developed a diversified power structure made up of various groups (government officials, civic leaders), the business elite never became a ruling group. However, business leaders had a significant input into decision making.[2] The business elite of the city consisted of the heads of a number of home-grown companies such as Coca-Cola, the executives of local banking, insurance, and utility companies, the leaders of department stores such as Rich's, and the senior members of the city's main law, real estate, and construction firms. These individuals made up the so-called Big Mules (the heads of the main indigenous companies), in contrast to the regional officers of large national corporations in the city, who had much less influence. The Big Mules were a fairly closely knit group with similar backgrounds. Most were born in or near Atlanta, went to Georgia schools, and were strong boosters of their city. In a sense their economic success was tied to the success of Atlanta. Most of the elite had their firms in the downtown business district. There was also a good working relationship among them, which made a solid business voice possible. This cohesion enabled the business elite to have more influence on city affairs than had they been a disparate group.[3] Their voice was heard through private channels as advice to politicians or through the public forum of the Chamber of Commerce.

One of the ways in which businessmen influenced policy was through the mayor at this time, William B. Hartsfield. Hartsfield had served in this position from the mid-1930s to 1961 and had as his main supporter Robert Woodruff, head of the international Coca-Cola Company. Hartsfield and Woodruff often worked closely together behind the scenes and very definitely were forces of moderation during the city's racial conflicts. They were influential in "persuading the business community of the need for peaceful social change."[4]

The main racial crisis was that of the lunch counter and school desegregation issues during the early 1960s. However, before these events Hartsfield had already, although slowly, moved in the direction of racial cooperation. For example, in 1948 Hartsfield was instrumental in putting black policemen on the force for the first time. In the mid- to late 1950s, the municipal golf courses and the bus and trolley lines were integrated peacefully with the mayor's help. Hartsfield's involvement in helping blacks achieve equality was partly the result of his concern for the future of the city and partly self-serving. A 1944 Supreme Court decision had stated that blacks had to be allowed to vote in Southern Democratic primaries since victory in these contests was equivalent to election. Once blacks began voting in this important primary, Hartsfield became concerned about their needs. This was particularly true after the mayor won with black support and realized that he needed their votes.[5]

How Hartsfield handled the golf course and bus and trolley integration is important for understanding the mood of those deeply concerned for the future of Atlanta. In the golf course situation in 1955, the mayor carefully tried to avoid any publicity that might besmirch the city's racially moderate reputation. The bus and trolley integration of 1957 brought with it Hartsfield's special appeals to the business community. The theme in this crisis was that, if racial violence erupted in Atlanta, the city would decline with particular economic impact on the downtown businessmen.[6] A concern with Atlanta's reputation and the special interests of the business community in avoiding racial violence served as the prime moving forces in the resolution of the more serious racial confrontations of the early 1960s.

Sit-ins began in Atlanta in March 1960 and were part of the general desegregation movement sweeping the South at this time. In February 1960, black college students in Atlanta organized the Committee on Appeal for Human Rights (COAHR) under Lonnie King, a student at Morehouse College (one of the six black colleges of the Atlanta University complex). Before any sit-ins started, the students first issued a list of their grievances in a manifesto called "An Appeal for Human Rights." Finding little desire by the city's white leadership to deal with their complaints, COAHR held the initial sit-in on March 15 at public transportation depots and government office buildings. The thrust of these sit-ins was to secure desegregation of lunch counters and cafeterias in public buildings. After some arrests, the sit-ins were only held sporadically through the spring of 1960. It was not until October that constant sit-ins and picketing began. The demonstrations were now directed at the downtown merchants, particularly Rich's Department Store, in an effort to desegregate lunch counters in the central business district. During the October protests there were many arrests, including that of Dr. Martin Luther King, Jr. The arrested civil rights demonstrators refused to post bond and as part of their protest stayed in jail. After a short truce period in which the sit-ins were suspended and the jailed protestors released, the demonstrations began again in late November. Coupled with the sit-ins and picketing was a black boycott of the entire downtown area. After months of negotiations between the black leaders and the white business elite, a settlement was finally reached in March 1961. The black leadership agreed to end the sit-ins, picketing, and boycott, and the white businessmen agreed to desegregate the lunch counters by the fall of 1961 and to rehire black workers fired during the controversy.

The main reason for the desegregation delay was that another civil rights issue paralleled the lunch counter dispute. Federal courts, after some delays, had ordered the integration of Atlanta's schools by September 1961. The settlement of this issue received prime attention among the white leaders. Therefore it was decided to delay lunch counter desegregation until after the school issue was peacefully resolved in September 1961.

The above description represents merely the bare framework for the events. Intimately involved in both disputes were the business leaders. Not only were they part of the white power structure, but it was their businesses that were being picketed and boycotted. An analysis of the businessman's role in the crisis as well as that of Mayor Hartsfield and the press will fill in the necessary detail.

However, before these roles are studied, it is essential to consider the impact of civil rights activities in other Southern cities. Atlanta business leaders were as much reacting to the situation in nearby cities and the region in general as they were to the crisis in their own community. An important assessment of the effect of the racial situation on business in the South appeared in a 1961 article in the *Wall Street Journal*. It described what many businessmen were aware of and feared already. The article concentrated on a few cities, particularly Little Rock, Arkansas, Birmingham, Alabama, and Jacksonville, Florida, that had witnessed racial conflicts. It was noted that industrial growth had virtually stopped in Little Rock after the 1957 school desegregation problems.

The Arkansas capital city had attracted an average of five new plants a year...between 1950 and 1957. In the early months of 1957, before the outbreak of violence over school integration, eight new plants were opened. But, according to Everett Tucker, director of Little Rock's Industrial Development Commission, in the nearly four years since the start of the school troubles there has not been a single major industrial expansion.

Not only was the city affected, but the state saw an immediate and serious drop in the building of new factories since 1957. The attacks on freedom riders in Birmingham in 1961 brought similar statements of economic decline. Alabama businessmen were reporting that out-of-state companies were deciding not to build in the state after earlier planning to come to Alabama. A senior official of one of Birmingham's major banks told of the loss of a big Ohio company, which decided to locate instead in New England. He concluded that the loss was due to the "unrest down here." The president of the Birmingham Chamber of Commerce, Sidney Smyer, correctly noted, "These racial incidents have given us a black eye we'll be a long time trying to forget. We're now in as bad a situation as Little Rock." The school desegregation issue was a problem even if no violence erupted. A Jacksonville businessman commented that regional plants were having great difficulty in retaining executives because this occupational group did not want to remain in an area where their children's schools might be closed due to the racial crisis.[7]

Warnings to Atlanta businessmen came from other sources also. Malcolm Bryan, president of the Federal Reserve Bank in Atlanta, stated that if the South did not control violence and support the laws, the effect on job opportunities and on the wealth of the region would be disastrous. There was a general business consensus that industry would not come to a troubled area. One Alabama real estate leader aptly commented, "You have to have a healthy climate to attract industry."[8]

As the desegregation issue in Atlanta developed, it was clear that the business leadership was fearfully aware of the economic impact of the racial crisis. This awareness was fortified by General Lucius Clay, chairman of the Continental Can Company, who noted in a speech to Georgia businessmen in 1961, "None of us [big businesses] wants to locate in areas where there is a serious risk of conflict between local custom and federal law."[9] Earlier the head of the Little Rock Industrial Development Commission spoke in Atlanta about the terrible effect on economic growth the school integration dispute had on his city. He warned other city leaders to do all they could to keep their schools open.[10]

Despite these warnings, Atlanta's business leaders at first resisted any racial changes. The attempt to gain desegregation of downtown lunch counters was unanimously opposed. After the sit-ins had begun, the presidents of Atlanta's black colleges contacted the white merchants in an effort to secure desegregation before the issue exploded into more serious disturbances. Their suggestion was ignored. The early efforts of the student leaders to have the Chamber of Commerce consider their demands did not meet with a serious response.[11] There were no negotiations yet on the issue. Therefore the demonstrations continued. The main target of the sit-ins and picketing was Rich's Department Store. The civil rights advocates felt that, if they could get the influential Richard Rich to agree to integrate, the other merchants would follow his lead. Rich, however, rejected the desegregation demands. Partly this was due to Rich's idea that integration should come slowly, occurring only a step at a time. School desegregation, according to Rich, was the first step, and other matters had to wait. Also, Rich did not want to be the individual deciding the lunch counter issue; he did not want to be the first merchant to give in. As Thomas C. Cochran has noted in his *Business in American Life*, "Entrepreneurs are inclined to be wary of external political or social change. Unless such change is essential to their success, they would sooner make their plans on some other basis." Rich and the other business leaders apparently did not yet feel that the success of their businesses was in immediate jeopardy. Therefore Rich held firm, as did the rest of the business community, who watched his moves carefully.[12]

Negotiations first began in the fall of 1960. The fact that talks between the business elite and the black leaders could begin at all was the result of a number of pressures on the business community. After the desegregation of the municipal golf courses in 1955, Mayor Hartsfield had made his often quoted statement that Atlanta was "a city too busy to hate."[13] The reputation of the city as a New South center, a progressive, forward-looking, racially moderate metropolis was one the business leaders wished to enhance. It was good for economic growth for Atlanta to be viewed in this way. As the number of sit-ins increased in the fall of 1960 and as the racial situation became more tense, the business elite slowly began to reconsider their earlier refusal to discuss seriously the grievances of the black community. A major incident at this time was the arrest of Martin Luther King, Jr., which resulted in unfavorable national publicity for the city. Hartsfield, serving as mediator and trying to calm the explosive situation, was able to secure a thirty-day sit-in truce and open up negotiations. King's rearrest by neighboring DeKalb County on violation of an earlier suspended sentence for driving without a license and his harsh treatment brought further national criticism and the intervention of John F. Kennedy into the dispute. Kennedy, campaigning for the presidency, helped secure King's release.[14] The arrest of a prominent civil rights figure and the involvement of a presidential candidate put Atlanta into the national spotlight.

Meanwhile the negotiations stalled. The business community was concerned about the possible loss of white customers if the lunch counters integrated, or if it looked like they were giving in. An organization called Georgians Unwilling to Surrender, formed by Lester Maddox, urged whites to boycott stores that agreed to integrate. To further complicate the situation, the Ku Klux Klan soon began to counterpicket the downtown stores.[15] With the negotiations stalled and after the short truce, the sit-ins commenced again on November 25, 1960. A black boycott was also instituted against the entire downtown area. During the truce period, the blacks had asked for face-to-face conferences with the merchants. They were refused. Hartsfield continued to serve during this time as a go-between for the two groups. In late November, after the sit-ins started again, Rich set up a direct meeting with some black leaders. However, when newsmen arrived, the meeting was quickly adjourned. Rich did not want publicity for any face-to-face negotiations with the black community. Efforts to revive the talks during December also failed. Reverend William Holmes Borders, one of the black leaders, contacted the Chamber of Commerce, the Junior Chamber of Commerce, and the Atlanta Merchants Retail Association and asked that representatives be sent to meet with the officials of COAHR, the black student group leading the sit-ins. The time was not yet right for serious compromise.[16]

The business leaders were in a difficult position. They were caught between the threats of some in the white community to disrupt the city's businesses if integration was accepted and the continuing civil rights demonstrations, which were already beginning to affect adversely business and Atlanta's economic growth and image. Faced with a conflict between established racial practices and a drive for social change, the business community was reluctant to take decisive action and play a leadership role. Eventually, as the civil rights pressures proved more menacing, the business elite were forced into a leadership position and into a serious effort to resolve the dispute.

The sit-ins and boycott soon had their effect. The Federal Reserve Bank in Atlanta reported in January 1961 that department store sales in central Atlanta had declined 11 percent from the previous year. In the metropolitan area as a whole, sales were down only 1 percent whereas in the entire federal reserve district (Georgia, Florida, Alabama, and part of Louisiana, Tennessee, and Mississippi), where the civil rights demonstrations had less of an immediate economic impact, sales were up 1 percent from 1959. For the four-week period ending December 31, 1960, sales in downtown Atlanta were down 8 percent when compared to the same period in 1959. The metropolitan area only saw a 2 percent decline during the same time, and the federal reserve district had sales equal to that of the 1959 four weeks.[17]

Even before the boycott, concern had been expressed that Atlanta's economic future was in jeopardy. The economic growth rate in the city had perceptibly slowed in 1960 after years of rapid expansion. It was felt that new industry had to be attracted to Atlanta to ensure future growth.[18] However, as one senior vice president of a large Atlanta bank later noted in 1961, "There is no way of measuring how many plants we've lost or how many we will lose because of racial conditions, but we know the number has been substantial."[19]

Pressure increased to end the racial disputes. Branch executives in Atlanta were being urged by their bosses to deal with the racial conflict. The national headquarters were concerned about the business decline and the uproar caused by King's arrest. However, the nationwide chain stores affected by the sit-ins such as Woolworth's had a policy of following local custom on racial matters.[20] The local executives of these firms therefore could not be expected to take a leadership role in ending the crisis. It fell to the business elite (the Big Mules) to settle the disputes.

The continued battering of the city's reputation, the concern for Atlanta's economic future, and the sales decline had two effects on the business elite. As one Atlanta business leader noted, "Businessmen realized that these things [civil rights protests] could ruin the town." The newly elected (fall 1960) president of the Chamber of Commerce, Ivan Allen, Jr. (head of the Ivan Allen Company, an office equipment firm), called for a Forward Atlanta program in late November. The chamber agreed to finance a special advertising and public relations effort to promote the city. As part of this program, a full-time traveling representative was hired by the chamber to further the city's economic growth by calling on industrial and business prospects.[21] Secondly, the business leaders agreed to a reopening of negotiations in February 1961.

These negotiations were preceded by contacts between A. T. Walden, a black community and business leader, and Robert Troutman, Sr., Rich's general counsel. Walden and Troutman contacted Allen in mid-January in an effort to break the stalemate. After a number of meetings between these individuals, Allen, who had earlier refused to set up biracial negotiations, now agreed to do so. As president of the Chamber of Commerce, he called together twenty-five business leaders to discuss the racial situation. The businessmen supported the reopening of negotiations and the appointment of Allen and Opie Shelton, executive vice president of the chamber, as representatives of the business community. Not only were negotiations revived, but the business leaders had agreed to face-to-face meetings. Allen noted that the reasons the business community was supporting talks at this time were economic, moral, bad publicity, and home office pressure. The main point in this decision, according to Allen, was business pragmatism. Another factor was that the school desegregation issue was nearing settlement. The reluctance and disgust of the business elite is best expressed by Rich's comment at this meeting: "Get the damned thing over with, even if it means integration." A settlement was reached soon afterward.[22]

Following the announcement of an agreement, the mayor, reflecting business concern, proclaimed March "Shop Downtown in Atlanta Month." In the subsequent months, Troutman, Walden, and Allen served as a planning committee for desegregation. They carefully worked out the details by selecting the initial stores to be integrated and preparing publicity for the event. When the day came, September 28, there were no incidents.[23]

The business community had totally opposed lunch counter desegregation at first. Then, slowly and reluctantly, due mainly to economic pressures, they conceded. Yet, although their shift was self-serving, one must also remember that the business leaders were forging a new desegregation policy and aiding social change. Atlanta, significantly, was the first Deep South city to desegregate its lunch counters.

The business leaders, although again slowly, took a more racially moderate position in the school crisis that paralleled the lunch counter issue. The prospect that the schools would close worried the businessmen more than the lunch counter problem did. Evidence of this concern is that a settlement of the school dispute was given top priority. Lunch counter desegregation was even delayed until the schools were peacefully integrated.

The business community's prime motivation was again clear. As one businessman stated, "Nobody here—at least no white person— wants integration. Life is too comfortable the way it is." However he continued by noting, "We know what happened in Little Rock after the mob took over and disrupted the school system. For a period of two years, not a single new business of any consequence moved there."[24] Allen, as the new chamber president, outlined a six-point program in his inaugural address that included opposition to closing the schools. Pointing to what had happened in Little rock and other cities, he urged the chamber and the general business community to work for open schools. Allen warned that the uncertain school situation had already become "a negative factor in Atlanta's future economic picture." The chamber supported his position.[25] Fear of losing business was strong. The examples of the other cities was evident. As the school dispute grew more intense, rumors spread suggesting even more dire happenings. For example, W. A. Palmer, general manager of Lockheed's Georgia division, had to deny publicly the rumor that the giant aircraft firm was going to leave the state due to the school controversy.[26] The business leaders, particularly the Chamber of Commerce, therefore belatedly but finally threw themselves into the school fight by late November 1960 in an effort to avoid violence and any bad publicity that might retard the city's economic growth.

The business community had to deal not only with public opinion on this issue but also with the determination of the state legislature and many prominent state political leaders to resist integration. The federal courts had ordered the Atlanta School Board to prepare a desegregation plan in 1959. Although the board developed an acceptable plan by January 1960, a delay in implementing it was allowed in order to give the state legislature time to change its laws barring school integration. Conflict between state and federal law would have closed the schools.

Atlanta's business leaders were active in breaking this deadlock even if they disagreed with integration. John A. Sibley, chairman of the Trust Company of Georgia, was asked in February 1960 to head a commission that would hold public hearings on the school issue and offer recommendations to the legislature. The Sibley Commission was supposed to resolve the dispute or at least to open up public debate. Sibley, who felt that segregation was the best system, realized the seriousness of this crisis. He made it clear at the beginning of the hearings that the federal law stated that segregated schools could not continue. Therefore the choice was either to agree to the law and end segregation or to close the schools and suffer the consequences. The commission advised in May that the state school segregation laws be eliminated and the legislature permit local community option on desegregation.[27] After much discussion and delay, the recommendations were finally accepted as being the only realistic alternative available.

Sibley represented a very personal and direct business involvement in the resolution of this issue at a time before the business community had officially declared itself. The other business leaders were later vigorously involved in behind-the-scenes legislative work and with public opinion in an effort to win support for the Sibley Commission suggestions and to settle the dispute peacefully. They became an important part of a large school integrationist element that included the League of Women Voters, church groups, civic associations, and PTAs.[28] The Junior Chamber of Commerce, for example, was an active member of a citizen's group called OASIS (Organizations Assisting Schools in September), which tried to prevent school desegregation violence. On one payday more than 50,000 Atlanta workers found notes in their pay envelopes reading, "Atlanta is a great city, too busy to hate. Let's keep it that way." The Junior Chamber of Commerce provided the message.[29] The Atlanta Chamber of Commerce kept up a steady barrage of statements supporting peaceful desegregation. Shelton, the chamber's executive vice president, noted in July 1961 that these were troubled times for Southerners when basic decisions had to be made. "Social changes that are steadily and surely moving over the South are not changes that most Southerners welcome." Shelton, however, continued by calling for reason and an acceptance of the inevitable changes.[30] The chamber also played on Atlanta's pride to foster school integration. When the schools did peacefully integrate in September 1961, a full-page message from President Kennedy appeared in *Atlanta Magazine*, the publication of the Chamber of Commerce, congratulating the city and urging other areas that had desegregation disputes to study how Atlanta was dealing with the crisis. Shelton later noted how "Atlanta is pointed to as the city in which courageous leadership is helping to shape the future not only of Atlanta, but of the whole South as well." It was emphasized how members of chambers of commerce from elsewhere in the South were coming to Atlanta to see how desegregation was handled so well.[31]

After school desegregation was begun, the chamber continued to support strongly the public schools and condemn violence.[32] The objective in this position always remained clear. High-quality public education was needed to attract new industry. The chamber was so concerned about the city's reputation in this crisis that it wrote to all the out-of-town newsmen who had come to Atlanta to cover the school desegregation story urging that they treat the city fairly.[33]

In both the lunch counter and school desegregation issues, Mayor Hartsfield partly reflected and partly guided the business community. Woodruff of Coca-Cola continued to have influence on the mayor's policies. Hartsfield was strongly opposed to violence and used the few violent incidents to awaken the business leaders to their proper role. After a black school was bombed in December 1960, the mayor angrily commented that "such senseless destruction is the work of the lowest element...encouraged by the silence of most of our substantial civic leaders." Hartsfield continued by noting, "It is time for the substantial citizens of Atlanta—the people who own its great stores, office buildings, plants, and factories—to assert themselves. Otherwise a few little, loud-mouthed racial demagogues will be mistaken for the voice of Atlanta." The mayor made it very certain that violence would not be allowed. He ordered the police to keep a close surveillance of the anti-integration groups. As the mayor said, "When racists come to *this* town, they know they're going to get their heads knocked together." During the various controversies, it was evident that Hartsfield was trying to preserve the image of the city. When the lunch counter dispute first emerged, the mayor stated that in Atlanta, in contrast to Birmingham, where the government was against the black community, there was no need for the blacks to demonstrate. All they had to do was to come into city hall and speak to him. The mayor was critical of the sit-in and boycott tactic because it would hurt business and endanger the city's good race relations. During the uproar over King's arrest, Hartsfield tried repeatedly to emphasize that DeKalb County and not Atlanta had issued the arrest orders. The mayor endeavored to present a favorable view of all incidents. On one occasion he noted, "Atlanta is the only city in the country where Negroes and the Klan can picket on the same street—to music by the Salvation Army." Hartsfield's main role, however, was to serve as mediator for the black civil rights leaders and the white business elite, particularly in the early stages of the negotiations. He reflected the business community's desire for a peaceful solution to the disputes that would maintain the city's image, and he guided them toward that end.[34]

The newspapers also tried to maintain a favorable image for the city, while at the same time noting the dangers inherent in the crisis. They also reflected the business leader's concern. For example, after King's arrest by DeKalb County, an editorial in the Atlanta *Constitution* urged the state to pardon the civil rights leader. "Any ends of justice that could be served by holding Dr. King in prison would be minor indeed compared to the wreckage of this community's reputation for racial restraint and forebearance." The editorial continued by noting that it is "important for us to be seen to be fair." Early in the desegregation controversy, an Atlanta *Journal* editorial urged blacks not to use the boycott since "any effort that threatens to set this community back economically should be discouraged." What happened to Atlanta's economic growth was of great concern. Ralph McGill, publisher of the *Constitution*, emphasized the decline that other cities had faced due to racial conflict. He warned that businesses want calm climates and political stability. "Investment money does not want to run the risk of mobs, boycotts, and the strife which so damaged Little Rock." He urged southerners to accept reality. A 1960 *Journal* editorial referred to a report that Atlanta was one of the cities expected to boom in the next decade. The editorial commented that whether this economic growth occurred depended to a great extent on how the racial situation was handled. The paper argued against violence, closed schools, demonstrations, and anything else that might give the city a bad reputation. After the lunch counter settlement, the business leaders approached Jack Tarver, editor of the *Journal*, and asked him to play down the agreement in the newspaper so as not to upset the white community. Tarver agreed. McGill had already supported limited publicity for any settlement.[35] The businessmen were very concerned that

Atlanta would be faced with white counterdemonstrations and wanted to treat desegregation quietly. The newspapers reflected this concern.

The Atlanta business community did help to end the two desegregation disputes peacefully. In contrast to the violence that rocked other Southern cities, Atlanta remained a model of peaceful change. The motivations of the business leaders have been explained, but the limitations of their type of social leadership and reform have not. It is time to ask why the business elite took so long to act, even when faced with the results of inaction in other cities, and also to determine what was really accomplished in Atlanta.

The business community was reluctant to get involved in these controversial issues for fear of jeopardizing its businesses. As long as economic growth was assured and segregation could be maintained peacefully, there was little questioning of racial policies. Business leaders were pulled into the controversy due to the sit-ins and boycotts directed against their stores and thrust into a leadership role in this dispute due to their influence in the community. It was a very reluctant role, but one brought about by the new social setting created by the civil rights movement. As Cochran has noted in another context, "Existing business roles were altered by new social environments." However, once it was accepted that the state's and city's economy was going to be hurt by continued conflict and that their businesses would therefore be seriously affected, the business leaders used their influence and took the lead in bringing about social change. It was at this point that "business institutions reacted upon American society." The self-interest that kept the business community out of the dispute at first was eventually responsible for pushing them into it. They came to understand the consequences of inaction and as a result worked for a peaceful solution. As one 1960 study of community leaders in five Southern cities has noted, "Those [leaders] who expressed the strongest awareness of the dangers of racial controversy tend to be more 'moderate.'" Moderation meant only what was necessary to prevent extreme prosegregation actions such as violence or school closings, which might convince new industries not to locate in the area.[36] Moderation therefore was based on awareness, and certainly the Atlanta business elite was cognizant of what had occurred in other cities. Still, they were very careful to move slowly toward social change, trying to avoid antagonizing the white community or the powerful state political leaders. There were, of course, other factors that influenced the business leaders' role in the two racial disputes. The profit motive was not the only one. Businessmen were also affected by the prejudices of the times. Many surely opposed integration and moved slowly partly due to that factor.

The more important point in both controversies is that the business leaders were only reacting to the immediate explosive situation—trying to resolve the conflict quickly and peacefully. If the blacks would have been satisfied with less than lunch counter and school desegregation, then surely the business community would have supported less. There was in general no commitment to integration, only to limiting the conflict. As the earlier noted study on white community leaders in five Southern cities concluded: "The movement for equal rights for Negroes will have to receive its impetus from sources other than recognized white community leadership." These leaders, the study continued, will probably be helpful only in crisis situations and will support some integration "when they feel they have to. But these leaders should not be expected to join the equal rights movement itself or to provide any major active and continuing support for civil rights in general."[37] As a result, the social changes in Atlanta were limited and planted the seeds for future racial unrest.

The limitations of the business-oriented resolution of the two disputes was quickly evident in various areas. Rich's Department Store after the lunch counter settlement still did not employ any black sales help. The Kennedy administration made a determined effort to secure the signatures of a number of industries to a voluntary equal employment program called Plans for Progress. The firms agreed to eliminate job discrimination in their businesses. Twenty-four signers who had plants, offices, or regional headquarters in Atlanta were later surveyed to determine compliance with the agreement. With the exception of a few firms, there was little adherence to the accord. Only three of the twenty-four firms were really fulfilling the program. In education, after the schools were officially desegregated in September 1961, black students in Atlanta remained overwhelmingly segregated.[38] The changes, at least in the years immediately following the two crises, were token. Real social change did not come.

An awareness of the lack of real change or the desire for it existed in both the black and white communities. Julian Bond, one of the student leaders of COAHR, noted later that Atlanta "nationally. . .had a progressive image on racial matters. Sometimes, it is clear, that progressive image is more image than progressive."[39] Ivan Allen, Jr., who became mayor after Hartsfield retired in 1961, stated, "There was substance to the charge that the liberalism of the white business community was motivated purely by pragmatism—if Atlanta didn't solve its racial problems it would suffer economically just as Birmingham had—rather than by a genuine sympathy toward the suffering of the Negro."[40]

Allen's statement is verified by two events. After the lunch counter desegregation, there was pressure on the hotels and restaurants in the city to do the same. They refused. In 1963 the Chamber of Commerce issued a declaration asking all businesses in Atlanta to desegregate. A number of hotels and restaurants agreed at this point but mainly in the downtown area, where the tourist trade was centered. The hotels consented to desegregate only for conventions. This controversy erupted during the time that Kennedy's Civil Rights Act, including a provision for desegregation of public accommodations, was being discussed in Congress. Allen noted that despite the Chamber of Commerce declaration, he felt that he would find few or no supporters for the public accommodations provision in the chamber.[41] When Martin Luther King, Jr., was presented a Nobel Prize in 1964, there was much resentment in the business community toward acknowledging the award. However, the business elite finally decided to plan and attend a biracial dinner honoring the civil rights leader. As Allen commented, "I don't think you could say there was overwhelming, enthusiastic endorsement for the planned dinner. They [business leaders] were for it primarily on pragmatic grounds: that it would look bad for Atlanta's image if we did not honor Dr. King."[42] In Atlanta, the mayor, the press, and particularly the business community were much more concerned with image than with substance.

Therefore, although it can be said that Atlanta's business leaders aided social change, although slowly and reluctantly, and helped forge a new policy, the motives were self-serving, and the results were limited. Atlanta was not a city too busy to hate but rather a city where hating was not good business.

NOTES

1. On Atlanta's and Georgia's economy, see Virgil A. Hartley, "Atlanta: Industrial Center of the South," *Atlanta Magazine* (August 1961): 17-18; *City Builder* (March 1960): 1; Atlanta *Journal*, December 12, 1960, p. 1; Atlanta *Constitution*, February 9, 1960, p. 4.

2. Floyd Hunter, *Community Power Structure: A Study of Decision Makers* (Chapel Hill: University of North Carolina Press, 1953), p. 81; M. Kent Jennings, *Community Influentials: The Elites of Atlanta* (New York: Free Press of Glencoe, 1964), pp. 166, 168.

3. Seymour Freedgood, "Life in Buckhead," *Fortune* (September 1961): 110; Jennings, *Community Influentials*, pp. 56, 58-59, 166-67; Ivan Allen, Jr., *Mayor: Notes on the Sixties* (New York: Simon & Schuster, 1971), pp. 30-31.

4. Freedgood, "Buckhead," p. 183.

5. Joseph B. Cumming, Jr., "Last Hurrah for Hartsfield," *Atlanta Magazine* (November 1961): 30, 47; Douglas Cater, "Atlanta: Smart Politics and Good Race Relations," *Reporter* (July 11, 1975): 18-19.

6. Cumming, "Last Hurrah," p. 47; Carter, "Atlanta," p. 18.

7. *Wall Street Journal*, May 26, 1961, pp. 1, 21.

8. Ibid.

9. Jack Patterson, "Business Response to the Negro Movement," *New South* 21 (Winter 1966): 69.

10. Helen Hill Miller, "Private Business and Public Education in the South," *Harvard Business Review* 38 (July-August 1960): 77-78.

11. Benjamin E. Mays, *Born to Rebel* (New York: Scribner's, 1971), p. 291; Stanley S. Jones, Jr., "Atlanta Politics and the Sit-In Movement, 1960-61" (Senior Honors Thesis, Harvard University, 1971), p. 53; Allen, *Mayor*, pp. 34-35.

12. Howell Raines, *My Soul Is Rested: Movement Days in the Deep South Remembered* (New York: Putnam's, 1977), p. 87; Freedgood, "Buckhead," p. 184; George B. Leonard, Jr., "The Second Battle of Atlanta," *Look*, April 25, 1961, p. 34; Thomas C. Cochran, *Business in American Life: A History* (New York: McGraw-Hill, 1972), p. 5.

13. The mayor repeated this statement or variations of it a number of times. See, for example, Atlanta *Constitution*, March 10, 1960, p. 14.

14. Atlanta *Journal*, October 21, 1960, p. 1; ibid., October 23, 1960, p. 18; Atlanta *Constitution*, October 24, 1960, p. 1; ibid., October 27, 1960, p. 10; Jones, "Atlanta Politics," pp. 72-73.

15. "South's Race Disputes Involve Businessman," *Business Week* (December 17,

1960): 32, 34; Atlanta *Constitution*, November 26, 1960, p. 1; Jones, "Atlanta Politics," pp. 75-76.

16. Atlanta *Journal*, November 25, 1960, p. 1; Atlanta *Constitution*, November 23, 1960, p. 1; ibid., November 29, 1960, p. 7; Jones, "Atlanta Politics," p. 78.

17. Atlanta *Journal*, January 8, 1961.

18. Ibid., November 8, 1960, p. 18; Allen, *Mayor*, p. 22; Atlanta *Constitution*, March 31, 1960, p. 46; ibid., July 8, 1960, p. 4.

19. *Wall Street Journal*, May 26, 1961.

20. Chattanooga *Times*, March 15, 1960; ibid., May 19, 1960; Allen, *Mayor*, p. 37.

21. Although Allen's call for a Forward Atlanta program took place before the report of a sales decline, it coincided with the start of the boycott that was expected to have an economic impact. Patterson, "Business Response," pp. 70-71; Curtis Driskell, "The Force of 'Forward Atlanta,'" *Atlanta Magazine* (August 1964): 37-38, 40; Atlanta *Constitution*, November 29, 1960, p. 1.

22. Allen, *Mayor*, pp. 37-39; Atlanta *Constitution*, March 9, 1961, p. 4; Jones, "Atlanta Politics," pp. 88-91, 93; Atlanta *Constitution*, March 8, 1961, p. 1; Raines, *My Soul*, p. 91.

23. Jones, "Atlanta Politics," p. 99; Atlanta *Constitution*, March 8, 1961, p. 1; ibid., July 27, 1961, p. 5; ibid., July 28, 1961, p. 16.

24. Freedgood, "Buckhead," p. 186.

25. "Year-End Report of the Atlanta Chamber of Commerce—1961," *Atlanta Magazine* (December 1961): 42; Atlanta *Constitution*, November 29, 1960, pp. 1, 10. Allen's statement on the school crisis came in the same speech calling for a Forward Atlanta program. His position on the school issue was also motivated by the sit-ins and their effect on Atlanta during the fall 1960 period. School and lunch counter desegregation were seen as interrelated issues.

26. Miller, "Private Business," p. 87.

27. Jack E. Patterson, "The Unruffled Mr. Sibley," *Atlanta Magazine* (February 1962): 38-39, 59; Atlanta *Journal-Constitution*, August 6, 1977.

28. Allen, in his November 29 speech, had urged the chamber to endorse publicly the Sibley Commission recommendations. The chamber agreed to do so. Numan V. Bartley, *The Rise of Massive Resistance: Race and Politics in the South During the 1950s* (Baton Rouge: Louisiana State University Press, 1969), p. 333.

29. Richard M. Shapiro, "Atlanta: The Deep South Says 'Yes,'" *ADL Bulletin* (October 1961). The *ADL Bulletin* is a publication of the Anti-Defamation League.

30. *Atlanta Magazine* (July 1961): 5.

31. Ibid. (September 1961): 15; ibid., (December 1961): 78.

32. Ibid. (October 1961): 7; ibid., (November 1961): 21; ibid., (September 1962): 19.

33. Ibid. (October 1961): 19.

34. Atlanta *Journal*, December 12, 1960; Cumming "Last Hurrah," p. 47; Leonard, "Second Battle," p. 34; Atlanta *Journal*, March 9, 1960; Atlanta *Constitution*, March 31, 1960; ibid., October 27, 1960; Leonard, "Second Battle," p. 31.

35. Atlanta *Constitution*, October 26, 1960; Atlanta *Journal*, March 31, 1960; ibid., January 8, 1961; ibid., November 25, 1960; Jones, "Atlanta Politics," p. 94; Atlanta *Constitution*, May 14, 1960.

36. Cochran, *Business*, p. 3; M. Richard Cramer, "School Desegregation and New Industry: The Southern Community Leaders' Viewpoint," *Social Forces* 41 (May 1963): 386-89.

37. Cramer, "School," p. 389.

38. *The Negro and Employment Opportunities in the South: Atlanta* (Atlanta: Greater Atlanta Council on Human Relations, Atlanta Council for Cooperative Action, Southern Regional Council, 1962), p. 5, in Atlanta Historical Society, Negro Community File; Southern Regional Council, "Plans for Progress: Atlanta Survey," Special Report, January 1963, pp. 1, 7-8, 12, in Atlanta Historical Society, Southern Regional Council File.

39. Julian Bond, *A Time to Speak—A Time to Act: The Movement in Politics* (New York: Simon & Schuster, 1972), p. 73.

40. Allen, *Mayor*, p. 93.

41. Ibid., pp. 103, 107-8.

42. Ibid., p. 97.

Fate, Flux, and Good Fellowship:
An Early Virginia Design for
the Dilemma of American Business

MICHAEL ZUCKERMAN

By the beginning of the summer of 1709, William Byrd was so worried that he was even watching his wife's spending. Her regular "invoice of things" from England suddenly seemed "enough to make a man mad." The articles themselves, on arrival, appeared indecently "extravagant." And so, after some days of disgruntlement, he acted. Without a word to her until the deed was done, he sorted through her purchases and sold off all that he decided she "could spare."[1]

His wife did not esteem her losses as lightly as he did. He soon found her "in tears" and, quite likely, bewildered as well, unable to fathom why the wife of the richest man on the James River could not indulge herself a little. But she never did appreciate the pressure he was under nor realize that her misfortune was little more than a shadow of his larger-looming troubles.[2]

For at that season Byrd's affairs were in a distinct descendent. The price of tobacco was plunging. Conflicting rumors of war and peace confused his impotent speculations on the prospective effects of the international situation on trade. An enemy privateer had been seen hovering off the Virginia shore. A vessel with sixty hogsheads of his best tobacco and seven hogsheads of his furs had foundered in a storm in Margate Roads, a "very great" loss. Another, with another thirty-six hogsheads of his leaf, would be "run down" at sea within the next two weeks and all its cargo sunk.[3]

Since his own American fortune went back no further than his father, Byrd could hardly have been unmindful of the fact that estates were made with remarkable rapidity in the New World, and unmade at much the same rate. Among the planters of the early eighteenth-century Chesapeake, none were so secure as to be beyond such mutability, not even William Byrd. Indeed, the bad luck that befell him in the spring and summer of 1709 was not the worst that he suffered in his enterprises.

Storms struck not just at sea but also at home, decimating herds, destroying buildings, and maiming men and women.[4] Thieves threatened not just in privateering expeditions off Cape Charles but also in ill-protected merchants' warehouses.[5] War reared its unruly head not just with the far-off French but also with the Indians at home.[6] And commerce was so unpredictable that when a ship carrying his consignments did get safely to its destination, Byrd rarely failed to rejoice.[7]

In his liability to such perils of premodern business he was, of course, anything but unusual. Every businessman of his era had to contend with those uncertainties and a host of others as well. The essence of the advantage of the entrepreneur over more traditional holders of more secure assets was the flexibility that was the other side of that coin of insecurity. Yet, exactly on that account, enterprisers were caught in cruel and connected dilemmas.

Their capital was the fluid capital of the early modern world. It gave them an effective wealth altogether disproportionate to their actual resources. But by the same token the very liquidity of their entrepreneurial assets imposed on them an inevitable impermanence. As Richard Grassby has put it, "Businessmen had power over money, but not over time." Their fortunes were too supple to establish a new class. Their money was too mobile to sustain family continuity. Their estates were too dependent on their own personal management to pass down intact from generation to generation. Yet every effort to make their holdings more stolid and secure forfeited to some degree the fundamental advantage inherent in their dynamism.[8]

Problems of securing business assets and perpetuating business fortunes were already evident in England by the beginning of the eighteenth century. But they were acute and inescapable in America, where men could not take traditional refuge in landed ease. Byrd himself, with all his tens of thousands of acres,[9] could never have lived off the revenues of his lands at rent; and for decades after, to the time of the Revolution and beyond, men made and maintained fortunes in America by land speculation, political speculation, or otherwise active careers in merchandizing, smuggling, or government contracting rather than by passive receipt of income on inheritances or acquisitions.[10]

Even the most prominent men of wealth in the colonies therefore confronted the dilemmas of endemic insecurity and enforced dynamism. And, not unnaturally, they sought strategies to relieve the strain. Merchants in Boston had recourse to trading networks of kinsmen who could be trusted to serve the family interest faithfully. Quaker businessmen in Philadelphia relied on their far-flung religious connections in the Atlantic community of Friends to facilitate transactions. And Jewish traders in Newport and New York took advantage of what Lord Chancellor Hardwicke called "the correspondence they have with their brethren in other parts of America" to become, as Addison once said, "the instruments by which the most distant nations converse with one another."[11]

But for all that such bonds were the best that men could call upon, they were never powerful enough to dissolve the central dilemma itself. They could secure the honest attachment of a captain or an agent to his employer's interest, and they could provide a flow of well-meant information, but there was more to provincial business than that. They could not still the storms that sent ships down or deter the depredations of privateers and pirates. They could not arrest the rotting of crops in dank holds or provide any satisfactory sort of storage of commodities and assets. They could not assure the persistence of the market conditions they described in correspondence across the long lags in communication or even be confident that the letters and commercial papers they dispatched would reach their intended recipients at all. They could not, in short, avert uncertainty.

More than that, they could not hold forth any prospect tending to that end. They were all essentially traditional solutions that looked backward to traditional terms of family life and religious community. Even the limited assurances they conferred pointed no way to any wider future because such assurances were becoming less and less adequate in an American environment increasingly corrosive of extended kinship connections and intense religious ties.

Expansive familial networks simply could not maintain themselves intact in the face of abounding American incentives to mobility and widespread Western demands for heightened privacy within the isolated nuclear family.[12] Religious reliances diminished with the decline of the persecutions that underlaid separatism and the rise of the tolerances that made shared religious affiliation a less automatic bond of brotherhood.[13] By the beginning of the eighteenth century, neither nephews nor fellow sectarians could be counted upon for fidelity on those accounts alone. And the very attenuation of those ties of clan and congregation inevitably exacerbated the problems of trustworthiness that such links had once served to alleviate.

In any case, the clannishness that enabled a few Quakers and Jews to ease uncertainty could never have afforded similar solace to the rest of the population. For that clannishness was as much imposed by the rest as elected by the few. It reflected a traditional consignment of the suspect work of business to some of the society's suspect if not lowly orders in a world in which the great majority went about other and more honorable work. Accordingly, it could never have modeled a culture pervaded by business activity and business values.

In the evolution of such a culture, a pariah class of Quakers or Jews was not nearly enough. A whole people had to be impelled by business ambitions, imbued with business attitudes, and engrossed in business schemes. And exactly insofar as it was, a whole people had to be exposed to business insecurities.

The emergence of a business civilization demanded, then, a palliation of an unprecedented predicament. It required relief of uncertitudes far more sweeping than those that had already proven all but irremediable, and it required relief on terms that precluded even such limitedly successful solutions of the past as dense kinship connection and shared sectarian allegiance.

In William Byrd that emergent civilization found a herald of the sort of solution it would one day embrace.

***

It is hard to think of Byrd, the great Virginia planter, as a businessman at all, let alone as a prototypical and pioneering one. Other colonial businessmen did not command a half-dozen languages and rise routinely before dawn to read at length in one or another of them. Others did not, in advanced middle age, set off on arduous surveying expeditions across uncharted frontiers. They did not go on gambling binges that went on for weeks at a time. They did not gather great personal libraries or labor lengthily over their own literary essays.[14]

But for all that, Byrd was indeed a businessman, by birth and education alike. His father's father was a London goldsmith. His father was, before everything else, an Indian trader. Byrd himself spent his youth and early adulthood in mercantile apprenticeship in Holland and in legal study at the Middle Temple in London. After he returned to Virginia to take over his father's magnificent plantation trading post at Westover, he never did depart from the commercial calling for which inheritance and instruction had prepared him.

If recent revisionist historians have rather exaggerated his unremitting attachment to regimens and ethics of work, they have nonetheless been more perceptive of his essential bent than earlier students who saw in him and his fellow planters the leisured gentlemen of Southern legend. The plain truth is that Byrd worked at his enterprises, and worked hard and often, even if rarely systematically.[15]

The more intriguing truth is that his enterprises as he actually pursued them were so often commercial and so infrequently agrarian. Remarkably little of the work he did or described in his diaries was concerned with planting per se. On his own account of it in those diaries,[16] his planting activity paled beside his commercial operations in terms of the time, energy, and ingenuity he devoted to it. He literally never occupied himself with questions of crops to plant or calculations of yields. He hardly ever even concerned himself with the grind of getting the crops into the ground, or the arduous tasks of tending to them, or the hurry of harvesting them, or the niceties of curing them. He simply had other things to do and other interests to attend to.

From February 1709 through September 1712, for example, he recorded specific commercial transactions or relations almost 350 times on almost 300 different days. Of these references, less than one-tenth pertained to tobacco. The others ranged over an extraordinary variety of undertakings and involvements. He contracted debts and collected them. He bought and sold everything from wheat and wine to shingles and rope and iron. He purchased Negroes and books and sold a sawmill. He negotiated notes and bonds and bills of exchange and wrote wills and conveyances and contracts. He weighed gold and discounted the difference between money and sterling. He acquired a quarter interest in a ship, pursued his partnership in a store in Williamsburg, and maintained faithfully his father's Indian trade. And these were but the ventures he specified. On hundreds of other occasions he spoke of having "settled [his] accounts" or of having done "a great deal of business," without giving any further details. Taking all these commercial references together, barely 3 percent reflected his dealings in tobacco.[17]

Moreover, Byrd's meager attention to the marketing of his broadleaf was paralleled by his virtual unconcern for its cultivation. Over a span of almost five years he troubled to record his observation of the planting, progress, or curing of his tobacco crops only about once every other month. Such consideration was roughly one-twenty-fifth of what he gave to his commercial activities and, even more revealingly, hardly half of what he accorded his industrial operations.[18]

Although Byrd was by no means an earnest industrialist, his industrial initiatives exhibited a rich inventiveness and variety and stirred in him an authentic excitement that planting never did. He threw himself eagerly into schemes for mines, a tannery, mills, an iron works, a quarry, and a lime kiln. He took favored guests to see his projects and exuded an unbridled pride when the governor observed one of his ventures "very nearly" or when his various visitors declared themselves "much pleased" with his undertakings.[19] He made social events out of wagers on the speed or power of his sawmill, and he exulted immodestly when he won his bets, "to the confusion of" his doubters.[20]

Indeed, the capacity of his industrial enterprises to arouse him emotionally and engage his sporting instincts stood in marked contrast to his relative disinterest in such supposed planter passions and gentry prerogatives as hunting and horse racing. He wagered on his sawmill almost as often as he ever did on horses, and he referred to the races with aversion about as often as with relish.[21]

If the racing horse was the supreme symbol of aristocratic agrarian orientations and the sailing ship the ultimate emblem of the mercantile mentality, Byrd attached himself unmistakably to the mercantile side. He spent no notable efforts or energies raising horses and expressed scant admiration for the animals, their handlers, their breeders, or their owners. Race meets rarely afforded him an occasion for serious social visiting and never presented him a pretext for extensive entertaining. On the other hand, he was eager to see ships being built, he threw himself avidly into parties for ship launchings, and he attended gladly the dinners and social evenings that were often given on board one ship or another on the river.[22] He observed the pageantry of shipping festivity—the craft's guns and the salutes it fired—as carefully as he disdained to discover the ritual panoply of the race course.[23] He had ship captains as house guests on many occasions, accepting them as his social peers and confidants quite as clearly as he ever did his fellow planters, and in fact it was a pair of captains whom he invited to be godfathers of his own first-born son.[24]

He had ships of his own as well, a sea sloop for more extensive operations and a smaller sloop that plied the James between Williamsburg, Westover, and his outlying plantations. Interestingly, even in the dispatch of their cargoes, which might have been conceded most completely to tobacco, only a third of the sloops' specified shipments were of the weed. By far the larger part were of a great range of other trade goods, staples, and supplies: sugar and salt; cider, wine, and rum; wheat; port; copper and coal; shingles, planks, clapboards, and building frames; tar and canvas; chains, ammunition, and powder; books; skins and hides; and even fig trees.[25]

Likewise, he noted news of the price of tobacco on but a baker's dozen days in all the years of the diaries, whereas he reported news of other sorts more than ten times that often.[26] He recorded his reading in his law books, a marginal aspect at best of his commercial round, four times as frequently as his reading of tobacco prices. He had occasion to draw upon his legal reading and research, in cases in the courts of law, three times as frequently.[27] And he appeared on the other side of the bar, as a judge of the General Court of the colony, a dozen times and more.[28]

Moreover, Byrd's extensive allocation of time to his judicial duties was but a fraction of his far larger engagement in politics. He sat in the council about as often as he sat in court. He served as receiver general of the colony, governor of the college, director of the town of Williamsburg, officer of the militia, and vestryman of the church. He pursued still other governmental appointments avidly, for himself and for his friends. And in all these activities he played his part the more ardently because his political powers enhanced his economic options. The information he acquired and the acquaintances he made in the assembly and in other public positions were always more valuable to him even than the salaries and stipends those positions paid. The steady succession of opportunities for personal advantage and enrichment that public office afforded was very nearly as dear to him as the status and respect such office signified. Politics was one of the preoccupations of his life, in part, at least, because it was rarely irrelevant to his business endeavors and interests.[29]

Yet politics was, if anything, even more precarious a calling than business, and a politics so inseparable from business was more precarious still. The very extensiveness and intensity of Byrd's participation in public affairs exacerbated his insecurity about his sacred honor, his fortune, and, on occasion, his life itself.[30] His political entanglements left him anxious about his standing with governors, fearful lest he fall out of favor with them or, for that matter, their female consorts. His political commitments and obligations left him susceptible to rage, suspiciousness, and self-doubt when he could not get positions for friends whose candidacy he promoted. His political ambitions left him exposed to frustration when he discovered his impotence to advance his own candidacy for governorships of Maryland and Virginia.[31] And the risks he ran and the enemies he made in politics only compounded his economic vulnerability. They heightened his liability to setbacks such as those that forced the disposal of his wife's long-fancied fineries. They redoubled the danger of real catastrophes such as the one that followed his taking on his father-in-law's hopelessly encumbered estate, in which the repayment of the dead man's debts exhausted him through the last three decades of his own life.[32]

Byrd stood in serious need, therefore, of a means of mitigating the uncertainties of his situation. Much like other colonial men of affairs, he required a way of reducing his anxiety in a world he could neither control nor predict. And as it happened, he hit upon not just one but two of them.

***

Byrd's first way was essentially religious. It was not founded in religious fellowship, as were the ways of the Quakers and Jews, so much as in a profoundly fatalistic acceptance of God's will in the world. Even in the sorest of circumstances, personal as well as pecuniary, he found a very private source of reassurance in his conviction of God's ruling providence and gracious design. When gusty winds blew down three of his plantation houses, he bore it "with a submission to God Almighty who knows best what to do for us." When his linen chest was plundered on its way to Williamsburg, he resolved to "try to bear" his bad fortune "with patience till God shall please to better it." When his slaves fell sick, he prayed that God would "restore them to their health if it be consistent with His holy will." When he was himself sick, when his slaves died, when his nearest neighbor and best friend died, he reconciled himself to such fate with a laconic "God's will be done." Even when his only son died in tender childhood, he resigned himself to the divine wisdom in which he trusted so utterly. "God gives and God takes away," he confided to his diary on the day of the boy's death. "Blessed be the name of God."[33]

Tested and tempered as it was in such straits, Byrd's ability to abide in the Lord's providence was authentic and absolute. But on exactly that account it was unavailable to vast masses of Americans who could not steel themselves to such self-control. Some American businessmen, then and thereafter, did surely draw on spiritual sources rather like his. Most, however, had neither his stoic strength nor his margin for error. His religious recourse could hardly, then, have sustained the business system or made bearable the strains of a business civilization.

Byrd's second strategy was more widely accessible and far more fundamentally prefigurative of the subsequent shape of American business life. It was at once traditional, in its dependence on social relations to soften the strokes of destiny, and starkly modern, in its deliberate creation of such social contexts of consolation and congeniality. For no communal network was anciently established among eighteenth-century Virginians. No social circles were deeply described, and few friendships were ascriptively given by kinship, coresidence, or intensely shared religiosity.

Instead, in the very teeth of the inherent isolation of his circumstances, Byrd set about to surround himself with—indeed, immerse himself in—a fellowship of his own making. By frenetic visiting and unremitting rounds of fraternizing, he achieved what those who remained in the Old World simply inherited. And in achieving it he achieved something both exceedingly old and daringly new. He perpetuated the primacy of associational activity even as he contrived an associational activity essentially independent of familial and religious givenness. His was a social life shallower in many ways than the Old World round, yet wider as well and, above all, willed.

Several commentators have seen how central the question of community was for Byrd and other Southern colonists. But such commentators have, on the whole, taken the thinness of the settlers' society as an immutable fact, and they

have thereby misconceived much that was most intriguing in the adaptation of
Byrd and his provincial peers.

Kenneth Lynn viewed Virginia's social deficiencies as irremediable for someone of Byrd's sensibility, simply because neither Westover nor Williamsburg
was London. "The awe of provincial tobacco-farmers was hardly sufficient for a
man who had been the friend of Congreve," and Rotten Row was not to be
transplanted to the silent rows of broadleaf in the fields of the Chesapeake. On
Lynn's account, the reassurance that Byrd required could have come only from
metropolitan admiration and acceptance, and therefore it could not come at all.[34]

David Bertelson saw Southern social failings less largely and unyieldingly
given by location on the wrong side of the Atlantic Ocean, but no less real for
that. In his interpretation, isolated planters like Byrd suffered from an absence
of redeeming meaning in their lives that derived from the absence of "rational,
purposeful, socially oriented labor" on a social stage sufficiently rich and complex for meanings to be mounted and made visible.[35]

Either way, such commentators conceived of the colonial Southerner as a man
mutilated by his estrangement from any sustaining social milieu, a flawed and
ultimately failed figure. Either way, they took Byrd as a type of that failure.

But as they did, they betrayed their forced reading of the man. Byrd's diary
reveals no anguish at the infirmity of institutions or the absence of conviviality
along the James. On the contrary, it exudes an acceptance of provincial society
that was profound and even complacent.[36] Bertelson and Lynn both projected
onto Byrd a modern academic consciousness that was never his, and in so doing
they misconceived much that was most formative for community life in the New
World.

They missed entirely the emergent American sense that a social matrix may be
made as well as given. They took no account of the propensity of men to
establish their own distinct communal orbits within the same social constellation.
They failed to understand that there could be a myriad of personal communities
in uneasy relation to the structures of a more widely shared social existence. And
above all they did not see that William Byrd was building just such communal
configurations.

By his energetic visiting and entertaining and by the priority that he placed on
his public life over his more narrowly domestic cares, Byrd arranged, for himself
and for those within the compass of his fellowship, a dense social experience
amid the dispersed settlements of the Tidewater. Where no community was
conferred by history and geography, he animated a regular and reassuring bustle
of camaraderie. In a corner of the globe haunted by uncertainty, he helped clear
an area of comparative security.

Diffusing his dependence on others and spreading his emotional as well as his
economic investments, Byrd diminished his vulnerability to the loss of any
crucial few. For in a world in which buildings blew down and shiploads of
tobacco sank and sons died before their first birthday and wives went to their
graves in the bloom of youth, his far-flung affiliations and the flattening of affect

that attended them enabled him to accept his sufferings and losses and adapt to instability as equably as he did.

***

Disease, death, and natural disaster were never far from Byrd's thoughts. But then, they were rarely remote from his everyday experience either. The diary simply shows that he devoted his most private musings to the immediate realities of his environment rather than to self-doubt or social criticism.

He observed unfailingly the unfathomable weather of the Southern seaboard, as if by ceaseless attention he might somehow wrest order out of the erratic elements. And he occupied himself even more urgently, if less regularly, with his illnesses and afflictions and those of his family, friends, and neighbors.

Indeed, he evidenced no more absorbing interest in his diary than his interest in sickness and dying. His medical references dwarfed his allusions to his children and accounted for the vast preponderance of the notice of his offspring that he did take. His discussions of medicaments and mortality far overshadowed his attentions to matrimony and similarly stood responsible for a fair proportion of the mention of his wife that he made.[37]

His entries on ailments and fatalities eclipsed even his marking of his participation in public affairs. They exceeded, easily, the entirety of his allusion to politics. They surpassed, though more narrowly, the sum total of the attentions he paid to his business endeavors.[38]

Byrd's obsession with doctors, disease, and dying in Virginia contrasted strikingly with his comparative unconcern for such matters in the mother country. During the London years of his diary, he made medical observations only about a third as often as he did when he was at Westover.[39] And of those, almost none evoked the threat of death. The mortality that haunted his Virginia diary, accounting for nearly a fifth of its multitudinous medical references, reared its fearsome face in little more than a fiftieth of such notations in the London diary. The acknowledgment of the way of all flesh that appeared so routinely in the Westover record, every four or five days, issued forth irregularly in the metropolis, every four or five months.[40]

The medical entries Byrd made in England were, on the whole, of minor moment. He often noted that his friends were "indisposed." He occasionally regretted the inconvenience of visiting and finding someone "sick, so I could not see her." He worried through the recurrent "running" of his own venereal disease, though never sufficiently to desist from his pastimes with prostitutes.[41] Even when he did discuss disease in England, he generally did so in a manner that made clear how little he conceived the course of the illness or its outcome to lie in his own hands. He rarely did the doctoring or registered any interest in how it was done. He hardly ever took the trouble to follow the progress of the infirm or comfort the convalescent. On learning that his landlady was "extremely ill," he abandoned her to her own devices for the next three weeks. On discovering that his own daughter was unwell with what her custodian "feared. . . would be a smallpox," he went fully a week—without any word about her in the interim—before he paid her a perfunctory visit. On finding a friend "very sick," he simply proceeded to the next stop on his sociable circuit. Affliction impinged on him only as it disrupted his social rounds. It stirred nothing in him of curiosity, concern, or a caring to cure.[42]

In Virginia, on the other hand, Byrd was incorrigibly curious, absorbedly concerned, and earnestly engaged in efforts to cure. He strove to enlarge his pharmacological competence. He gathered an extensive store of medications and dispensed them freely to all who sought his help. He cultivated the company of doctors, learned from them, and applied his learning for the benefit of family, slaves, gentry friends, and neighbors alike. And he mixed such medical expertise with attentiveness and devotion. It was not only with his closest companion, Benjamin Harrison, that he stayed up night after night in hours of need. It was also with as insignificant a servant as the one denoted in the diary merely as L-s-n. Byrd ministered to him day and night for several days. When finally he had to go off to Williamsburg he "left the best directions [he] could about him." And when he arrived at the capital, he "went to the Governor's to consult the doctor about L-s-n," pressed the doctor for "directions in writing" about the case, and forwarded them at once to Westover.[43]

In London, Byrd would never have done remotely so much, because in London he held himself subtly apart from a society that exercised its watch over others without his complicity. In Virginia, he could not hold himself so aloof. Social life did not run on as if of its own accord. Community had to be consciously created and cared for. It had to be purposefully fostered or scarcely exist at all.

Byrd therefore behaved very differently in the Old World than in the New, and the difference appeared, symptomatically, in his dealings with disease and death. In the mother country, Byrd worried primarily about his own health. Relatively few of his medical references paid any regard at all to the suffering and dying that surrounded him. But in the Old Dominion, he expended the preponderance of his concern on others. Less than a fifth of his allusions to illness were self-centered in Virginia, whereas more than three-fifths focused on himself in England.[44]

As Byrd went from private preoccupations in the metropolis to solicitude for his fellow colonists along the James in matters of morbidity and mortality, so he shifted more generally. Among the sophisticates of the great city, awash in their ceaseless whirl of playgoing and coffeehouse rounds and parties at the Spanish ambassador's, he showed no sense of anchored attachments or any evident feelings of fondness or steady affections. Even when he courted an eligible widow or believed himself in love with a fine lady, he did not desist from frequenting his favorite whorehouses or kissing his chambermaid until he "polluted" himself.[45] Even when he went to receptions and stayed for hours, he knew that there was "nobody [he] liked" there. Even when he went to masquerades and did not go home until five in the morning, he realized that he was "but indifferently diverted."[46] He simply had no connection of consequence to London and its life.

Among his servants, slaves, neighbors, and fellow planters of the Chesapeake, however, he rarely complained of the social scene. He had with them an unspoken understanding of relatedness that he never had with his worldly peers in England—a relatedness of his own deliberate contrivance and determined maintenance—and he had toward them and the community they constituted a real sense of responsibility that he could never even have conceived across the Atlantic. In the metropolis he just looked after his own business and pursued his own personal pleasures. City society went on well enough with or without him. But in Virginia he acted unceasingly to knit his friends and fellows together and articulate their ties.

Perhaps the most graphic indication of his purposes and priorities came when he returned from his lengthy stay in London in February of 1720. He had not been home for five years. He had not taken stock of the state of his plantation in all that time, nor walked its once-familiar fields, nor spoken with his retinue of retainers. And yet, when his ship touched shore after almost two months at sea, he did not start straight for home. He made his way to Williamsburg, visiting and receiving visitors as he went. He spent several days at the capital, renewing old acquaintances and refreshing old alliances. And he wended a dawdling course up the James, enjoying the hospitality of friends and favored guests. Altogether, he was in Virginia for nine days of politicking and neighboring before he set eyes on his own acres at Westover.[47]

In the manner of his return, he at once recapitulated his wandering ways of an earlier decade and prefigured his resumption of them. Quiet life at home had never been his bent and would not be when his wife was dead and his daughters were with relatives in England. For him, Westover was never a refuge from the rigors of the wider world. On the contrary, it was itself a representation of that world, teemingly peopled with apprentices, artisans, servants, and slaves as well as friends, flunkies, and veritable strangers. And insofar as it was not, insofar as he could not bring all the affairs of Chesapeake society within its walls, Byrd went out willingly from its confines. At home and abroad, he was an utterly public man, happy in company and happier still amidst "abundance of company."[48]

At home he was hardly ever without such company. From 1709 to 1712 he had visitors almost two days out of every three. Month in and month out for the better part of four years, he entertained at least fifty people a month at his plantation or his quarters in Williamsburg. And from the time of his return in 1720 until the middle of the following year, he still received guests at least every other day and still fed or bedded more than forty men and women a month, although he no longer had his wife's help in the management of the household.[49] People stayed for days and even weeks at a time, and an unremitting parade of people trooped through for shorter periods. Doctors and ministers remained while they tended members of the family who were seriously sick. Women of the neighborhood were put up while they took charge of deliveries and miscarriages. Friends from far away stopped on the way to or from funerals and court days. Fellow church-goers came back from services for dinner. Men with business dealings dropped in. Even the Indians of the area passed through and found food and drink freely given.[50]

In the midst of all this bustling going and coming, Byrd also made time for his own inveterate visiting. From 1709 to 1712 he imposed upon the hospitality of others at least one day of every three, and from 1720 to 1721 he partook of their entertainment almost two days of every three. Since in each period alike he made a couple of stops on each day out, he tarried at about twenty-five homes a month in addition to welcoming a full fifty guests at Westover.[51]

Day after day after day, then, he maintained his hectic social schedule. Week in and week out, unabatingly, for five years, he spent six days of every seven visiting or being visited.[52] Month in and month out, he was away from Westover about one night out of every three, and hardly more when his wife and children were all dead or distant than when his lovely young bride waited for the pleasure of his company in their nuptial bed.[53]

The plain truth was that Byrd put no premium on privacy and displayed no desire for domestic intimacy. Even when he was at home, he immersed himself in the affairs of his wider plantation family rather than retreating into the shelter of his narrower nuclear family. Even amid the multitudes already on his estate, he stood ready to take in more. He took the sons and daughters of his social peers who sought to serve for a while at Westover. He took the relatives of the gentry who had fallen on hard times, such as a sister of Mr. Digges who "had nobody to take care of her." He took his own hapless kin, such as his marginally mad uncle and his orphaned nephews. He took a feckless friend of his wife whose clergy-man husband beat her, "threatened to kill her, and abused her extremely." And he attempted to take total strangers too. He promised "a poor woman" whose name he did not know that he would "endeavor to cure" her daughter, who was "troubled with vapors," if the woman would let the girl "come and stay [at Westover] for two months."[54]

All these extensions of his household into wider reaches of Chesapeake society enabled Byrd to build alliances and deepen associations around him. They enabled a community to augment its access to itself, and they did so by deliberate design, for Byrd had no higher priority than the sustenance of sociability in what he once called that "silent country." His relentless round of visitings and entertainments showed as much, and so, sometimes, did specific events. When he got word one morning that sixty Virginians had been killed by Indians, he did not spring into action. When, a little later in the day, he received orders as military commander of Charles City County to proceed to an immediate rendezvous with the governor, he delayed his departure for a full day. He "could not go till tomorrow because [he] had invited company to dine." Confronted with a choice between responding appropriately to the crisis of the most catastrophic Indian massacre of his generation and serving dinner to a few promising "young men" of the province, Byrd chose to serve his dinner.[55]

***

In such choices, and in his allocation of time and energy more generally, Byrd helped to establish an American style in the New World. Along with his fellow settlers, he promoted a supercharged sociability that alleviated isolation and anxiety on those lonely plantations. In confederation with his neighbors and the other nabobs of Virginia, he fashioned a code of congeniality that allowed men to move in a social world that could be controlled as well as in the natural one that could not.

Indeed, he not only constituted a social milieu but also in a sense reconstituted the natural environment itself. For his canons of casual conviviality actually altered the experience a man might expect in the woods and along the trails. They provided a stranger a fair prospect of passing safely through great swaths of the colony since, as one of Byrd's contemporaries put it, the traveler had "no more to do, but to inquire upon the Road, where any Gentleman or good House-keeper Lives, and there he may depend upon being received with Hospitality." Significantly, such domestication of danger did not obtain in "hardly inhabited" areas where conventions of easy association did not prevail. Another contemporary, voyaging on the Eastern shore of the bay, discovered that there, so far from supporting each other, people "made it their business to rob all passengers."[56]

On both the hospitable mainland and the forbidding peninsula, Virginians lived at a distance from their nominal neighbors on scattered plantations. But they lived very differently despite their similarly sparse settlements, and the difference reflected the extent to which social mobilization on the mainland overset the geographically given pattern of habitation. By their strenuous construction of networks of facile and far-flung friendships, Byrd and his fellow planters of the Piedmont and Tidewater made their light presence on the land humanly heavier. And by their perseverance in keeping up such friendships they made plain that they found the entailed effort refreshing and the achieved end rewarding.

Their casual yet constructed familiarity prefigured the fuller and more formal institutionalization of such networks and nodes in the nineteenth century, when the vast lattice of voluntary associations that still set the style and ambience of American business first took shape. Joint stock companies, corporations, workingmen's unions, trade associations, chambers of commerce, fraternal lodges, private clubs, boarding schools, benefit societies, country clubs, and a proliferous host of other organizations evolved to offset the uncertainties of the marketplace. And they were all predicated upon the same capacity for shallow sociability that Byrd brought into play to relieve his own somewhat different inquietudes.[57]

Amid the alterations of the economic environment that the twentieth century has wrought, there have been still further shifts in the sources of uncertainty in the business arena. But through them all, cultivation of congeniality and sensitivity to the opinions of others have continued steadily at the center of the successive adaptations of American thought and behavior.

They have quite controlled our workaday world. Businessmen and laboring men alike have entered easily and increasingly into the large corporate aggregations in which autonomous and idiosyncratic identities are subordinated for the sake of the security that the collective social context affords.[58]

They have shaped our most celebrated outward expressions of our most compelling ambitions for ourselves. Dale Carnegie has told millions of aspiring Americans how to win friends and influence people. Spock has taught even more how to help their children "belong completely" by living exactly like "the other average children in the neighborhood."[59]

Above all, they have informed our inward sense of propriety and priorities. According to the survey data, Americans already believe what their favored preceptors preach. Asked, for example, to indicate their agreement or disagreement with the proposition that "parents should be guided primarily in what they do by what other parents do in their neighborhood so as to avoid bringing up their child differently," American mothers and fathers agree resoundingly, whereas Austrian and English parents disagree vehemently. Queried on whether "the negative opinion of others often keeps me from seeing a movie or play I had planned to attend" or whether "my political opinion is easily swayed by editorials I read," Americans answer even more affirmatively than Germans.[60]

Such distinctive susceptibility to the opinions and prejudices of others has been essential in countless ways to the conduct of contemporary American business. It has obviously sped the emergence of a national market undisturbed by intense local loyalties. It has manifestly underlaid that market's most remarkable institution, national advertising. It has plainly preconditioned the success of the great corporations in making managers over into organization men. And it has also, more subtly and perhaps more profoundly, affected other attitudes on which institutional behaviors depend.

In one study, for example, American managers disagreed almost to a man— and far more forcefully than managers in any of the other countries sampled— with the statement that "in business you can only really trust friends and relatives." Such impersonal acceptance of strangers has abetted such preeminently American business practices as uniform pricing and such preeminently American business practitioners as the traveling sales representative and the professional consultant. Such tacit trust of unknown others and its attendant assumption of the interchangeability of individuals have sustained our distinctively high degree of mobility of personnel and our innovations in the delegation of managerial responsibility. For in other cultures, as Thomas Cochran has shown so brilliantly in his study of the Puerto Rican businessman, men more insistent on their own unique individuality do not delegate authority at all, lest it limit their own personal control. Men less concerned for the opinions of others do not join clubs where they might mutually promote their business interests or communicate new ideas. Men disinclined to submerge themselves in larger entities for mere material betterment do not merge their own companies into large combines or enter into middle management.[61]

And yet, the ironic outcome of this special American genius for organization may well be the erosion of its psychological substrate. The very success of the great corporations and unions has, as attitudinal surveys show, enabled individuals to come to a conception of their own worth that does not depend on the vagaries of the economy and their own vulnerabilities in it. The emergence of a welfare bureaucracy under corporate auspices has allowed individuals to make choices about the conditions of their lives and livelihood that they were rarely so free to make before.[62]

The consummation of the corporate state has, in effect, altered American modes of meeting uncertainty and offsetting instability by dramatically diminishing uncertainty and instability themselves. And as it has done so, codes and conduct have been palpably changing. Interesting and rewarding work has come to count for more than mere income in people's estimation of a job. Quality of life has become a prime consideration in locational decisions for firms and individuals alike, sometimes in strange fashion. An unemployed accountant spurns a coveted berth on his astrologer's warning that the month is unpropitious. A bank cashier declines a promotion to a branch too far from a McDonald's. An executive turns down a position with a manufacturer who will not pay for his weekly acupuncture appointments. And these excesses simply emphasize the more general transformation they attend. Sober executives of all sorts now refuse relocation in one-third to one-half of all cases, against a rate of refusal of just one in ten a decade ago.[63]

Increasingly, the associational values and behaviors that gave shape to American enterprise at least as long ago as the early eighteenth century—the cultivation of extensive circles of frothy friendships, the relentless socializing with interchangeable others, the obligations to get along by going along—have come to seem a hindrance more than a means to fulfillment. Increasingly, in a society in which such personal fulfillment presents itself as the highest good, submergence in far-flung fellowship has come to seem a constraint more than a comfort.

The attentiveness to others that provided Byrd and his successors something of a solution to their isolation and insecurity has now become a part of the problem, in an inner revolution that has left modern Americans with little else to value than the private pursuit of happiness.[64] When the intricate social round of created communities of busy men comes to seem an interference with that pursuit, it is hard to see how a society built on that intricate round can conserve itself. Broad, shallow sociability has been so long at the core of American character and conduct that to turn away from it is to turn away from much that has been most formatively and distinctively American for three centuries. Indeed, it is to turn away from an entire bourgeois business style.

If the problems posed by such a turning are evident, their solution is not yet in sight. It is permissible to guess, however, that a successful solution will succeed on terms illuminated profoundly by William Byrd. Just as Byrd's solution differed decisively from previous patterns, just as the business civilization he helped initiate was truly a new thing under the sun, so will any culture that emerges out of the new ethos be decisively discontinuous with American civilization as we have known it.

NOTES

1. Louis Wright and Marion Tinling, eds., *The Secret Diary of William Byrd of Westover 1709-1712* (Richmond, Va.: Dietz Press, 1941), June 14, 15, 27, 1709. Hereafter cited as *Diary*.

2. Ibid., June 27, 1709.

3. Ibid., June 15, 16, 17, 1709; July 26, August 27, 31, September 2, 3, 1709; May 30, 6, 1709; July 10, 1709. During those same distressing days, Byrd suffered social and political setbacks that weighed even more heavily on his mind than his economic adversities. A jury of his neighbors awarded him damages of but a shilling in a lawsuit he had pressed for far more, and the county court rebuffed his determined drive to secure a clerkship for a favorite friend (Ibid., June 3, 1709, May 8-June 21, 1709, *passim*).

4. Ibid., February 26, March 4, July 7, 1709; March 21, December 25, 1710; May 24, August 1, 4, 1711; June 10, July 24, 31, 1712. For other damages by fire, falling trees, and the like, see April 24, October 8, 1709; November 29, December 17, 1711; January 5, March 27, September 15, 1712. Byrd's friend and neighbor Benjamin Harrison, owner of a plantation adjacent to Westover and member of the House of Burgesses from 1736 to 1744, was, along with his two youngest daughters, struck dead by lightning on July 12, 1745; see Maude Woodfin, ed., *Another Secret Diary of William Byrd of Westover, 1739-1741, with Letters and Literary Exercises, 1696-1726* (Richmond, Va.: Dietz Press, 1942).

5. *Diary*, July 5, 1710; May 11, September 26, 1712.

6. Ibid., March 26, 1711-August 18, 1712, *passim*. See esp. October 7-21, December 2-19, 1711; April 18-26, 1712.

7. For example, ibid., March 22, 1711; April 22, 1712; William Byrd, *The London Diary (1717-1721) and Other Writings*, ed. Louis Wright and Marion Tinling (New York: Oxford University Press, 1958), April 21, 1718.

8. Richard Grassby, "English Merchant Capitalism in the Late Seventeenth Century: The Composition of Business Fortunes," *Past and Present* 46 (1970): 87.

9. On his return to Virginia in 1705, Byrd inherited 26, 231 acres; see Alden Hatch, *The Byrds of Virginia* (New York: Holt, Rinehart and Winston, 1969), p. 70. In 1718 he had, by his own reckoning, "about" or "above" 43,000 acres; see Marion Tinling, ed., *The Correspondence of the Three William Byrds of Westover, Virginia 1684-1776* (Charlottesville, Va.: University Press of Virginia, 1977), pp. 312, 313. At his death in 1744, he owned not less than 179,440 acres; see Woodfin, *Another Secret Diary*, p. xlii.

10. On conditions at the Chesapeake, see Aubrey Land, "Economic Base and Social Structure: The Northern Chesapeake in the Eighteenth Century," *Journal of Economic History* 25 (1965): 639-54. For evidence of a very few who did, rather late in the eighteenth century, wax wealthy on rents, see Rowland Berthoff and John Murrin, "Feu-

dalism, Communalism, and the Yeoman Freeholder: The American Revolution Considered as a Social Accident," in *Essays on the American Revolution*, ed. Stephen Kurtz and James Hutson (Chapel Hill, N.C.: University of North Carolina Press, 1973), pp. 256-88, though the evidence is embedded in an argument based on a very strange notion of feudalism. For perhaps the best indication of the instability of fortunes in early Virginia, compare the one closest to home: Byrd's own only male heir, William Byrd III, dissipated an inheritance far larger than the one Byrd himself began with, concluded his career of dissolution both broken and broke, and committed suicide.

11. Bernard Bailyn, *The New England Merchants in the Seventeenth Century* (Cambridge, Mass.: Harvard University Press, 1955); Frederick Tolles, *Meeting House and Counting House: The Quaker Merchants of Colonial Philadelphia* (Chapel Hill, N.C.: University of North Carolina Press, 1948); Jacob Marcus, *The Colonial American Jew* (Detroit: Wayne State University Press, 1970), pp. 519-852, quotations at pp. 792: 801-2.

12. For a suggestive study of the fate of far-flung community in one of the earliest of business-oriented American communities, see Stephanie Wolf, *Urban Village: Population, Community, and Family Structure in Germantown, Pennsylvania, 1683-1800* (Princeton: Princeton University Press, 1976), chs. 7, 8. For wider Western developments, compare Philippe Ariès, *Centuries of Childhood: A Social History of Family Life* (New York: Knopf, 1962); Edward Shorter, *The Making of the Modern Family* (New York: Basic Books, 1975); and Lawrence Stone, *The Family, Sex, and Marriage in England, 1500-1800* (New York: Harper & Row, 1977).

13. The transition from sect to church has long been a dominant theme in the sociology of religion. For some of the most effective American applications, see Perry Miller, *The New England Mind: From Colony to Province* (Cambridge, Mass.: Harvard University Press, 1953), on the New England Puritans; Bruce Steiner, "Anglican Officeholding in Pre-Revolutionary Connecticut: Parameters of New England Community," *William and Mary Quarterly* 31 (1974): 369-406, on the New England Anglicans; Deborah Gough, "Pluralism, Politics, and Power Struggles: The Church of England in Colonial Philadelphia, 1695-1789" (Ph.D. diss., University of Pennsylvania, 1978), on Philadelphia Anglicans; Sydney James, *A People Among Peoples: Quaker Benevolence in Eighteenth-Century America* (Cambridge, Mass.: Harvard University Press, 1963), on Philadelphia Quakers; and, in the nineteenth century, Donald Mathews, *Slavery and Methodism: A Chapter in American Morality* (Princeton: Princeton University Press, 1965), on Methodists; and Dickson Bruce, *And They All Sang Hallelujah: Plain-Folk Camp-Meeting Religion, 1800-1845* (Knoxville, Tenn.: University of Tennessee Press, 1974), on Methodists and Baptists.

14. The biographical data in this paragraph and the next are drawn from the diaries and correspondence already cited, especially their introductions, and from Hatch, *The Byrds of Virginia*.

15. The decisive figures in the revisionary appreciation were Carl Bridenbaugh and Louis Wright; see esp. Carl Bridenbaugh, *Myths and Realities: Societies of the Colonial South* (Baton Rouge, La.: Louisiana State University Press, 1952), ch. 1. At least since the publication of Arthur Cole's seminal essay, "The Tempo of Mercantile Life in Colonial America," *Business History Review* 33 (1959): 277-99, it has been clear that an erratic pace of enterprise was neither distinctive to the South nor an effective impediment to commercial practice in the North; but a host of studies following upon E. P. Thompson's decisive article, "Time, Work-Discipline, and Industrial Capitalism," *Past and Present* 38 (1967): 56-97, have made Byrd's departures from a Weberian ideal-typification of the Protestant Ethic even less consequential in and of themselves.

16. All three published portions of the diary have been examined for this study, but only the two earlier ones are here analyzed. By the time of the final fragment, Byrd was a very old man by contemporary Virginia standards and barely three years from his death-bed. His diary displays a much-diminished level of economic activity of all sorts, and even its editor concedes that Byrd's "more strenous years were behind him" by then; see Woodfin, *Another Secret Diary*, p. xli. Apart from these three published fragments of what was apparently a lifelong labor, no other parts of the diary have been unearthed.

17. There were 348 specific commercial references on 286 different days, of which 26 on 23 different days dealt directly with tobacco. That is, 9.1 percent of the daily refer-ences and 7.4 percent of the total references were to tobacco. On another 367 occasions on 292 different days, Byrd spoke of settling his accounts, and on still another 94, on 81 different days, of doing a great deal of business or something of similar import. Taking all of these commercial references together, tobacco accounted for only 3.2 percent. For 1720-21, the Virginia period of *The London Diary*, there was but a single transaction pertaining to tobacco among 28 explicitly commercial operations, or but 3.9 percent. Including another 70 statements of settling accounts and another 4 dealing with the extent of business Byrd did, tobacco accounted for a bit less than 1 percent of all the commercial reckonings of that later period. Hereafter, specific dates cited will refer to Byrd's diary for the relevant years.

18. There were 31 references to tobacco planting operations of all sorts, on 28 different days, from 1709 through 1712, and 5 others in 1720 and 1721. The references to tobacco planting were therefore only 4.2 percent of the references to commerce in daily terms and only 3.8 percent in total terms for the period 1709-12, and 5.4 percent in terms of days and 4.9 percent in terms of total references for 1720-21. Tobacco planting did not even predominate among Byrd's sporadic references to planting in his diary. From 1709 through 1712, other crops—wheat, corn, oats, hay, and fruits—accounted for 47 references on 45 different days, or about half again as many as tobacco did during the same span. There were 59 references to industrial ventures, on 50 different days, in the 1709-12 segment of the diary, and 9, on 8 different days, in the 1720-21 portion.

19. March 27, 1711. See also February 17, August 19, December 23, 1709; October 5, 1711; February 16, May 13, 1712; April 1, 10, 1721.

20. November 29, 1709. See also March 30, 1710.

21. For his betting on horse races, see October 17, 1710; September 8, 9, 1720; May 11, 1721. For his attendance at them, August 19, 1710; August 6, 1720. For adverse comments and cautionary tales, August 27, 1709; September 17, 18, 1711; June 30, 1720. On planter affection for fast horses and absorption in racing meets, see Rhys Isaac, "Evangelical Revolt: The Nature of the Baptists' Challenge to the Traditional Order in Virginia, 1765 to 1775," *William and Mary Quarterly* 31 (1974): 345-68: and T. H. Breen, "Horses and Gentlemen: The Cultural Significance of Gambling Among the Gen-try of Virginia," *William and Mary Quarterly* 34 (1977): 239-57.

22. There were 57 references to such nautical occasions in the period 1709-12, another 11 in 1720-21.

23. See June 14, July 23, 1709; March 12, April 14, August 18, September 20, 1710; February 27, March 12, June 14, 16, 1712; March 9, 21, April 18, 29, May 9, 25, 1720; May 16, 1721.

24. Byrd recorded 231 visits or other encounters with ship captains, on 189 different days, from 1709 to 1712. Fifty-four of these occasions included a sharing of meals, and 13 included overnight stays, some of several days' duration. Byrd gave the captains

presents (September 26, 1710; May 16, July 21, 1711; January 5, 1712), played billiards with them (September 1, October 24, 1710; January 5, 1712), and showed them about his library (June 9, 1711). They gave him presents (March 2, May 2, 1710; June 14, September 13, December 8, 1711) and offered him a variety of favors (April 13, May 26, June 29, 1710; April 14, June 14, July 17, August 31, 1711; May 23, 1712). The reference to the captains as godfathers is on September 27-28, 1709.

25. From 1709 to 1712, there were 44 references to the sloops carrying tobacco and 86 to the transport of other commodities. For 1720-21, there were 3 references to tobaccos on the vessels and 8 to other freight. For the two sequences combined, the entries pertaining to tobacco were precisely one-third of the total of specified shipments. There were also 57 references to unspecified cargoes in the period 1709-12 and 8 such references for 1720-21. Virtually all of these entries referred to the river sloop; the sea sloop accounted for none of the transit of tobacco, 1 shipment of other goods, and 9 of the unspecified passages. On 20 other occasions in the years 1709-12 and 7 more in 1720-21, Byrd noted items that came to Westover from the plantations without specifically saying that they came by sloop. The items were, for the most part, foods—wildfowl, game animals, domestic stock, and fruit—although on June 4, 1710, a coffin came.

26. There were 13 references to news of the price of tobacco, and 149 references on 137 different days to the news more largely, in the 1709-12 section of the diary. There were no references at all to news of tobacco prices, and 20 references to news in general, in the 1720-21 fragment.

27. Byrd referred to his reading in the law 53 times on 40 different days from 1709 to 1712 and on 2 other occasions in 1720. He mentioned his involvement in court proceedings 33 times on 28 different days in the period 1709-12 and 7 times in 1720-21. These figures do not include another 29 instances on 28 different days in the earlier diary and another 4 on 3 different days in the later one when he attended or otherwise alluded to county courts without himself having a case at stake there.

28. Byrd discussed court sessions 116 times on 93 different days from 1709 to 1712 and 40 times on 38 different days in 1720-21, a total of 156 times on 131 different days for the two periods together. These figures do not include 8 other references on 3 other days to his participation in military tribunals.

29. Byrd mentioned his appearances in council 85 times on 81 different days in the years 1709-12 and 40 times on 40 different days in 1720-21. He referred to political machinations and deliberations, primarily pertaining to patronage appointments on everything from governorships for himself to a sinecure as sexton for old Higbee, on 143 occasions on 118 different days for the period 1709-12 and on 84 occasions on 66 different days for 1720-21, a total of 227 references on 184 different days. He discussed his official disbursements and his preparation or settlement of government accounts 65 times on 47 different days in the period 1709-12 and 23 times on 17 different days in 1720-21, his responsibilities in checking the government accounts of others 17 times on 14 different days from 1709 to 1712 and 11 times on 9 different days in 1720-21, and his salary 7 times for the years 1709-12 and 4 times for 1720-21; all told, he adverted to such matters 127 times on 98 different days. And he referred to governmental and quasi-governmental agencies and affairs of direct business import 50 times on 39 different days in the years 1709-12 and 33 times on 29 different days in 1720-21, a total of 83 times on 68 different days. Taking all his political engagements together—the court, the council, the patronage chasing and policy making, the accounting and executive attending—he recorded 736 references on 615 different days, or well over two references for every five days of the diary.

30. Byrd literally declined to come back to Virginia in the midst of one dispute with Governor Spotswood. "I shall hardly perswade myself to return," he wrote to his brother-in-law in 1717, "til I can get it determind whether a governor may hang any man he takes to be his adversary or not. For if it be in his power to appoint me my judges I am sure I won't come within his reach." Byrd to John Custis, October 4, 1717, in Tinling, *Correspondence* pp. 305-6. See also Byrd to Philip Ludwell, October 28, 1717, in ibid., pp. 308-9; Byrd to Philip Ludwell, January 31, 1718, in ibid., pp. 309-11; Byrd to Commissioners of Trade and Plantations, February 24, 1718, in ibid., pp. 314-15; and, for the resolution of the dispute, Byrd to Commissioners of Trade and Plantations, March 24, 1719, in ibid., pp. 320-22.

31. For Byrd's close attention to the attitude of the governor, almost any month affords illustrations. For his still stronger solicitude for the favor of the governor's lady, and his unease when he did not have it, see July 18, August 11, October 21, 28, November 8, 30, December 9, 1710; March 30, April 1, 2, 3, 5, 8, 16, November 2, December 9, 1711; January 25, April 1, July 20, August 18, September 21, 23, 1712. For his fury at his inability to deliver a position he had promised a friend, see esp. February 9, 11, 27, March 1, 4, April 13, May 8, 11, 17, 18, 19, 24; June 1, 6, 8, 19, 21, 1709. For his failure to gain the executive chair in each of the Chesapeake colonies, see September 16, 19, 1709; March 31, April 17, 1710; February 8, April 14, June 13, December 23, 1718; February 26, April 20, 1719.

32. See the biographical introductions to the diaries and correspondence, and see Hatch, *The Byrds of Virginia*.

33. March 21, 1710. July 5, 1710. December 29, 1710. July 6, 7, 10, August 5, 1711; June 4, 1712. April 19, 1709; January 3, 14, February 3, 15, 17, March 4, 17, May 28, 1711. April 10, 1710. June 3, 1710. See also May 6, July 10, October 8, 1709; March 31, June 24, July 31, 1710; January 1, 2, April 21, July 5, August 7, December 3, 1711. Byrd's resignation to God's will was so strong that he rarely even prayed for the outcome he preferred. For the few instances of appeals as innocuous as "L-s-n was very ill, God preserve him," see December 2, 3, 1711; February 19, July 23, 1712.

34. Kenneth Lynn, *Mark Twain and Southwestern Humor* (Boston: Little, Brown, 1960), ch. 1; the quotation is on p. 12.

35. David Bertelson, *The Lazy South* (New York: Oxford University Press, 1967), ch. 4; the quotation is on p. 82.

36. For more genuine alienation, from self and society alike, a generation later, see Jack Green, ed., *The Diary of Colonel Landon Carter of Sabine Hall, 1752-1778* (Charlottesville, Va.: University Press of Virginia, 1965).

37. From 1709 to 1712, Byrd made 1909 references to infirmity and fatality on 833 different days. Over the same span he made 158 references to his children on 107 different days, or only 8.3 percent as many references on only 12.8 percent as many days. At that, 135, or 85.4 percent, of the references to his children were to their sicknesses and, in the boy's case, their death. Over those years, too, he made 850 mentions of his wife on 562 different days, or 44.5 percent as many references on 67.5 percent as many days; 336, or 39.5 percent of those were similarly to his wife's medical troubles and treatments. From 1720 to 1721, Byrd made 207 medical references on 139 different days. Over that stretch he made but a single reference to his daughters, whom he did not even have at home with him, having left them in England when he returned to Westover. His wife was, by then, several years deceased.

38. From 1709 to 1712, Byrd made 736 references to politics and 1,009 to commerce,

or 38.6 percent and 52.9 percent, respectively, as many references as he made to disease and death, For the year 1720-21, he made 180 references to politics and 149 to business, or 87 percent and 72 percent, respectively, of his rate of reference to perils of poor health.

39. From December 1717 to December 1719, Byrd made 214 medical references on 166 different days, or 8.9 such references a month on 6.9 different days a month. By way of contrast, he made 44.9 medical references a month—almost exactly five times as many—on 19.4 different days a month—a bit less than three times as many from 1709 to 1712, and 14.8 references a month on 9.9 different days a month—about half again as many—from February 1720 to May 1721. Combining the Virginia portions of the two segments of the diary, he made 37.2 medical references a month—more than four times as many as he did in London—on 17.1 different days a month—two and a half times as many.

40. Byrd discussed death 356 times in the earlier Virginia segment of the diary, an average of 8.3 times a month and 18.6 percent of all his indications of physical ills. He discussed it 30 times, or slightly more than twice a month, in 1720-21, but even that reduced reference still acounted for 14.5 percent of all his medical allusions. Taking the two Virginia fragments together, he made some notation of mortality 6.8 times a month, and those notations added up to 18.2 percent of all allusions to mortality and morbidity combined. By way of contrast, he mentioned death only 5 times in the two years of the London fragment of the diary, or less than once every four months. Such reference amounted to barely 2.4 percent of the relatively meager attention he paid to all manner of ailments. It might be added that Byrd was haunted literally as well as figuratively by the specter of death in Virginia; 58.3 percent of the 20 dreams he described in the Virginia logs pertained to death and other ill-defined calamities. Women and sex figured in 16.1 percent, business in 11.9 percent, politics in 10.1 percent, and a neighbor in 3.6 percent. The relative place of death and sex was almost exactly reversed in the 13 dreams he recounted in the London entries. There 53.8 percent revolved around women and concupiscence whereas only 23.1 percent involved death and danger; another 23.1 percent were vaguely specified "bad dreams."

41. For "indisposition," see, for example, April 22, June 10, July 9, 1718; January 23, June 30, September 27, October 15, December 10, 1719. For sickness upsetting his social schedule, see May 12, September 5, 1718; January 23, 1719; the quotation is from September 5, 1718. For venereal disease, see March 11, June 13, 19, 20, 21, 25, 30, July 25, 26, 27, 28, 29, 31, November 3, 4, 20, 21, 1713; June 1, December 12, 1719. For his persistence with women despite his sometimes "violent" running, see, for example, July 31, August 1, 1718.

42. December 10, 1718, January 3, 1719; June 17, June 24, 1718; May 12, 1718. Byrd's disregard of his daughter appeared again and again. When he learned that she had the measles, he did not come to look after her, or even to comfort her, for three days, and then for fully a week again after that. August 1, 4, 11, 1718. And when, some months later, she showed signs of smallpox once more, he did visit her briefly but then resumed his regular rounds that afternoon and evening at the coffeehouse, the theater, the places of prostitutes, and the alehouse. January 8, 1719.

43. For Byrd's efforts in pharmacology, see his recurrent ad hoc appropriations of local herbal lore and especially his expenditure of almost two months after buying the books and medical cabinet of a deceased doctor in ordering and mastering the man's "closet." February 8-March 25, 1710, and sporadically thereafter. For his own stock of medications and his dispensation of it, see, for example, March 1, 15, May 18, 19, June

14, August 20, September 2, 7, 8, 26, November 6, 1710; February 18, April 10, June 7, July 29, August 14, September 28, October 22, 1711; March 8, August 5, 12, 31, September 1, 2, 7, 9, 20, 25, 1712. For his death watch over Harrison, see March 22-April 10, 1710. For his ministrations to L-s-n, see December 1-4, 1711. For his sustained attention to others of all statuses, see (to take only those of a single year) March 1-6, May 21-31, September 12-16, September 24-October 1, November 26-December 2, December 19-22, 1720.

44. During the days of the London diary, 136 of his 214 medical references—63.6 percent—were to his own infirmities. During the days after his return to Westover, only 48 of 207 such references—23.9 percent—were similarly self-centered. And earlier, from 1709 to 1712, only 358 of 1909—18.8 percent—articulated his own ailments. Taking the earlier and later Virginia segments together, 19.2 percent of all his medical references were self-referring, 80.8 percent were attentive to others.

45. For Byrd's divertissements while paying court to the widow Pierson, see March 3-July 7, 1719, *passim*. For his persistence with mistresses and maids even in the midst of his proclaimed passion for Mary Smith, see December 22, 1717-June 7, 1718, *passim*. (For his goings to them on the very days in which he carried on his campaign, see December 22, 1717; February 7, 20, 22, March 25, 29, 30, April 17, 18, 26, May 1, 8, 9, 10, June 7, 1718.) For allusions to his having "polluted" himself or otherwise "committed uncleanness" with these women and others encountered even more casually, see February 7, 21, 24, April 17, 26, May 1, 8, 1718. It should be added that Byrd's blithe infidelity was reciprocated. Women with whom he made assignations failed to keep them—for example, May 13, 17, 26, 1718—and his own mistress "had commerce with another man"—June 14, 1718, for which he forsook her for having "played the whore" (June 16, 1718).

46. January 15, December 16, 1718. See also, for example, January 16, 17, 21, March 20, April 14, May 25, 28, 1718; January 12, 27, February 27, March 16, April 1, 22, October 17, 20, 1719. A suggestive measure of Byrd's disconnection from any circle of authentic intimacy and assured acceptance was the frequency with which, when he paid his visits, he found people "from home." There were days when he had to resume his forlorn rounds four, five, once even nine times before discovering anyone at home to admit him. All told, he failed to find his intended company on 356 of his 1,497 visits, or fully 23.1 percent of them.

47. February 4-13, 1720.

48. April 12, 1712. I have written much more elaborately about the limited significance of the immediate nuclear family for Byrd in "William Byrd's Family," *Perspectives in American History* 12 (1979): 253-311.

49. From 1709 to 1712, Byrd received 49.7 visitors on 19.9 days a month. From 1720 to 1721, he had 40.9 visits on 16.1 days a month. For the two periods together he entertained 47.5 visitors on 19.0 days a month. And these figures do not include Byrd's own overseers, servants, and slaves when they came in from the outlying plantations, or his friends and the children of his friends whom he installed in long-term residence, or artisans attached to his operations. They do count artisans on specific short-term employment on the days they are explicitly cited in the diary; but even such a procedure understates the extent of their visitation, since such artisans stayed until their task was complete, often a month or more, but were commonly recorded only on their arrival and/or departure. The figures do not, indeed, count anyone except on days he or she was specifically mentioned, although on literally dozens of days people were demonstrably at Westover

even if they were not actually named. (To take but the most egregious example, of the 84 units that should be attributed to the Cock-Catesby party that arrived May 24, 1712, and departed June 17, only 25 were in fact credited since only those were explicitly declared in the diary.) The figures also discount many groups of visitors referred to in the diary merely as "many" or "abundance" or the like; all such indeterminable references were tallied as 3 visitor units, even when such locutions clearly pointed to far larger numbers. In other words, these figures underrepresent in half a dozen different ways the actual extent of entertaining that Byrd undertook.

50. For entertainments of Indians, see, for example, August 13, 1709; March 11, 1712; March 23, 24, 1721. The others recurred too often to cite specifically.

51. From 1709 to 1712, Byrd made 20.5 visits on 11.3 days a month. Through 1720-21 he made 37.1 visits on 18.6 different days a month. Over the entire time he averaged 24.2 visits on 13.1 different days each month.

52. From 1709 to 1712, Byrd averaged 4.6 days a month neither visiting nor visited; from 1720 to 1721, 3.7. For the two stretches together, he averaged 4.4 days per month, or almost exactly one day a week, without his customary company.

53. Nights away from Westover were not necessarily nights counted as visiting, since such nights included those spent in sporadic military expeditions, occasional stays on his outlying plantations, and frequent and often extended excursions to Williamsburg, where he rented his own lodging. From 1709 to 1712, he spent 28.8 percent of his nights away from home; from 1720 to 1721, 38.7 percent; and for the two segments of the diary combined, 31.2 percent.

54. April 11, June 7, 1709; January 4, 15, 31, February 10, 11, March 7, 10, 1710; February 24, April 11, August 14, 1711. March 10, 1711. February 10, 11, June 28, 1710. March 31, 1711. June 14, 1710. See also April 12, 1710; August 14, 1711.

55. October 7, 1711.

56. Robert Beverley, *The History and Present State of Virginia*, ed. Louis Wright (Chapel Hill, N.C.: University of North Carolina Press, 1947), pp. 312-13; Edward Alexander, ed., *The Journal of John Fontaine: An Irish Huguenot Son in Spain and Virginia, 1710-1719* (Williamsburg, Va.: University Press of Virginia, 1972). p. 120.

57. The literature on voluntary association in a "nation of joiners" is virtually inexhaustible. The classic source is, of course, Alexis de Tocqueville, *Democracy in America*; interesting empirical investigations particularly pertinent to the conceptualization advanced here are E. Digby Baltzell, *Philadelphia Gentlemen: The Making of a National Upper Class* (Glencoe, Ill.: Free Press, 1958) and Robert Wiebe, *The Search for Order 1877-1920* (New York: Hill and Wang, 1967).

58. See, among many, Thomas Cochran, *The American Business System: A Historical Perspective, 1900-1955* (Cambridge: Harvard University Press, 1960); Daniel Miller and Guy Swanson, *The Changing American Parent: A Study in the Detroit Area* (New York: Wiley, 1958); David Riesman, with Nathan Glazer and Reuel Denney, *The Lonely Crowd: A Study of the Changing American Character* (New Haven: Yale University Press, 1950); and William Whyte, *The Organization Man* (New York: Simon and Schuster, 1956).

59. Benjamin Spock, *Baby and Child Care*, 3rd ed. (New York: Meredith Press, 1968), pp. 392, 589; for an extended interpretation of Spock's child-rearing advice in this vein, see Michael Zuckerman, "Doctor Spock: The Confidence Man," in *The Family in History*, ed. Charles Rosenberg (Philadelphia: University of Pennsylvania Press, 1975), pp. 179-207.

60. David McClelland, *The Achieving Society* (Princeton: Van Nostrand, 1961), pp. 197, 203. For further discussion of the centrality of peer orientation and the need for affiliation among Americans, who "are certainly among the most other-directed people in the world" (p. 197) see ch. 5.

61. McClelland, *Achieving Society*, p. 291; Thomas Cochran, *The Puerto Rican Businessman: A Study in Cultural Change* (Philadelphia: University of Pennsylvania Press, 1959), esp. chs. 4, 6, 8. For other instances of cultures in which an intense familistic individualism precludes or impairs impersonal trust and busines consolidation, see David Landes, "French Business and the Businessman: A Social and Cultural Analysis," in *Modern France*, ed. Edward Earle (Princeton: Princeton University Press, 1951), pp. 334-53; John Sawyer, "The Entrepreneur and the Social Order: France and the United States," in *Men in Business: Essays on the Historical Role of the Entrepreneur*, ed. William Miller (New York: Harper & Row, 1962), pp. 7-22.

62. Louis Banks, "Here Come the Individualists," *Harvard Magazine* 80 (September-October 1977): 24-29, esp. p. 27; Miller and Swanson, *Changing American Parent*, esp. pp. 42-60; Larry Hirschhorn, "Post-Industrial Life: A U.S. Perspective," *Futures* 11 (1979): 287-98.

63. *International Herald Tribune*, June 1; *Time* 111 (June 12, 1978): 73-74. Although they have accelerated sharply in the past five or ten years, these trends have been noted at least since the 1950s. See, for example, Daniel Bell, "American as a Mass Society: A Critique," in *The End of Ideology: On the Exhaustion of Political Ideas in the Fifties*, rev. ed. (New York: Harper & Row, 1961), pp. 21-38; Clyde Kluckhohn, "Have There Been Discernible Shifts in American Values During the Past Generation," in *The American Style: Essays in Value and Performance*, ed. Elting Morison (New York: Basic Books, 1958) pp. 145-217; Seymour Lipset, *The First New Nation: The United States in Historical and Comparative Perspective* (New York: Basic Books, 1963), ch. 3, esp. pp. 137-39; David Riesman, "The Found Generation," *American Scholar* 25 (1956): 421-36.

64. The term *inner revolution* derives, of course from the title essay of Thomas Cochran's *The Inner Revolution: Essays on the Social Sciences and History* (New York: Harper & Row, 1964). Cochran is one of a remarkably small band of historians who have wrestled earnestly with the problem and its implications, but the problem itself has been implicit in Western culture for at least the last two centuries. It has had a host of acute analysts, from the day of de Sade and Blake down to the present.

The Anatomy of American Reform

ROBERT H. WALKER

One way of viewing American history is as the consequence of two conflicting "permanent" revolutions. One has been created by the inventors and entrepreneurs who transformed the United States from its primarily bucolic character to its present shape as an urban nation dominated by large-scale entities: "governments" of corporations and states. The other permanent revolution has resulted from the fear that the concentration of wealth and power would lead the innocent new nation straight into a hell that closely resembled worldly, hierarchical Europe. Thomas C. Cochran is well recognized for improving perceptions of the first of these revolutions; he has also told us more about the other revolution than is commonly known. The point of this essay is to approach the study of the second revolution in a way that has less to do with the moral imperatives of a Cotton Mather and much to do with Cochran's familiar frontier between history and social science.

In calling attention to the antebellum force of industrial growth, Professor Cochran has implicitly added meaning to the antimaterialism of reformers like Henry David Thoreau and explained the instant elevation of economic issues (land, money) to primacy on the reform agenda.[1] At the other end of the chronological spectrum, Cochran provides a singular intellectual history of twentieth-century America drawn against the shifting role of the individual and making possible a more precise evaluation of all varieties of social change.[2]

One reason for studying the second revolution is to learn the difference between self-interest and public interest. This question has engaged Thomas Cochran from early in his career. He showed that business leaders were quick to expand the definition of corporate self-interest as they discovered the extent to which their enterprise was linked to the health of the community in which it operated.[3] As this community grew from local to regional to national, the definition of self-interest on the entrepreneurial side approached the functional altruism of the more astute reform leaders.

The ultimate purpose for studying any broad aspect of history is to come to grips with the fundamental patterns and values that define the nation. Cochran has constructed a number of useful models for this kind of enterprise, none more concise and useful than a seven-point list delivered only in lecture form.[4] There is little in the study of American society that is outside the scope of Professor Cochran's work; an effort to provide a structure for a historical approach to social change seems particularly to reflect the spirit of his teaching and scholarship.

***

This essay is part of a longstanding effort to discover usable patterns in the history of American reform. As an "anatomy" it is of course useless without a body to test its accuracy. This function may be largely served by a document collection, already published, that was compiled with most of the categories described in this essay in mind.[5]

For all its prominence, reform has been underused as a general source for understanding American society. There are many excellent studies of specific topics, leaders, and epochs; but there are no accepted terms or categories that allow for their effective accumulation and synthesis.[6] Variables have been dramatized; continuities, overlooked. Little wonder the search for national character turned to social psychology or popular culture, or the frontiers of technology, wilderness, and abundance. Its pervasiveness, coupled with its relative neglect, make reform the truly neglected American frontier.

A major step toward overcoming this neglect would be the development of a set of terms useful in transforming particular knowledge into general wisdom. The terms must grow out of the way reform really works. They must allow for the true taxonomic function: the collection of similarities and differences. They must point toward distinguishing constant from variable traits. They should be as clear and simple as possible. This proposal attempts to meet these criteria by offering an outline of five major headings.

Modes are the large categories of reform defined mainly by their objectives. These categories improve on the customary division of reform into "social," "humanitarian," "political," "economic," and so forth: descriptors that have never been used precisely, consistently, or with mutual exclusivity. Each mode has its distinctive *actors*, *forms*, and *dynamics*. Major differences in reform activity occur across modal lines.

Social *actors* designate the agents—individuals and groups—responsible for initiating and perpetuating the momentum for change. Their proportions and alignments vary with time and topic.

Potentially, every *form* of social expression has been utilized in the reform process. This category allows for the discussion of changes in the prominence and effectiveness of various expressions as well as the affinity of certain forms for certain movements and eras. The progress of a particular movement often has much to do with the forms available to it as well as with the competence developed within a particular form.

Dynamics call attention to the fact that reform moves through important, recognizable stages. In identifying reform only in its more mature stages, historians have often overlooked the importance of crucial, early activity. The terms under this heading not only describe how social movements evolve but also identify patterns that constitute crucial differences among the three main modes.

Arguments used to persuade the reformer's constituency are remarkably constant, even though the assumptions that underly them vary drastically. This category allows for the accumulation and consideration of that aspect of reform that is most consistent and most directly indicative of cultural values.

Taken together, these terms indicate how reform works as well as how it can be studied. Under each *mode* the identification of the *actors* indicates "who," the *forms* "what," the *dynamics* "when," and the *arguments* "why."

MODES

The improvement of politicoeconomic democracy.

The improved treatment of specific individuals and groups.

The alteration of society by reference to a substantially different model.

To bring even a modest logic to a subject as sweeping as social change requires at least one great leap toward control. This insight, for me, came with the crucial realization that all important reform activity fell into one of three very broad yet clearly recognizable modes. This discovery, along with the realization that reform arguments had a certain predictable character, became the backbone for the hopeful assumption that American reform could be treated as a single subject.

The term *mode* indicates that this largest of reform categories can be defined not by substance, method, or philosophy alone but by a combination of several traits. Modes represent generalized goals. Within each is a distinctive combination of actors, forms, and assumptions. Each mode follows a notably different dynamic pattern.

One of these modes has been designated the "mainstream" because it has involved the greatest number of actors, the largest of groups and institutions, and the most inescapable of all issues. Here are the most fundamental political and economic questions: who can vote, and for whom; who can work and for how much; and where the public interest lies in the struggle between the great politicoeconomic entities. The theme that unites this mode is the belief that the purification of the political process will at least remove the extremes of economic want and privilege and may even bring a measure of economic democracy. Actors in this mode often express radical discontent, yet they generally assume that the system can be successfully revised through modification, refinement, and extension—as opposed to revolution.

Large as this mode is, it cannot be narrowed without losing its essential attributes. It is impossible, functionally, to separate the political thrust from the concern for economic consequences. In some areas of investigation, it may be necessary as well as proper to separate political from economic considerations. When scholars have attempted to deal separately with political reform as distinct from economic (often called "social") reform, however, they have failed to make connections essential to the understanding of social action. Movements can be understood distinctively in terms of place or time or philosophy or personnel; but the mainstream movement cannot be appreciated with any completeness unless the political means have been connected with the economic ends. These linkages are not accidental; they are *vital*.

The national history of this mode opens with that famous Revolutionary battlecry, "Taxation without representation is tyranny!"—an ideal paradigm for this topic. It does not claim that lack of representation is tyrannical or that taxation is wrong. It connects the two. It demands that a political means—in this case an extension of representative democracy—be used to correct an economic injustice (inequitable taxation). This is the message of mainstream reform in a ringing five-word summation.

A second mode of reform activity is more limited and more complex. It contains those movements on behalf of special groups within the population that have been denied, for one reason or another, full participation in the politicoeconomic mainstream. Under this heading are movements that both question and extend the assumptions of the first mode. If the mainstream could be seen as flowing smoothly along, broadening inevitably to include all citizens, then there would be no need for the second mode. To launch a special crusade on behalf of native Americans or residents of Appalachia is to admit that the mainstream has swirled around some prominent islands without bringing them the nourishment of its waters. On the other hand, most of these movements share assumptions and methods with the mainstream: that is, they seek to insert the group into full political participation, assuming that representation will produce economic equity and that social benefits will follow. If the propertyless were given the vote, they would then have the political power to assure their economic place in society. Social equality would ensue. Seen in this way, the second mode is not so much an attack on the first mode as an extension of it.

This question is complicated by the fact that some of the special groups have opposed the direction of the mainstream altogether: for example, some of the Afro-American and native American voices. It is not that these citizens reject their fair share of the nation's wealth and productivity; it is just that they are reluctant to accept the dominant values and mores as a price for sharing the product. For better or worse, however, most groups have eventually found their remedy in working for full politicoeconomic rights while maintaining aspects of cultural or subcultural distinctiveness.

In this category comes the protection of individuals who may be only temporarily outside the mainstream, for example, professed communists during a period of anticommunist hysteria. Some are placed outside the mainstream by an act of choice or will: pacifists or atheists, for instance. Even though such individuals have not accepted all the mores of the mainstream, they have sometimes generated social action to protect their rights. Also a part of this mode are movements on behalf of some very large groups that, up to this point in American history, have elicited the continuing attention of reformers. Women, Afro-Americans, native Americans, and other racial, religious, and national groups have all been the subject of longstanding movements. So have the physically and mentally handicapped. Still other groups have been singled out on the basis of occupation (coal miners, for example) or place of residence (slumdwellers).

Between this category and the first mode there are differences beyond ambivalence toward the mainstream. If all the efforts on behalf of special groups were considered as a single social crusade, then this activity would appear to be almost as large, as widespread, and as continuous as the mainstream of politicoeconomic reform itself. But these movements are in no functional sense united. Many are isolated in time or in place. The treatment of the Chinese in the 1880s was largely a local matter, although the nation's attention was often attracted. The defense of civil liberties has occurred during postwar periods when other crusades have languished. Activity may depend on the work of a peculiarly gifted leader, as in the case of Dorothea Dix's efforts on behalf of the handicapped before the Civil War. A few advances may be achieved and then, with the passing of the leader, a whole movement may slip into inactivity. Or, as in the case of the women's rights movement before 1920, there may be constant activity that is periodically overshadowed by more dramatic issues, thus giving the illusion of sporadic action.

Viewed as a mode composed of many varied issues and movements, some on behalf of individuals although most on behalf of large groups, this aspect of social change is reflective of the nation's limited attention span. Sympathy for any one viewpoint seems intermittent or cyclical when compared with the steady preoccupation with politicoeconomic issues. Because of this very quality, these movements are ideal for illustrating those aspects of reform which are importantly constant. For, if similar approaches dependably recur over a span of time that has seen the extremes of neglect and concern, then these methods will at least have proven their durability.

The first two modes share a further assumption: that the process of social change is basically remedial. A problem is discovered, discussed, and dramatized. Eventually a solution may be identified, proposed, and adopted or defeated. The third mode of social change rejects the idea that the basic process of change is corrective. Nor does this mode assume that the progress of mainstream reform will eventually respond to all reasonable social demands. Instead, the action begins with the vision of a new order dramatically different from the existing one. Were there not dissatisfaction with the status quo on the part of the originators of these ideas, of course, there would be no alternative proposal. Instead of first exposing the problems, however, the response takes the form of a new social design.

The history of this mode begins immediately after the Treaty of Paris with the hope that the new nation could be constructed to ideal specifications.[7] When the more sweeping of these proposals were not accepted, the focus shifted to a number of communitarian experiments in the wilderness, which cropped up in great numbers between 1820 and 1850, offering both secular and religious examples of alternative political and social systems. For interesting if predictable reasons, most of them were gone by the Civil War. In their stead, almost three decades later, came the utopian romances, pouring forth in a veritable deluge following the success of Edward Bellamy's *Looking Backward*. Roughly speaking, these utopias were a kind of urban, high-technology equivalent for the more rustic antebellum experimental communities.

With the twentieth century, this mode lost its evolutionary unity and split into three segments. Authors of what came to be called "social science fiction" produced works of the imagination that had much in common with the tradition of the utopian novel. A second, more limited and pragmatic version was the expanding science of urban and regional planning, which put into attainable dimensions some of the ideas of the communitarians and utopianists. A third group extended the concept of the model community to a global dimension, working toward a mechanism for peaceful world government in a spirit recognizably akin to those planners of smaller communities.

It is this third mode that is drastically set apart from the other two. By comparison, the reformers in the earlier categories are mere tinkerers blinded by a narrow problem and limited to a small quiver of programmatic arrows. Most of the planners and dreamers who make up this third mode have nothing less than a complete new social order as their agenda. Sometimes they invent new social philosophies; more often they abstract from experience. Edward Bellamy made a utopia from an inventive form of socialism. Bradford Peck made his by extending his experience as a department store entrepreneur to organizing the entire world. The International Workers of the World, although they often acted like labor agitators in a physical struggle for power, were also dreamers of their own utopia where all of civilization would be organized as One Big Union. These widely divergent presentations of alternative societies comprise mode III.

The separate consideration of these three modes of social activity is central and fundamental:

What is the important meaning of American reform? Most concisely and directly...it is the pursuit of economic equity through the extension of political democracy; the quest for full citizenship for all groups outside the dominant culture; and the conceptualization of models for a better society—*in that order*. Other reform activities exist; but, if they are not describable in the above terms, they are not of the first magnitude.[8]

ACTORS

Independent individuals.

Unorganized groups.

Voluntary associations.

Institutions, including all levels and branches of government.

Social change occurs for many reasons. Sometimes it seems an almost automatic response to events that happen outside social controls: inventions or shifts in the size and character of populations. Whatever the impetus, however, social change is usually directed. Reluctant institutions need prodding; alternative methods of change need debate; institutionalized changes need interpretation and enforcement. All such processes demand leadership. The agents that provide this leadership are often called social actors, in the sense that they seek to act upon society in order to change it. These actors come in only two large categories, individuals and groups, but there are a few important differences between and among these types of actors that are worth pursuing.

The most unusual and in some ways the most interesting social actors are the isolated individuals who work independently, without the aid of colleagues or a permanent organization, to protest a perceived social evil or to dramatize its solution. To work alone would seem to require some spectacular means for calling attention to a cause. One thinks immediately of John Brown's raid on Harper's Ferry or Henry David Thoreau's night in jail. Yet even Brown had his small band of raiders, and Thoreau's act might not have been memorable without the remarkable essay that followed it. There were a few lonely and desperate people who, during the latter days of the war in Vietnam, sat on a low concrete wall outside the Pentagon and protested the war by self-immolation. The impact of these actions—singly and cumulatively—is hard to judge. The perpetrators remain anonymous. Martin Luther King, Jr., spent some time in jail in a way that was deliberately reminiscent of Mahatma Ghandi and Thoreau, but he was wise enough not to let the act speak for itself. He made it immortal by writing a letter to eight of his fellow clergymen. On the other hand, the very act of publication sometimes constitutes a solitary gesture aimed at arousing society. David Walker's *Appeal* is one such isolated action, jarringly out of tune with the nonviolent measures advocated by the colonization and antislavery societies with which he shared the Boston reform stage. Aside from a few rare examples, some involving violence and martyrdom, it is difficult to find individuals who, unaided, successfully precipitated social action.[9]

What we know about social actors as a category of individuals is remarkably little, and we probably know even less than we think. The closest thing to a comprehensive treatment is Henry J. Silverman's analysis of the individuals listed in William D. P. Bliss's *Encyclopedia of Social Reform*, whose subtitle promised coverage of "political economy, political science, sociology, and statistics, covering anarchism, charities, civil service, currency, land and legislation reform, penology, socialism, social purity, trades unions, woman suffrage, etc." Silverman used the 1908 edition and based his generalizations mainly on the 166 individuals who had left substantial biographical records.[10]

In spite of its limitations, Silverman's analysis offers a useful picture of the reformer, a picture that diverges at many points from the stereotype. In 1908, these social actors were, on the average, but fifty-four years old. Silverman deduces that they began their activities rather early in life and achieved recognition while still in their middle years. Most of this group were from the Northeastern United States both by birth and by residence. They were born of middle-class parents, as far as is known, and, although they received better than average educations, they tended to remain middle-class themselves. Very few were wealthy. Their professions involved them heavily in writing and editing, teaching and lecturing, organizing, and government work. Clergymen stood in a median position and showed an interest in a wide range of activity, from Christian socialism to temperance; educators tended to express themselves through economic issues; businessmen worked unsurprisingly on economic causes but also for temperance and socialism; politicians, a fairly large group, showed the narrowest range of interests, centering on labor, populism, and temperance. The careers of these actors show clearly that the economic issues were by far the most prominent.

Perhaps the most important lesson to be learned from Bliss's compendium is that the reformer is virtually defined by the groups with which he works. Bliss did not concern himself with the John Browns and the David Walkers, if there were any. His reformers identified themselves with specific causes and organizations for substantial time periods. On the other hand, they were by no means limited to a single social issue; more than 60 percent of this group is readily identifiable with more than one issue. Moreover, there seemed to be some natural affinities among reform causes. If one began as an abolitionist, for example, he was most likely to go on into woman's rights and temperance. Other connections were: temperance with Christian socialism or with labor reform; socialism with labor reform or the single tax; and child welfare with philanthropy.

The overlapping interests connect with a motivation that Silverman finds similar in most of his subjects. Reformers are unusually drawn to both science and religion, which makes them argue simultaneously from moral, rational, and practical viewpoints. He suggests, although he never says as much, that even 166 disparate individuals make up something that can be described as a collective and surprisingly uniform temper. In addition to the affinities in substance and persuasion, there is geographic concentration, uniformity of class, and shared assumptions and goals. One might be tempted to go on from where Silverman leaves off to construct a composite picture of the era's prototypical social actor.

On the other hand, to read Silverman's conclusions along with other reform studies is to inveigh extreme caution. Chroniclers of reform, including this one, would be taken aback to note that but 11.7 percent of Bliss's entries are female. To the common stereotype of the reformer as a well-to-do patrician, Silverman offers a flat "no." There had been a widespread tendency to equate social agitation with immigrants, and it is true that many of the antebellum friends of the workingman were born outside the United States. But, by the Bliss generation, the immigrant had become but a negligible minority among the social actors, even if one looks at the socialistic reformers. Bliss may not be representative and Silverman may not be infallible, but there is enough debunking of former stereotypes to impede any rash generalizations about the American reformer. Thanks to Bliss's encyclopedic approach and Silverman's biographical analysis, however, one has the opportunity to view the social actor as an individual instead of an anonymous part of a group.

Like all serious studies of social change, Silverman's composite portrait shows genuinely disinterested individuals working, sometimes against their own economic self-interest, or the improvement of general conditions. History has many examples of opportunists who have used the watchword of reform in order to achieve selfish ends. There is also a gray area, including politicians and labor leaders, where it is sometimes impossible to separate social altruism from professional responsibility. But the admittedly little we know about social actors does strongly indicate that the effective majority has not engaged in reform for profit or power. The great army of antislavery crusaders stood to profit in no way from abolition; for some the contrary was true. Temperance advocates did not own sarsaparilla bottling plants. Horace Mann did not sell textbooks. Most reformers are volunteers; those who earn a livelihood from their social actions could, it would appear, have done better materially in other pursuits. Reformers may be misguided, and often are; it is hard to question their altruism.

Silverman's analysis is valuable because he attempted responsibly to answer all the obvious questions. Although Bliss's broad scope operates in Silverman's favor, the sample is really very small indeed. Lisle A. Rose, who spent much of his life collecting information about literature and reform between 1865 and 1915, compiled a manuscript biographical directory of American reformers in the period that contains well over 20,000 names.[11] The relatively small number of entries in Bliss's work indicates a sample more illustrative than representative.

The most important implication of Silverman's study is that the individual social actor is nothing compared to the association. The reasons for this are obvious. Social change is usually slow; therefore issues tend to outlast the effective career of an individual. Most social change involves large populations even when confined to the state or local level. To persuade a sizable group takes sizable resources, resources typically beyond the means of a single person. In causes that involve the whole nation, it is often necessary for the social actor to be present in several places at the same time. Finally, a democracy consistently applies the test of numbers. If the idea is worthy, it will attract many adherents, the nation assumes. Therefore the size of an organization becomes a kind of test of the merit of its program, and the existence of a large association becomes a testimonial to its efficacy.

There is not, in either historical or sociological literature, any consistent usage of the word *group* or its approximate synonyms that could provide automatic order to this discussion. From the viewpoint of the present subject, three types of groups need to be differentiated. The least formal of these collectives is roughly parallel to the individual social actor who works by himself and often makes his statement in a single, dramatic act. Thus, some groups have little or no permanent structure yet profoundly affect the course of social change. The 1960s, in the area of civil rights, witnessed a number of examples. The march on Washington of August 1963 was called by a number of well-organized associations. Their summons went out not only to their own members but to the public in terms that, many feared, would create a panorama of mass violence. The results were both peaceful and memorable; the group that defined this occasion was never again convened. At the other end of the scale were those group actions which resulted in the burning and looting of large parts of Detroit, Los Angeles, and Washington, D.C., as well as other cities to a lesser degree. Some were triggered by the King assassination. The nation saw these riots as astonishingly violent and destructive as contrasted to the serene and constructive spirit of the march on Washington. All these events had their impact; all were largely unplanned.[12]

Sensational as has been the impact of some of these minimally organized occasions, they have produced far less in the way of substantive results than those voluntary associations which have an extended life, an effective organization, a means of acquiring funds, a controlled set of objectives, and a competence in the techniques of achieving change. the major examples of these associations are well known. They are the bread and butter of reform. They include the early workingmen's organizations in New York and Philadelphia; the antislavery and temperance societies that began mostly in New York and New England; the assemblies devoted to the solution of monetary problems, resistance to railroad inequities, and other issues that were of particular concern to the Western and Southern farmers and that arose in those regions; leagues devoted to consumer and urban issues that were prominent in Chicago at the turn of the century; and on down to the famous twentieth-century associations that have a truly national constituency: the National Association for the Advancement of Colored People, the League of Women Voters, the American Civil Liberties Union, Common Cause, and many others.

To qualify as social actors, these groups must have a well-recognized social purpose that is perceived as serving the public good. Grangers wanted flexible currency and credit for self-serving reasons; but they sincerely believed that such measures would benefit the nation at large. Some members of the NAACP were hoping their activities would improve their own status, but they were also working for a large outside constituency to which many of the leaders did not even belong. A reasonable criterion for a reform association is that it seek to serve a group of people either outside the organization or else larger than the organization. Labor unions sometimes meet this definition, sometimes they do not. Minor political parties often meet this definition, major parties sometimes do.

There are groups, including labor unions and political parties, that qualify as social actors and that have for their purpose the overthrow or drastic change of the government. They are a distinct minority. Most associations accept the basic structure of government and society. They are not content with the status quo, but they seek social change within a range of established methods and limits tolerated by the society. They seek to change the society in some important ways without altering its fundamental assumptions.

If this is the accepted pattern of behavior for the associational actors, there is some reason to feel that it is not successful often enough. One work that studies the general characteristics of voluntary associations concludes that the "challenging group," as it is called, succeeds so infrequently as to refute the pluralistic notion of satisfactory social change within the system.[13] Effective change, when it occurs, results from a powerful and sustained, although not necessarily centralized, organization.[14]

The third type of group-actor could more appropriately be called the *institution*. This term would recognize the fact that formally structured, large, and long-lasting agencies often act to promote social change. This category overlaps with the foregoing to the extent that churches, political parties, labor and business unions, and other associations of such longstanding character as to be considered as institutions might be serviceably included in either category. This third category exists mainly to recognize the fact that government while often the target of protest, itself becomes a social actor as a movement enters its institutional phase. This occurs at all levels and in all branches.

City governments have offered the leading edge of experiment in proportionally representative voting and professional management. States have advanced such democratic devices as unicameralism, election of judges, initiative, referendum, and recall. Although legislatures are the common target of pressures for change and have responded more fully than the other branches of government, they have not acted alone. The executive, through its agencies, has often been responsible for social actions ranging from the assurance of credit, the protection of savings, and the provision of financial relief, to the control of impure food and harmful drugs. Sometimes these actions represent responses to pressure. Sometimes they represent initiative. The courts were traditionally thought to be the last fortress against change; New Deal battles dramatized this relationship. But the famous "Warren Court" startled the nation by taking the initiative in civil rights for minorities in education, voting, housing, and other areas. Students of the courts argue as to whether this aggressive attitude toward change was typical or not; surely it was not a unique instance.

Students of reform do not need to change their impression that the most important agent for social change is the voluntary association. It would be helpful to know much more than is now known about these groups, but it is clear that the more lasting of them have importantly aided the institutions of society in adapting to changing expectations, and conditions.[15] It would also be useful to know more about individual reformers. Except for some of the government programs and a few of the large voluntary associations, no class of social actor has been studied well enough to reveal a reliable and accurate pattern of behavior, if indeed there is one. Even the role of state and local governments in stimulating change seems largely understudied in spite of a few excellent exceptions. There are but two sweeping generalizations concerning social actors: that voluntary associations have been continuously important, and government increasingly so.

FORMS

Individual protest/martyrdom.

Speeches/sermons/debates/theater.

Meetings/conventions/campaigns.

Demonstrations/parades/deliberate violence.

Strikes/boycotts.

Articles/essays/verse/drama/fiction/biography/autobiography.

Pictures/motion pictures/cartoons/posters/pictorial symbols/music.

Medals/buttons/banners/3-dimensional symbols.

Model communities/plans/designs/social-impact technology.

Social actors, in order to induce change, have taken advantage of every form of expression available to groups or individuals. If one knew the whole history of civilization, he would surely find that actors for social change had at least refined and probably invented many such forms. Perhaps ballet began as a tableau protesting repression; the first parade could well have brought a petition to a ruler; and what is now called guerilla theater and taken as an aberration could instead easily be the parent of the formal stage. In any case, there is hardly a form of expression that is inappropriate for generating social change; all forms have been used for this purpose, whether originally or not.

To compile a complete list of the forms taken by social actions would be to catalog society's entire repertoire. The point of the modest list produced here is to put some stress on scope. Too often public issues are studied only through strikes or legislative acts, court decisions or mass demonstrations. To assemble the whole picture on any important aspect of social change requires attention to many forms of activity, some of which may have unusual weight in the American setting: the muckraking tendencies of the free press; the social involvement of imaginative literature; the ubiquity of technology; and perhaps even a special attitude toward violence. James Bryce was one of many students of America who found that a large difference between the New World and Europe was rooted in a combination of voluntarism and a militant press. Surely the press has done nothing to discourage this impression, from Peter Zenger through the Pentagon Papers. The press may be more effective in exposing problems than in solving them, but there is no doubt that social actors have used periodicals to attack land monopoly, slavery, trusts, bossism, imperialism, slums, and political chicanery. Several names could be matched with each of these subjects; some prominent ones would be George Henry Evans and the land question; William Lloyd Garrison on slavery; Joseph Pulitzer and William Randolph Hearst on the oil and sugar monopolies, Bosses Tweed and Hanna, and the Spanish oppression of Cuba; Jacob Riis and his verbal as well as graphic attack on tenements; and the Washington *Post*'s persistent investigation of the circumstances surrounding the forceful entry into Democratic party headquarters in 1972.

Cartoons and exposés are not designed to be fair or constructive. They are, by their nature, sensational and partial. They reflect the fact that newspapers are supposed to sell and that arousing emotions is more profitable than engaging in calm and often dull considerations of remedial measures. Naturally, the militant press specializes in underlining abuses. Sometimes the press also participates in posing solutions. In the late nineteenth century, for example, a rather extensive "greenback press" emerged to propose a flexible and generally expanding currency as a remedy for some of the nation's recurring economic problems. Although "greenbackism" was not a final solution, it was a stage in a classic social process. Journalism is capable of linking problems with solutions, and its role is more satisfying to the student of social change when this linkage occurs. Realistically, however, the press can typically be expected to function as a spotlight on problems—the more sensational the better.[16]

As hard-hitting as is good journalism with its uncompromising photographs, its mordant cartoons, and its short, muscular paragraphs of prose, it may not have the long-term impact of imaginative literature. A partisan of slum clearance would count himself fortunate to have a Jacob Riis on his side; he might be even more fortunate to enlist a Jack London or a Stephen Crane. Who knows how much newspaper coverage was given to the abuse of merchant seamen before Richard Henry Dana's novel swayed the legislature? Theodore Dwight Weld compiled an excellent compendium of journalistic accounts of abuses taking place under slavery. It was a best seller in its day. Yet Abraham Lincoln was never reputed to have accused Weld of causing the Civil War; rather, this distinction rests with Harriet Beecher Stowe and her novel, which combined realism and sentimentalism in a way that left no emotions untouched.[17]

Along with fiction, autobiographies have also been effective vehicles for social change, especially as they have touched on the lives of black Americans from Frederick Douglass through Malcolm X. There is no question that all genres of imaginative literature are involved. To demonstrate this point one study examined that literary form (verse) held to be most severely separated from social concerns during the era when writers were, as a class, held to be out of touch with contemporary reality (the Gilded Age) and found a quite substantial commitment.[18] This trait, when combined with a muckraking frame of mind, produces some strikingly negative American literary vistas. Usually, although by no means always, the writer is not turning his back on his native land but hoping to provoke some remedial action. Upon Sinclair's *The Jungle* depicts an ugly situation. His expectations were more than realized when the novel led promptly to a Pure Food and Drug Act. He did not expect Chicago to be obliterated.

Novels may in fact be better designed to produce constructive results than are the products of the daily press. Not only did the novels of Dana, Stowe, and Sinclair seem to lead directly to positive results, but even minor novels continue to have a kind of immediate consequence disproportionate to their permanent literary value. One popular novel of the Cold War era, for example, convinced the foreign service that it needed a much more extensive training program in foreign languages and cultures for Americans going overseas, and another novel reputedly prompted the military to install additional safeguards against the accidental initiation of a nuclear attack.[19] It would seem that imaginative literature— on all levels and in all its forms—is a normal part of the process of social change in the United States, perhaps more so in this country than elsewhere.

America has been accused of having technology as its national religion. Whether this is a fair indictment or not, technology has been intertwined with social change in myriad ways. All schoolchildren are taught that a single invention, the cotton gin, caused the Civil War by making cotton grown with slave labor profitable. They are also taught that emancipation sprang from a victory by the North made possible through superior technology. They are less likely to be aware that the Rappites, who built model communities in Pennsylvania and Illinois, were among the first successful functional planners and prefabricated builders. From these points a strong, if zigzag, line can be traced to Buckminster Fuller, who not only is the ultimate prefabricator but would save democracy by allowing all citizens to vote on all important issues through a system of computer-tabulated phone calls.[20]

Most reform energies in the Western world went to coping with the impact of industrial technology throughout the nineteenth and into the twentieth century. This was true in America as well, although the relatively sparse population mitigated some of the social problems spawned in the more crowded industrial cities of Europe. More than in other nations, perhaps, reformers in America have been prone to look to technology for social remedies. Many of the antebellum experimental communities placed heavy stress on improving the human lot through efficiency and technical innovation. The Shakers could hang their furniture on the walls, thus not only simplifying housecleaning but also making floor space for their ceremonial dances. At Oneida, special pantries were built to store food prepared only once daily. Superior technology gave communities valuable products to sell to travelers. A clean, well-run community would attract converts as well as sales and admiration. To solve social and spiritual problems, one had best start with a smooth technological deployment of the unavoidable physical problems.

When model communities left the woods to reappear on paper, technology again was graphically described as that miraculous agent that would allow men and women to rise above the destructive impulses of unrestrained competition and furnish that harmonious setting which would make the most of human potential. This was the message of Edward Bellamy's incredibly popular utopia; it influenced the others and leaves a clear mark to this day. The evolution of the utopian solution into urban and regional planning and into science fiction obviously lessened the stress on technology not one whit.

Whether or not it is distinctively American, the stress on technology as a solution to social problems persists through a rising tide of antitechnological sentiments. The main cure for urban problems is still improved architecture, engineering, and design. Efficiency is the answer to the energy crisis, just as the ecology movement has stressed new techniques for recycling products formerly regarded as waste. The advocate of social change still looks for help from new products and processes; but, as the calendar has turned toward the present, he has come to regard technology as something less than a panacea. Less than an end in itself, less than a means to an end, technology is now seen as a prime source of social problems.

It had also been generally assumed that, with the startling exception of the Civil War, American society had been able to accommodate social change without violence. During the last decades this assumption has been increasingly questioned. Is violence un-American or routinely American? The films of military violence in Vietnam, the experience of domestic riots in urban ghettoes, and the assassinations of Martin Luther King, Jr., and John and Robert Kennedy all combined to produce considerable new attention to this subject. Readers were reminded that the history of their nation was not as continuously peaceful as they would like to remember it.

In its more controlled forms, violence is not uncommon: demonstrating without a permit, destroying property, provoking confrontation and arrest. William Gamson found that 25 percent of his challenge group sample had made use of one or more of these techniques. Although its effectiveness is extremely difficult to appraise, violence is one tool in the reformer's kit.

DYNAMICS

Random negative (unorganized protest).

Structured negative (organized protest).

Random positive (various remedies).

Structured positive (organized movement with constructive aim).

Watchdog (surveillance of institutionalized reform).

Social scientists are more prone to identify "stages" than are historians, which, if it is true, may explain why historians have been guilty of grossly oversimple contrasts between alleged ages of reform and eras of apathy. The tendency has been to judge a time period by the presence or absence of a certain kind of achievement, forgetting that each fulfillment carries a long history of agitation as well as a future of careful if less spectacular surveillance. Awareness that reform activity comes under many guises may help to mitigate some of the exaggerated profiles historians have sketched for their favored eras.[21]

The main point in listing stages is to stress the fact that social change is a complex process made up of a number of identifiable phases. It is hard to understand either the society or the issue unless attention is paid to the entire process. Although the beginnings of each process are generally similar, they are not so in detail. Subsequently, one movement may evolve smoothly through all five stages; another may bog down in midstream and disappear; a third may progress through a few stages and then revert; still another may complete one cycle only to generate another.

All social movements begin with discontent with the status quo. Some do not then launch a specific protest but spring immediately to a sweeping solution (as with the utopians). But for most movements the process begins with complaint; hence "negative." At first the complaints come from miscellaneous sources; hence "random." Typical forms for this initial "random negative" stage would be an article in a journal, a letter to the editor of a newspaper, a small demonstration. These expressions have in common only that they oppose the same thing, say, the use of nuclear fission to generate energy. The reasons for the opposition will vary; there will be no organized attack.

The second stage, "structured negative," means that the opposition has become organized and that usually, although not by definition, the reasons for opposing the perceived problem will have been simplified or arranged into a hierarchy. The protesters will have decided that the dangers to marine life in superheated discharge are secondary and that the prime issue is the danger to human life. A campaign will be launched. This implies the formation of one or more associations. Memberships will be solicited. Funds will be raised, meetings held, publications issued. Political candidates will be asked to take a stand. At this stage, however, there is still no agreed-upon, positive remedy. The cry is simply to close down the nuclear power plants.

What happens after the second stage is often crucial. The nation has been organized, more than once, to oppose the despoilation of natural resources. Yet wide support has never been mustered for any adaptation of the system that would constitute an affirmative phase of the movement. Partial answers have been offered, supported, and institutionalized; but the absence of an accepted, comprehensive, positive program leaves the movement in the second stage.

Sometimes a movement achieves stage five without ever passing through either of the positive phases. A classic example is the temperance movement. Although there are positive consequences to the regulation of alcohol consumption, the public was never made to see these potential benefits as a direct outgrowth of prohibition. The movement thus leaped, with the passage of the Eighteenth

Amendment, from the second (structured negative) to the fifth (institutionalized) stage. Lacking a positive aspect, the prohibition issue sank quickly to a matter of enforcement and was probably doomed before it began.

It is equally common to see a movement faltering between stages three and four. At this point there is agreement on the problem; there are a number of remedies before the public; but there is no consensus as to a single positive answer or a hierarchy of answers. The protest against the use of nuclear fission as a source of energy has presently reached this point. A number of alternatives have been proposed: conserve energy; process oil shale; intensify oil and gas exploration; subsidize the development of solar and tidal sources. Before the attack on nuclear power can proceed much further it will probably have to develop a single positive alternative or at least an agreed-upon list of priorities.

There are reform movements that proceed through all five stages only to encounter problems in the watchdog phase. An example is the antimonopoly impulse that was born with the republic, gradually singled out specific targets, organized itself, attracted associational support, and evolved into a positive movement for federal regulation. Partially institutionalized under the Sherman Act, the restraint of monopolies was enforced in a manner that frustrated the reformers. Corporations were prosecuted selectively and ineffectively while labor unions were found in restraint of trade. Thwarted in the watchdog phase, the foes of industrial monopoly began again with the Sherman Act as their target and eventually found a more congenial form of institutionalization in the Clayton Act.

Another problem at stage five is cooption. Before the antitrust laws were passed, there was some policing of the problem by reason of the very existence of adversarial interests. When the antitrust act is passed and the Justice Department takes over the regulative function, the antimonopoly leagues disband. The regulators talk only to the regulated. Without meaning to, each party acquires something of the other's viewpoint. The government is supposed to present the public case; the watchdog has the extremely difficult job of assuring himself that this process is indeed in the large interest and does not represent, instead, some form of inside bargaining between two entities, each familiar with the problems of the other, making a series of accommodations and compromises with the public interest in the remote background.[22]

Movements fail at all stages. Some succeed without passing through the normal development. In one mode (reforms on behalf of special groups), the sequence is routinely experienced twice; in another mode (alternative models), the pattern is severely truncated. There are even examples of reforms beginning with institutionalization (greenbacks). Nevertheless, the dynamic pattern described here is not only logical but, in the history of reform in America, is followed more often than any other pattern. One important consequence of establishing a pattern is to give weight to the exceptions.[23]

Another vital consequence is in the added precision available to historians who make social activity a criterion for periodizing the American past. An understanding of reform dynamics makes it possible to give appropriate weight to the earlier stages of protest instead of limiting an "age of reform" to those times when positive structured activity raised the question of institutionalization or no. An awareness of stages make the characterization of American eras more accurate and more subtle. The question is not simply, Was this a reform era? Rather, the historian can ask which issues were prominent and what stages they occupied. The resulting picture will see dramatic contrasts replaced by a stress on continuity, complexity, and a set of more useful distinctions.

That there are stages in the process of social change seems evident. Their recognition can correct a number of incomplete perceptions concerning the social character of American eras. It can also clarify the reform process itself and throw light on those important intersections where the more stable patterns of American life meet the forces for change.[24]

ARGUMENTS AND ASSUMPTIONS

Explicit appeals to: A higher law; reason and experience; and a sense of the practical.

Implicit assumption of: unacceptability of the status quo and the consequent need for gradual or drastic change; process as an essential means and end; sustained presence of civil liberties; preeminence of the general (over particular) good; unique importance of the United States as a social experiment.

To study reform is to see, at first, a bewildering variety of modes and arguments. It is in these two cardinal aspects that the subject seems so annoyingly resistent to control; hence, it is proportionately reassuring to discover that both of these headings can be reduced to a few dominant categories. Three modes describe all important reform activity; similarly, three explicit arguments, coupled with a few implicit assumptions, characterize the vital philosophical underpinnings utilized by the advocates of social change. It is tempting to link certain modes or topics or periods with certain dominant rationales. In the end, however, these correlations do not prove decisive. Moral arguments are just as prominent as rational arguments in economic reform; practical appeals are as central as moral appeals in humanitarian reform. Even though certain worldviews lend special stress to one or more of these justifications, still the main arguments exist side by side throughout the history of the republic. All three explicit arguments can be derived from the ideas of antiquity and reinforced in the experience and literature of the European Renaissance. Some of them have particular relevance to the religious debates of the seventeenth century both in Europe and the Colonies. Some are distinctly stressed in Enlightenment thought. Some have to do with the circumstances of America's setting and origin.[25] Throughout the history of American reform, social actors have sought to persuade their fellow citizens to favor a certain measure because it is in tune with moral law, because its wisdom can be demonstrated through reason, and because it is workable. Each social movement has its own characteristics, each era its own points of distinctiveness; but the explicit arguments for change remain constant. Every important cause in every period has been supported, at the root, by these arguments.

Underlying these explicit appeals are assumptions that often go unstated. One of them is universal: the assumption that the status quo is unacceptable. This becomes an explicit argument during the first and second stages of reform dynamics. At subsequent stages, and in certain types of proposals, it remains unstated. A utopian novel may never make an overt reference to the problems of contemporary society, for example; yet the author's discontent is an important part of the work's entire rationale.

Utopias, and other proposals for alternative social orders, often make a second assumption that is relatively rare. When the alternative model differs drastically from the current society, then the actor is proposing support for an abrupt movement to a new system without the benefit of the usual stages. Here is an ideal society, he is saying. Further social evolution may be unnecessary once the culture arrives at this state. Consider, therefore, a revolution—peaceful or not— that will discard the present system and substitute for it the one offered by George Rapp, Robert Dale Owen, Edward Bellamy, or the International Workers of the World.

A far more common assumption is that gradual change is inevitable and proper. This assumption, sometimes stated but more often implicit, constitutes one of the most fundamental attributes of reform. It assumes that reform is a process without permanent plateaus. A movement may have an apparent beginning, a series of landmarks publicly achieved, and even a stage that institutionalizes the concept. And yet, for all these distinctions, the most important thing about social change is that it is a continuing process. Shifting external conditions— new inventions, population growth—require constant adaptation of social mechanisms and public institutions. One achievement may beget another movement, as emancipation eventually generated a civil rights movement. The winning of a ten-hour workday served as a platform for pursuing a nine-hour day. Passage of laws to protect female laborers suggests a social evolution that would make special protection of women irrelevant. Far from being discouraged by the endless agenda of reform, most social actors welcome the perception of a dynamic society in which goals, if static, are but momentarily so.

The other assumptions—also usually implicit—will not surprise a student of the national character. They do help explain why certain prominent American values—freedom, liberty, achievement, self-reliance, individualism—are rarely encountered as a basis for reform persuasions. Many of these unstated values are enumerated in the Bill of Rights and taken for granted unless abridged. As fundamental guarantees, they provide the foundation on which the structure of reform is built. That people will prefer the general good over individual rewards is assumed, more or less, by advocates of social change in many cultures. This assumption is evident more in measures proposed than in arguments submitted. It is clear too that reformers, like Americans in general, feel that their own nation is special indeed. However, in an argument that makes dissatisfaction its opening salvo, it is difficult to move directly to an invocation of the promised land. One is more likely to encounter this assumption in a negative sense, as when a sordid reality is contrasted to the golden promise. Arguments and assumptions evident on the reform frontier support preconceptions of American values in some ways while directly contradicting them in others.

To summarize these ideas of order it is first necessary to bring the categories together:

MODES

The improvement of politicoeconomic democracy.

The improved treatment of specific individuals and groups.

The alteration of society by reference to a substantially different model.

ACTORS

Independent individuals.

Unorganized groups.

Voluntary associations.

Institutions, including all levels and branches of government.

FORMS

Individual protest/martyrdom.

Speeches/sermons/debates/theater.

Meetings/conventions/campaigns.

Demonstrations/parades/deliberate violence.

Strikes/boycotts.

Articles/essays/verse/drama/fiction/biography/autobiography.

Pictures/motion pictures/cartoons/posters/pictorial symbols/music.

Medals/buttons/banners/3-dimensional symbols.

Model communities/plans/designs/social-impact technology.

DYNAMICS

Random negative (unorganized protest).

Structured negative (organized protest).

Random positive (various remedies).

Structured positive (organized movement with constructive aim).

Watchdog (surveillance of institutionalized reform).

ARGUMENTS AND ASSUMPTIONS

Explicit appeals to: a higher law; reason and experience; and a sense of the practical.

Implicit assumption of: unacceptability of status quo and the consequent need for gradual or drastic change; process as an essential means and end; sustained presence of civil liberties; preeminence of the general (over the particular) good; and unique importance of the United States as a social experiment.

The main burden of this outline is the idea that the study of reform can be organized and, to a degree, controlled. The major step in exerting this control has been the establishment of modes within which activities share basic traits and among which they differ. Some essential points of similarity and contrast may best be seen by rearranging the outline as shown in Table 1. Outlines are best suited to dramatizing structural points. It remains to indicate the dynamic character of reform by summarizing the essential changes as seen against the time dimension.

The *modes* of reform have remained constant, although the forms of their interior workings have changed through time. The process of perfecting political democracy went on as obviously in 1980, when many worried about a constitutional crisis possibly created by the presence of three prominent presidential candidates, as it did in 1800, when Abraham Bishop railed against property qualifications for voting. The political issues remain as firmly tied to economic consequences. As for movements on behalf of special groups, the general issue prevails while the number of movements multiplies geometrically. Cotton Mather was worried about the treatment of but slaves and Indians. Today there are movements on behalf of dozens of groups based on everything from ancestry to geography. The nature of alternatives to the present polity has changed, but the habit of offering variant models continues as it did in the 1830s, an interesting minor form of social agitation.

Types of social *actors* are constant, too, but the shifts in their nature are important. As society has grown larger and more complexly arranged, it has become increasingly difficult for an isolated individual to make a serious impact. Edmund Wilson, in emulation of Thoreau, refused to pay his federal taxes in protest against the government's failure to live up to some of its treaties with Northeastern Indian tribes. He defended his action in prose that may not have been as special as Thoreau's but was hardly ordinary. Yet the impact of Wilson's action would be hard to compare with Thoreau's. The individual, competing for attention in a crowded culture, gives way to the organized group.[26]

TABLE 1
Modes for Reform

	Mode I Politicoeconomic	Mode II Special Groups	Mode III Alternate Models
Principal actors	Large associations Government: all levels and branches	Individuals Voluntary associations Federal government: all branches	Individuals Associations
Characteristic forms	Speeches, and tracts Campaigns and conventions Strikes and boycotts Cartoons and symbols	Speeches and autobiography Demonstrations Cartoons, symbols, and music	Plans and designs Fiction Model communities Social-impact technology
Dynamics	Five-stage cycle culminating in legislative act, court decision, creation of government agency	As with Mode I except the five-stage cycle is typically experienced twice: toward segregated equality, then toward integrated equality	Two-stage sequence moving from structured positive to institutionalization or rejection
Arguments and assumptions	All modes assume the unacceptability of the status quo and appeal to a higher law, reason and experience, and a sense of the practical. They vary only as to:		
	Inevitability and propriety of gradual change	Inevitability and propriety of gradual change	Necessity for drastic change

As the passive government favored by Jefferson has receded into the realm of bucolic nostalgia, the agencies of the government frequently have responded to pressures for social change and often have initiated changes themselves. Legislatures, once the prime target for reformers, have had to share the limelight with the courts and the executive agencies. With the institutionalization of increasing numbers of social movements through the years, the agencies of the executive branch—federal, state, and local—have become a major center of social action.

Political parties and other voluntary associations, which once seemed likely to revolve about single issues, have now become broader, more flexible, and more enduring. In the nineteenth century a party could sometimes be identified simply with abolition, free trade, or the coinage of silver. Steadily the major parties have struggled toward a broad consensus in the hope that their particular blend of programs would match the mood and priorities of the electorate. Multipurpose reform associations were not invented by Ralph Nader or John W. Gardner, but their "citizens' lobbies" reflect a general inclination to delegate priorities and techniques to the professional reformer. Like political parties, reform associations have evolved gently—and by no means exclusively—in the direction of a large-scale enterprise that assumes its existence will be permanent and, as a consequence, stands ready to shift its activities from one cause to another depending on the interests of its constituency and its leadership.[27] The modern voluntary association is probably better organized than its predecessor. Although it will typically be identified with a single powerful leader at its inception, it will probably rely more on delegation of power and on a broad plateau of financial support. It will probably live long enough to lose its strong identification with a single leader and assume its own collective profile as an interest group. The LWV, the ACLU, and the NAACP furnish examples of this kind of institutional history.

Forms of social action directly reflect technology. With the advent of high-speed printing and an effective mail service, the printed word became the leading agency for social change, not replacing the live event but serving to amplify it. However stirring a speech might have been in 1880, it probably did not move many people unless it also read well. Succeeding technical innovations have affected reform as much as they have affected politics, and in roughly the same way. Radio and recorded sound brought back the direct power of oratory and, to a lesser extent, the campaign song. Photography may have accentuated the importance of a candidate's looks, but radio stressed his voice and diction, while the motion picture (and later television) added importance to gestures, mannerisms, and physical grace. But radio and television bring into the home not just the voice and image of the individual but entire street scenes, conventions, riots, and demonstrations. Garrison was famous for his adroitness at handling hecklers and unruly mobs. But this was a skill known mainly by repute. Only if his famous confrontation with the Rynders mob had been televised could it possibly have rivalled the vision, shared by millions of viewers, of the Reverend Martin Luther King arousing his gigantic congregation in front of the Lincoln Memorial.[28] Events still play important parts in social change, but they tend to be important in proportion to their suitability for presentation to the public through the media.

Although not all reform movements share the same *dynamics*, there seems little shift within this category except as already noted. As time passes and large numbers of movements arise, some inevitably succeed in becoming institutionalized. The result is that yesterday's reform becomes today's regulatory agency. As the nation prolongs its history, consequently, an increasing proportion of reform activity will have advanced to the state that requires surveillance rather than agitation. In this setting, many questions become highly technical, which may, in turn, help explain the increasing involvement of lawyers in reform and related issues. One recourse of the watchdog is to take the agency to court, where he will try the public interest against a special interest. In this stage, reform may shift from social history to institutional or legal history. If it were not for the constant generation of new causes, the study of reform would pass steadily into the hands of scholars much more attuned to legal and procedural questions than to the transactions between the public conscience and its organizers.

Arguments and assumptions retain their central meaning although their setting shifts. The appeal to the higher law may be primarily religious at one time or, in another context, may invoke the secular "religion of humanity." In either case it is a moral appeal. Appeals to reason and experience once favored the deductive logic of the *philosophes*; with time, these arguments took on a more empirical character eventually buttressed by the emerging social sciences. But whether the model was Diderot or Thorstein Veblen, the appeal was from one rational mind to another, with evidence and theory neatly packaged in the foreground. Similarly, each age has produced its own variety of utilitarianism, pragmatism, instrumentalism, or feasibility.

To trace the cultural variables that have produced the shifting emphases within the reform arguments is interesting and important. At least as important, however, is the realization that these appeals and assumptions, explicit and implicit, have retained their general character as well as their intricate interdependencies throughout the national history. When one American has tried to persuade another— for over two hundred years—this is the way he has done it.

This outline, qualified by a time dimension, seeks to control and simplify the subject of reform in a number of ways. Foremost is the establishment of three large categories (modes) into which all important movements can be placed with the assurance that their main points of similarity and divergence will be justly and faithfully preserved in this tripartite definition. This typology offers a great, perhaps essential, constant.

The other major anchor may be less crucial for the analysis of reform than for the analysis of national character. It is the contention that the main and prevailing persuasions (arguments) used to promote social change are both limited and constant.

Within each mode, reform movements become susceptible to analysis according to variables recorded under three headings: the kind of social actors promoting the change (individual, group, associational, institutional); the kind of forms utilized (from cartoons to charters); and the stages through which the movement has passed (dynamics).

Thus armed, the scholar improves his understanding of individual movements, learns to compare and contrast more precisely, and discovers reform activity previously overlooked because of incomplete definition of the subject. The use of a consistent taxonomy can only extend awareness of the subject while encouraging more detailed and subtle appreciation of reform's internal history as well as its interaction with the society at large. The importance of continuities will supersede a sense of overly dramatized superficial fluctuations. Full of vital differences, the subject of reform will appear, in sum, as one of the great, central constants in American life.

***

There is a wide chasm between outlining a structure for reform and offering public policy recommendations. Yet, considering how thoroughly public policy is enmeshed with the pressures for change, an improvement in the appreciation of reform patterns and values could hardly help affecting policy. If the assumptions and arguments set forth in this essay are even partially correct, they would constitute important piers on which a roadway over the chasm might be constructed. Reform is anything but a dead subject; its history scuffs the heels of its current position. Bridging the chasm is more a problem in connecting understanding with application than in separating past from present.

With an apology for submitting assertions that are by no means demonstrated in the foregoing essay, one might identify three general areas in which an awareness of the historical configurations of reform would make for enlightened policy decisions. One such area is in the connection of means with ends. An innocent pride in America's democratic forms has led to satisfaction in the purification of democracy for its own sake. The history of reform shows that social change does not stop at the level of textbook civics. It hardly pauses. If the enforcement of a voting rights act helps open the path for the expression of political choice by a theretofore suppressed minority, this is good. But it is only a first step. If political expression does not lead to what is often called social (read: *economic*) justice, then nothing really meaningful will have occurred. Taxation without representation is still tyranny. If the political voice does not produce improved economic conditions, then it was not a reform.

Public policy could be improved with the realization of how consistently industrial democracies have come to rely on a growing bureaucracy at the national level to deal with social and economic problems. Theoretically there are choices. Problems can be solved at the local or regional level, by government or by the private sector or by quasi-official agencies. In practice, however, whether in the United States or in other similarly evolved nations, the responsibility inevitably ends with the national government. Much rhetoric and some policy decisions are based on the assumption that there is still a choice. History—both remote and recent—shows there is not.

This perception does not mean that the federal agencies in the United States cannot be improved through reorganization, the provision of clearer mandates, and the application of more realistic criteria to their performance. Indeed, things have become sufficiently confused in the bureaucracy so that advocates of a narrow cause may have to search through dozens of guidelines before they find a responsive office. Public agencies always need policing both to keep alive the true public interest and to maintain the difficult connection between real problems and real solutions. Energy expended in this direction, history tells us, will be better rewarded than energy expended in searching alternatives to federal responsibility.

Finally, an informed view of the past should show the policy maker the futility of temporizing with what he might take to be a temporary popular mood. The melioristic temper has been portrayed, by both sociologists and historians, as subject to drastic vicissitudes. Although no one denies that change and alternation are a part of life, still the close analysis of reform shows that continuities are at least as important as variables, however much they may have been overlooked. Once one learns to recognize reform in its varied applications, in its multiplicity of forms, and in its evolving stages, one perceives that this impulse rarely if ever disappears; it merely shifts from one topic or stage to another. Policy makers who observe this condition might save the cost of tactical delays— postponements in the hope of a pendulum swing in the public disposition—and come to grips with the reform agenda in the full realization that marking time has no future.

It is no revelation that the variables in the reform equation are constantly shifting: the roles of individual actors and voluntary agencies; the impact of changes in demography and technology. Nothing is static. Many of these variables need constant study and improved understanding. But the greatest and most helpful perception of all is that the reform impulse itself is essential continuous. Founded on appeals to morality, social logic, and feasibility, it comes so close to the heart of the national existence that public policy cannot ignore it for long and can temporize at its peril.

NOTES

1. Thomas C. Cochran, *Frontiers of Change: Early Industrialism in America* (New York: Oxford University Press, 1981); Cochran, *The Inner Revolution: Essays on the Social Sciences and History* (New York: Harper & Row, 1964).

2. Thomas C. Cochran, *Social Change in Industrial Society: Twentieth Century America* (London: Allen & Unwin, 1972).

3. Thomas C. Cochran, *Railroad Leaders: The Business Mind in Action, 1845-1890* (Cambridge: Harvard University Press, 1953).

4. The list was presented with typical economy in just a few minutes of a graduate lecture; I wish it were mine to pass along, and I hope readers will join me in urging Professor Cochran to put these thoughts into essay form.

5. Robert H. Walker, *Reform Spirit in America* (New York: Putnam, 1976), hereafter cited as *RSIA*. The present essay is also a version of a chapter in a forthcoming monograph on the same topic. To avoid overelaborate definitions, I have described my subject in both these works as consisting of that area where reform and social change overlap. Within the boundaries of this understanding, I use the terms interchangeably.

6. A more elaborate complaint against terminology and chronology, as generally set forth, is contained in *RSIA*, pp. xv-xx.

7. Ibid., part 4.

8. Ibid., p. xx.

9. Ralph Nader furnishes a good example of a reformer who moved from individual actions to the associational approach. He produced the Highway Safety Act almost singlehandedly and later turned to shaping voluntary organizations.

10. Henry J. Silverman, "American Social Reformers in the Late Nineteenth and Early Twentieth Century" (Ph.D. diss., University of Pennsylvania, 1963). Perhaps because political actor is a more limited concept than social actor, it has begun to attract more systematic analysis. The pioneer study of the voter as political actor, stressing the consequences rather than the causes of his behavior, is Angus Campbell et al., *American Voter* (New York: Wiley, 1960). Sidney Verba and Norman H. Nie have not only updated the work of Campbell and his colleagues at the University of Michigan Survey Research Center but have expanded the ways of measuring participation other than voting. Their basic work is *Participation in America: Political Democracy and Social Equality* (New York: Harper & Row, 1972). A considerable literature, with obvious relevance to reform, is growing out of these two books.

11. This is a portion of the Rose Bibliography, a partially computerized resource administered by the American Studies Program, George Washington University.

12. See *RSIA*, pp. 337-50, for a discussion of the march on Washington. The riots of the mid-1960s furnish an example of violence producing immediate political results. Violence may or may not be rare in American reform, and it may or may not be generally effective; but it is certainly unusual to find universal agreement to the effect that these riots led directly to the outpouring of civil rights legislation.

13. William A. Gamson, *Strategy of Social Protest* (Homewood, Ill,: Dorsey Press, 1975). Starting with 4,500 groups, Gamson ends up with a sample of 53; 17 of these he calls "reform"; but it is probable that some groups from his other categories would also meet my criteria. In deriving his basic list, Gamson for some reason ignored the source (Bliss) on which Silverman relied totally.

14. Gamson conducts a good argument with Robert Dahl, the prime spokesman for the pluralistic view of social change. Gamson's scope is from 1800 to 1945; his chronology reflecting the formation of challenge groups is expectedly high in the 1880s and 1930s but remarkably low for the whole Progressive era. The only active antebellum decade is the 1830s, whereas most historians would expect much more activity in the decades immediately preceding and following. Gamson feels that crises are the most important cause for the foundation of these groups, although his chronology hardly supports this assertion convincingly. This is not a historical study but is very useful to historians of social change both substantively and bibliographically. So are some of the political studies, including those of Robert Dahl and James Q. Wilson, *Political Organizations* (New York: Basic Books, 1973).

15. Some needed help has recently been provided by Ralph M. Kramer, *Voluntary Agencies in the Welfare State* (Berkeley: University of California Press, 1981). Kramer's study is comparative but uses data only from agencies serving the physically and mentally handicapped. His data correlate strongly with my experiences within mode II.

16. See *RSIA*, pp. 614-16.

17. Ibid., pp. 276-318.

18. Robert H. Walker, *Poet and the Gilded Age* (Philadelphia: University of Pennsylvania Press, 1963).

19. The books in question are: William J. Lederer and Eugene Burdick, *The Ugly American* (New York: Norton, 1958); and Eugene Burdick and Harvey Wheeler, *Fail Safe* (New York: McGraw-Hill, 1962). The "ugly American" is one of those epithets, like "Uncle Tom," that gets turned around. The "ugly" character was the hero who shed his Americanisms and fit in with his foreign setting, thereby accomplishing much more than the "enclave" foreign national whose main aim is the reproduction of a small homeland overseas. Although agency officials are reluctant to admit in print that novels could influence policy, conversations often reveal that they do.

20. *RSIA*, pp. 606-7, 653-55.

21. Somewhere in the literature of social change there must be a better and more usable analysis of the stages of social action. Most of the places I have looked have treated this subject in a more narrow setting and, hence, with so much specific detail as to make it inappropriate for a general summary. The closest general answer I have found is in Albion W. Small "Sanity in Social Agitation," *American Journal of Sociology* 4 (November 1898): 335-51. Small's stages are: discovery, persuasion, individual adjustment, and social adaptation.

22. My own Washington experience includes some months as a consultant for the Federal Aviation Agency. The director, Elwood R. Quesada, explained to me in our first interview that regulative agencies tended to be dominated by the industry they were supposedly monitoring. The leaders of the airline industry were not pernicious to Quesada; many of them were among his closest friends. He simply saw the process as inevitable, and he wanted to forestall it by keeping the public aroused to its own vested interest in the nation's airspace. My job was to help him keep the public alert. I would like to think that "Pete" Quesada made things a bit easier for the watchdogs of the airways. One only knows that the problem is perpetual.

23. Illustration of important variations in dynamic patterns cannot be provided here. It will be proposed, however, that reforms for groups outside the mainstream move first toward segregated equality; then, in a new sequence, toward integral equality. Alternative models (like New Deal planned communities) are sometimes institutionalized without preamble. Communitarian and utopian proposals seldom show a "random" stage, either negative or positive, and are typically offered as positive structure (stage four). The greenback idea had but a limited public history before their issue as the Northern financial instrument during the first days of the Civil War. Most reforms are within mode I (politicoeconomic), and here the standard sequence is the rule.

24. Examples of misleading labels abound. In the 1950s, the term *premuckraking* came into use. Functionally this word has no meaning. It was used to combat the firm characterization of the Progressive era as an age of reform preceded by an era of apathy. Thus, any protest discovered before 1900 must have been premuckraking!

25. See *RSIA*, p. xxvii, for a statement of this problem. Part 1 derives these arguments from colonial roots.

26. My colleague at the Hoover Institution, Dean Carl Auerbach, argues that, in the field of public interest, we have passed the era of laissez faire between individuals and can hope only for laissez faire among groups. He also has some interesting remarks on the transition from countervailing powers to government regulations. See Auerbach, "Scope and Objectives of Legislative Intervention and the Public Interest," *UCLA Law Review* 6 (1959): 516-32.

27. A beautiful example is the Christmas Seal campaign, which for years collected money to support research on a cure for tuberculosis. A cure having been found, the organization preserved its technique while adroitly switching its sights to a different disease.

28. *RSIA*, pp. 337-50.

Bibliography of Thomas C. Cochran

The following bibliography is a chronological listing by category of the publications of Thomas C. Cochran, excluding such publications as book reviews, interviews, and in-house publications.

Books

Auction Bridge Hints. New York: Holt, 1923.

Auction Bridge Handbook. New York: Holt, 1926

New York in the Confederation: An Economic Study. Empire State Historical Publications, no. 84. Philadelphia: University of Pennsylvania Press, 1932.

The Pabst Brewing Company: The History of an American Business. New York: New York University Press, 1948. Reprint. Westport, Conn.: Greenwood Press, 1975.

Railroad Leaders: The Business Mind in Action, 1845-1890. Cambridge: Harvard University Press, 1953. Gloucester, Mass.: Reprint. Peter Smith, 1965.

The American Business System: A Historical Perspective, 1900-1955. Cambridge: Harvard University Press, 1957. Reprint. New York: Harper & Row, Torchbooks, 1962.

The Puerto Rican Businessman: A Study in Cultural Change. Philadelphia: University of Pennsylvania Press, 1959.

A Basic History of American Business. New York: Van Nostrand, 1959; rev.ed. 1969.

The Inner Revolution: Essays on the Social Sciences in History. New York: Harper & Row, 1964. Reprint. Peter Smith, 1966.

The Great Depression and World War II 1929-1945. Glenview, Ill.: Scott, Foresman, 1968.

Social Change in Industrial Society: Twentieth Century America. London: Allen & Unwin, 1972.

Social Change in America: The Twentieth Century. New York: Harper & Row, 1972.

Business in American Life: A History. New York: McGraw-Hill, 1972.

American Business in the Twentieth Century. Cambridge: Harvard University Press, 1972.

The Uses of History. Wilmington, Del.: Scholarly Resources, 1973.

Business Enterprise in American Life: Selected Readings. Boston: Houghton Mifflin, 1974.

Two Hundred Years of American Business. New York: Basic Books, 1977.

Pennsylvania: A Bi-Centennial History. New York: Norton, 1977.

Frontiers of Change: Early Industrialism in America. New York: Oxford University Press, 1981.

Books Authored in Collaboration

and Miller, William. *The Age of Enterprise: A Social History of Industrial America*. 1942. Reprint. New York: Harper & Row, Torchbooks, 1961.

and Reina, Ruben. *Entrepreneurship in Argentine Culture*. Philadelphia: University of Pennsylvania Press, 1963.

and Bining, Arthur. *The Rise of American Economic Life*. 4th ed. New York: Scribner's, 1964.

Theory and Practice in Historical Study: A Report of the Committee on Historiography. Bulletin no. 54. New York: Social Science Research Council, 1946.

The Greater City. Edited by Allan Nevins and John Krout. New York: Columbia University Press, 1948.

The Social Sciences in Historical Study: A Report of the Committee on Historiography. Bulletin no. 64. New York: Social Science Research Council, 1954.

Generalization in the Writing of History: A Report of the Committee on Historical Analysis of the Social Sciences Research Council. Edited by Louis Gottschalk. Chicago: University of Chicago Press, 1963.

The Democratic Experience: A Short American History. 1963. New editions. Glenview, Ill.: Scott, Foresman, 1968, 1973, 1980.

Books Edited in Collaboration

and Clarkson, Jesse D. *War as a Social Institution: The Historian's Perspective*. New York: Columbia University Press, 1940.

with Andrews, Wayne. *Concise Dictionary of American History*. New York: Scribner's, 1961.

and Lloyd, Henry Demarest. *Wealth Against Commonwealth*. Englewood Cliffs, N.J.: Prentice-Hall, 1963.

Williams, Harry; and Dew, Charles B. *The Meanings of American History*. Vol. 2, Glenview, Ill.: Scott, Foresman, 1972.

and Brewer, Thomas B. *Views of American Economic Growth, Vol. 1: The Agricultural Era, Vol. 2: The Industrial Era*. New York: McGraw-Hill, 1966.

Contributions to Edited Volumes

"Social History of the Corporation." In *The Cultural Approach to History*. Edited by Caroline F. Ware. New York: Columbia University Press, 1939.

"Business Organization and the Development of an Industrial Discipline." In *The Growth of the American Economy*. Edited by Harold F. Williamson. 1944. New edition. Englewood Cliffs, N.J.: Prentice-Hall, 1951.

"The Role of the Business Leader." In *Problems of American History*. Edited by Richard Leopold and Arthur Link. Vol. 2. 1952. New editions. Englewood Cliffs, N.J.: Prentice-Hall, 1957, 1966, 1972.

"Role and Sanction in American Entrepreneurial History." In *Change and the Entrepreneur*. Cambridge: Harvard University Press, 1949.

"The Entrepreneur in American Capital Formation." In *Capital Formation and Economic Growth: A Report of the National Bureau of Economic Research*. Princeton, N.J.: Princeton University Press, 1955.

"An Historical Approach to Economic Development." In *First International Conference on Economic History: Contributions and Communications*. Amsterdam: Mouton, 1960.

"Foreword." In *The Norristown Study*. Edited by Sidney Goldstein, Philadelphia: University of Pennsylvania Press, 1961.

"The Social Scientists." In *American Perspectives*. Edited by Robert Spiller and Eric Larrabee. Cambridge: Harvard University Press, 1961.

"Role." In *American History and the Social Sciences*. Edited by Edward Saveth. New York: Free Press, 1964.

"The Sons of the Trustbusters." In *Twentieth Century Pessimism and the American Dream*, Edited by Raymond C. Miller. Detroit: Wayne State University Press, 1961.

"Business in American History." In *America as a Business Civilization*. Edited by James Soltow. East Lansing: Michigan State University Press, 1962.

"The Social Impact of the Railroad." In *The Railroad and Space Program*. Edited by Bruce Mazlish. Cambridge, Mass.: MIT Press, 1965.

"Cultural Factors in Economic Growth." In *Explorations in Enterprise*. Edited by H.G.J. Aitken. Cambridge: Harvard University Press, 1965.

"Industrialization." In *The Comparative Approach to American History*. Edited by C. Vann Woodward. New York: Basic Books, 1968.

"The Norristown Study." In *The Challenge of Local History*, Albany: New York State Department of Education, 1968.

"Entrepreneurship." In *International Encyclopedia of the Social Sciences*. Vol. 2. New York: Macmillan, Free Press, 1968.

"Introduction." In *Railroads: Their Origins and Problems*. Edited by Charles Francis Adams. New York: Harper & Row, 1969.

"On Historical Method." In *Society and History: Essays by Sylvia Thrupp*. Edited by Raymond Grew and Nicholas H. Schenck. Ann Arbor: University of Michigan Press, 1977.

"Recollections of Hermann Krooss." In *Research in Economic History*. Supplement no. 1. Edited by Robert E. Gallman. Greenwich, Conn.: JAI Press, 1977.

Articles

"The Faith of Our Fathers." *Frontiers of Democracy* (October 1939).

"Inquiries into American Wealth." *Virginia Quarterly Review* (April 1941).

"Some Social Attitudes of Railroad Administrators at the End of the Nineteenth Century." *Bulletin of the Historical Society* 17 (February 1943).

"Historical Aspects of Imperfect Competition: Theory and History." *Journal of Economic History, Supplement* 3 (December 1943).

"New York City Business Records: A Plan for their Preservation." *Bulletin of the Business Historical Society* 18 (June 1944).

"The Economics of the Future." Review article. *Virginia Quarterly* 20 (Autumn 1944).

"Business Manuscripts; A Pressing Problem." With Arthur H. Cole. *Journal of Economic History* 5 (May 1945).

"Plans for Internship in Business Archival Work." *Bulletin of the Business Historical Society* 20 (June 1946).

"The Economics in a Business History." *Journal of Economic History, Supplement* 5 (December 1945).

"A Plan for the Study of Business Thinking." *Political Science Quarterly* 62 (March 1947).

"Research in American Economic History: A Thirty-Year View." *Mid-America* 29, n.s. 18 (January 1947).

"The Presidential Synthesis in American History." *American Historical Review* 53 (July 1948).

"A Decade of American Histories." *Pennsylvania Magazine of History and Biography* (April 1949).

"Land Grants and Railroad Entrepreneurship." *Journal of Economic History* 10 (1950).

"Problems and Challenges in Business History Research." *Bulletin of the Business Historical Society* 24 (September 1950).

"The Legend of the Robber Barons." *Pennsylvania Magazine of History and Biography* 74 (July 1950).

"The Executive Mind: The Role of Railroad Leaders 1845-1890." *Bulletin of the Business Historical Society* 25 (December 1951).

"A New Era in United States History." *Revista de Historia de America* 33 (June 1952).

"The American-Hawaiian Steamship Company 1899-1919." with Ray Ginger. *Business History Review* 27 (December 1954).

"History and the Social Sciences." *Relazioni del X Congresso Internationale di Scienze Storiche*. Vol. 1. Rome, September 4-11, 1955.

"Business in the Domestic Tradition." *Harvard Business Review*, (March-April 1956).

"Business in the Social Sciences." *American Jewish Historical Society, Publications* 46 (March 1957).

"The Research Center in Retrospect." With Hugh G. J. Aitken and Fritz L. Redlich. *Explorations in Entrepreneurial History* 10 (April 1958).

"United States: Industrial Development." *Encyclopedia Americana*. Vol. 27. 1958.

"The Organization Man in Historical Perspective." *Pennsylvania History* 25 (January 1958).

"Recent Contributions to Economic History: The United States, The Twentieth Century." *Journal of Economic History* 9 (March 1959).

"Cultural Factors in Economic Growth." *Journal of Economic History* 20 (December 1960).

"Did the Civil War Retard Industrialization?" *Mississippi Valley Historical Review* (September 1961).

"The World of Business." *Harvard Business Review* 40 (September 1962).

"The Entrepreneur in Economic Change." *Behavioral Science* (April 1964).

"The History of a Business Society." *Journal of American History* 54 (June 1967).

"Economic History, Old and New." *American Historical Review* 74 (June 1969).

"History and Cultural Crisis." *American Historical Review* 78 (February 1972).

"The Business Revolution." *American Historical Review* 79 (December 1974).

"The Paradox of American Economic Growth." *Journal of American History* 61 (March 1975).

"The Sloan Report: American Culture and Business Management." *American Quarterly* (1975).

"Early Industrialism in the Delaware and Susquehanna River Areas: A Regional Analysis." *Social Science History* 1 (Spring 1977).

"Philadelphia the Industrial Center." *Philadelphia Magazine of History* 106, no. 3 (September 1982).

Index

About the Editor and Contributors

Stanley Bailis is Professor and Chair of the Program in Social Science (Interdisciplinary Studies) at San Francisco State University, where he has been teaching since 1963. He is mainly interested in developing integrations of the social sciences that can be used to account for processes of change.

Ronald H. Bayor is Associate Professor of History at the Georgia Institute of Technology. He has published a number of articles on urban and ethnic topics and is the author of *Neighbors in Conflict: The Irish, Germans, Jews and Italians of New York City, 1929-1941*. Recently he has edited an anthology, *Neighborhoods in Urban America*. He is also editor of the *Journal of American Ethnic History*.

James J. Flink was a Woodrow Wilson Fellow (1958-1959) and received the Colonial History Prize, Colonial Society of Pennsylvania (1960). Dr. Flink is author of *America Adopts the Automobile, 1895-1910* (1970) and *The Car Culture* (1975). He has been consultant to the Smithsonian Institution, United States National Museum, 1972-1973, and has served on the Advisory Council, Society for the History of Technology (1978-1983). Dr. Flink has taught at San Francisco State University, the University of Pennsylvania, and Douglass College, Rutgers University. He is currently Professor of Comparative Culture and Social Sciences at the University of California, Irvine.

Bernard Mergen is Professor of American Civilization at George Washington University. In 1982 he was a Fulbright Professor at the Kennedy Institute of the Free University of Berlin. He has published articles and books on American cultural history, including *Play and Playthings* (Greenwood Press, 1982). He is also Senior Editor of *American Studies International*.

Harold Issadore Sharlin is the author of *Lord Kelvin: The Dynamic Victorian* (1979), *The Convergent Century: The Unification of Science in the Nineteenth Century* (1966), and *The Making of the Electrical Age: From the Telegraph to Automation* (1963). After teaching history of science and technology for twenty-five years, he resigned and moved to Washington, D.C. At present, Dr. Sharlin is a consultant and specializes in conducting seminars, conferences, and colloquia on regulation, technological innovation, and energy policy.

James H. Soltow, Professor of History at Michigan State University, is coauthor of *The Evolution of the American Economy: Growth, Welfare, and Decision Making* (1979) and author of *Origins of Small Business: Metal Fabricators and Machinery Makers in New England* (1965), *The Economic Role of Williamsburg* (1965), and a number of articles on economic history and business history. He is also editor of *Essays in Economic and Business History: Selected Papers from the Economic and Business Historical Society* (1976-1978, 1979, and 1981). He was president of the Economic and Business Historical Society in 1982. He has served as Business History Fellow at Harvard University (1958-1959) and as Fulbright Fellow at the University of Louvain in Belgium (1965-1966). His interest in the history of business began with his doctoral dissertation on the role of manufacturing in Norristown, Pennsylvania, supervised by Professor Cochran.

Robert H. Walker has been at George Washington University since 1959 and he has been continuously involved in developing a graduate program in American civilization suited to the resources of the national capital. On a brief leave of absence he helped establish the National Endowment for the Humanities, serving as its first director of education and public programs. For two years he was president of the American Studies Association. His publications include *The Poet and the Gilded Age* (1963), *Life in the Age of Enterprise* (1967), and *American Society* (1980). Dr. Walker has edited the *American Quarterly, American Studies International, American Studies: Topics and Sources* (Greenwood Press, 1976), and *The Reform Spirit in America* (a document collection, 1976).

Michael Zuckerman has been teaching history at the University of Pennsylvania since 1965 and has taught as a visitor at the University of Oregon, Johns Hopkins University, the University of Richmond, and the Hebrew University of Jerusalem. He has written *Peaceable Kingdoms: Massachusetts Towns in the Eighteenth Century* and articles on a range of topics including identity in early modern Europe and America, Horatio Alger, and Doctor Spock. Most recently, he has edited a collection of essays on the middle colonies, *Friends and Neighbors: Group Life in America's First Plural Society*, and he has been working on a book on the southern colonial family.